Buy Yourself the F*cking Lilies

BUY YOURSELF THE F*CKING LILIES

And Other Rituals to Fix Your Life
from Someone Who's Been There

TARA SCHUSTER

THE DIAL PRESS   NEW YORK

Copyright © 2019 by Tara Schuster

Published in the United States by The Dial Press,
an imprint of Random House, a division of
Penguin Random House LLC, New York.

THE DIAL PRESS is a registered trademark of Penguin Random House LLC.

LIBRARY OF CONGRESS CATALOGING-IN-PUBLICATION DATA
Names: Schuster, Tara, author.
Title: Buy yourself the f*cking lilies: and other rituals to fix your life,
from someone who's been there / by Tara Schuster.
Other titles: Buy yourself the fucking lilies
Description: First edition. | New York: Dial Press, [2019]
Identifiers: LCCN 2019007307 | ISBN 9780525509882 (hardcover) |
ISBN 9780525509899 (ebook)
Subjects: LCSH: Self-acceptance.
Classification: LCC BF575.S37 S38 2019 | DDC 158.1—dc23
LC record available at https://lccn.loc.gov/2019007307

Printed in the United States of America on acid-free paper

randomhousebooks.com

4 6 8 9 7 5

Book design by Diane Hobbing

The entire year I was twenty-six, I told people I was twenty-seven. Not because I wanted to be older (I did *not*) but because I simply forgot my exact age. I am terrible with time, dates, and numbers. This is my way of telling you that I tried my best to be accurate with my timeline, relying on my journals, my Google Doc, Instagram, friends, and family to help suss out the correct order of events during my self-care journey, but there's always the chance I screwed up along the way. In some cases, when it served the narrative or when I felt like you didn't need to hang around for the tenth time as I repeated the same fucking mistake in my life, I rearranged or compressed the timeline.

Additionally, I changed names and identifying characteristics and used composite characters when I thought it was the gentle, respectful thing to do. If, however, you somehow recognize yourself in these pages in a way that makes you think, *Ugh, that wasn't my finest moment,* welcome to how I felt.

I tried to show myself, fully. In all things, I let truth, vulnerability, and kindness guide me.

—TARA SCHUSTER

For you.
On your way.
About to set the world on fire.

Mrs. Dalloway said she would buy the flowers herself.

—Virginia Woolf, *Mrs. Dalloway*

CONTENTS

III: THE RELATIONSHIP RITUALS
You Can't Control How Others Treat You, but You Can Control What You'll Accept

THE
CHAOS RITUALS
And the Day I Decided To Grow Myself Up

So *This* Is Rock Bottom

It's three P.M. and I've just woken up on top of my aggressively floral duvet, fully dressed. I'm in my best "Girls' Night Out" ensemble: black Spanx, black tights, and a black sequined Forever 21 number that looks particularly cheap in daylight. I'm sweaty AF. I pull my hair as hard as I can to offset the pain of my crushing migraine. There is an uneaten, unexplained grilled cheese sandwich lying next to me. This is not a good look.

This is the wreckage after my twenty-fifth birthday. I can't recall the night before beyond a haze of dancing and some of the usual light sobbing. *I should smoke weed,* I think. *I should blur this moment out and drift away on a cloud of smoke.* But recently, weed has been making me sick. I think I've smoked my lifetime's allotment, and now my once trusty crutch gives me heartburn and paranoia. *Plus,* the weed is all the way in my bathroom-slash-closet-slash-study, which I can see just beyond the kitchen-slash-hallway-slash-dining-room of my studio apartment. That ten-foot walk seems like too much right now.

I grab my iPhone—THANK THE LORD I have not lost it again!—to Yelp "breakfast sandwich delivery." I see I have three missed calls and voicemails from my therapist. The therapist who seemed to be the only doctor on the isle of Manhattan, and possibly on planet Earth, willing to take my insurance. Why would she be calling me on a Saturday night? Supz weird. I listen to the messages.

Message one:

"Hi Tara, it's Dr. Goldstein. I haven't heard back from you so I'm recommending you go to the hospital, okay? Are you listening to me? There is no shame in that. You need to be around people right now. Nothing matters except for your safety, okay? Please, call me when you get this."

Whaaat? What an extreme message. Why would Dr. Goldstein leave something so creepy and ominous? Why would I go to the *hospital*?!

Message deleted.

Message two:

"Tara, it's me again, Dr. Goldstein trying to reach you. Listen, I'm going to bed soon, but I need you to call me. Okay? I'm concerned. Really, really concerned. Are you alone? Do you have friends you can be with? Please call me as soon as you get this."

Okay, what the actual fuck? Why was she trying to reach me last night? *Think, Tara, think!*

Message deleted.
Message three:

"Hi Tara, it's Dr. Goldstein. I got your message, and, through the tears, I could hear how much pain you're in. I'm so sorry you are feeling this way on your birthday. I'm really worried about you. You said you feel unbearably sad and that you hate yourself. You said there is nothing left to hope for and you don't see a way out, but Tara, I just have to say, there is so much to live for. There *is* a healthy part of you. *That* part of you called me and reached out. The healthy part wants to survive and shine. Are you thinking of hurting yourself? That's what's really concerning me. I've just never heard you this desperate. Please don't do anything rash. I promise, you *will* get through this. Call me back as soon as you get this."

Oh my God. Ohmygodohmygodohmygod.
I drunk-dialed my therapist.

I drunk-dialed my therapist and apparently wanted to hurt myself, and she, a woman who is perma-calm, whom I have never seen without a cup of tea and a placid smile, was so disturbed that she thought I should check myself into a hospital. WHAT HAVE I DONE?

The memories of the past night come flooding in like a tall wave I can't swim over. Here I am at my birthday dinner with my BFF drinking an unknown number of dirty martinis. Here she is ditching me early. Here I am dancing alone in a museum feeling sorry for myself. Here is a security guard telling me "The party is over, miss" before escorting me out. Here I am feeling super pathetic. Here is . . . a blur . . . and . . . I don't know how I got home exactly? Here I am taking drunk, sad selfies, posing in front of my bathroom mirror. Here I am in said bathroom alternating between crying and vomiting over the toilet.

I feel a shame that sparks in my belly, creeps up my chest, and sets my heart on fire with hate. I hate myself. I hate the things I do. I hate my body. I hate this double life of being "good" at work and "bad" at life. I've always been dogged about getting ahead, in school and in my job, so it's always looked like everything is okay, but things are decidedly *not okay*. I'm humiliated that I'm the type of person who is so out of control that she drunk-dials her therapist. I'm exhausted in my guts. I'm worn down from the hate and the drinking and the smoking and the crying and the just living from one crisis to the next crisis and I am SoTiredSoAshamedSoDesperate. This is a life I can no longer live. This is a life that will kill me.

Here Are Some Jokes

Okay, I don't really have any jokes. I'm not a great joke-teller, I'm sorry to say. I just feel like that got real dark real fast, and I want to have a moment with you where I can tell you directly that you have nothing to worry about. That mess of a girl no longer lives here. She grew up. She healed.

I am, in fact, stable now, and on a perfect day, when I am drinking a latte and wearing a feather-light, perfectly layered Zara scarf, I am joyful. Blissed-out even. I have a schmancy job in comedy that I adore. I have fulfilling friendships with people I find both fascinating and kind. I'm no longer crippled by the fear that I will a) become one of my parents, b) murder one of my parents, or c) go crazy and do all of the above. Because guess what? *I am going to do none of the above!* What a victory!

The book you are currently holding in your hands is the

story of how I grew myself up from a self-hating-mess-wreck-disaster-out-of-control person to a happy-stable-grateful-gleeful-let's-go-on-an-adventure person. I wrote it because I think that within my stories of learning how to take care of myself you will find tried and true, practical, enjoyable tools for your own self-care and healing. By sharing my discoveries, I think I can save you a little hurt and give you some direction on what can be a confusing, frustrating road. Why should you trust me, tho? For all you know I've never faced a real challenge in my life beyond getting too wasted and being kicked out of a museum party. For all you know I had a perfect white-picket-fence childhood where my mom and dad fully supported me and a cloud never blew past our home. And in some ways, you're right. I *was* privileged. I went to private schools where I excelled (still paying off that debt, tho, *yikes*), I had a roof over my head, and there was always food on the table. But I also spent the majority of my childhood either neglected or emotionally abused by my parents. I had no capable adults to show me how to grow up, much less nurture me. I was privileged, but I was not parented. And by the time I turned twenty-five, the only dependable habits I had learned were figuring out new and interesting ways to spend my days anxious, scared, and constantly on the verge of emotional implosion. I needed to find a way forward. I wanted a life I could enjoy—or at least deal with—but I didn't understand how I might build that life.

I think there are *a lot* of us out there. People who didn't have THE *WORST* CHILDHOODS EVER, people who had it "pretty good" but nevertheless find themselves regularly crying in their cubicles at work. We've achieved the outward markers of a happy, lucky life, but underneath it all, we're terrible at truly *living*. We walk around with overwhelming anxiety and emotional pain, and then we feel guilt and shame because "I didn't have it *that* bad—I should be fine!" My answer to you is *No. You do not have to be fine.* If you went through some shit, even if it was "minor," and it's affecting your life, then you deserve to deal with that shit. Period.

That is why I am with you now: because I've been there. I've been in that sunken, wretched, sad place. I worked like hell to climb out and bathe myself in the sunlight of healing. I spent years creating a blueprint for emotional recovery, and now I believe I can offer you lifesaving tips on self-care and how *not* to treat your mind and body like a flaming human garbage can. I think it would help if you knew a little more about me, though, so, as briefly as I can, let me explain where I began.

Things Came to My House to Die

When I was growing up, a family of deer died in our lap pool. Since we lived in a canyon full of wildlife (or as much wildlife as Los Angeles has to offer), it was not unusual to see a deer, a coyote, or a rattlesnake in the backyard. The assumption—with the dead deer—was that the papa deer put his head down to drink some water, lost his balance, and fell in. The mama deer probably tried to help him, and the baby deer followed suit. They couldn't find a way out of the pool, so they all drowned. My dad made the unhappy discovery the next morning while stepping into the pool to swim his daily laps. As a four-year-old, I remember seeing the waterlogged deer laid out on a blue tarp as animal control services tried to figure out how to get them out of our backyard.

Coco the Himalayan cat died. Light, our next Himalayan cat, died and so did her litter of three kittens. Iggy the iguana died just days after we brought him back from Petco. It took us a while to notice, though; we thought iguanas were just really still. My parakeet "disappeared" the way a dissident might in a

South American country. One day she was there squawking too loudly and the next, my parents told me she had "gone to a better place." The mice from my science experiment died. All of the plants died: the fig tree, the bougainvillea, the nursery of orchids that had come free with purchase of the house. The home was not under some mysterious hex—plants, animals, and children alike were shamefully neglected, unloved, and undernourished. My sister, Diana, and I somehow made it out alive.

Our house was built on a literally shaky foundation. An earthquake-prone, landslide-endangered foundation. There was always some construction project to "save the house" under way—some new retaining wall that needed to be installed or a new pylon to erect. The roof had been built too flat and without proper drainage, so whenever it rained, there was the threat of the whole ceiling collapsing. A thick, water-buckled crack in the middle of the white plaster above our heads served as a daily reminder that the seams of the house were vulnerable.

My mom and dad, a busy doctor and lawyer, never really noticed how dire the condition of the house was because they were rarely home. They only made visits to HQ long enough to drag my little sister and me into the fog of war that was their marriage. Much like Vietnam, no one was really sure why they were in it or what victory would mean, but for thirteen years they soldiered on.

Let me paint you a picture: Saturday nights were reserved for "family" outings to see a movie. Deciding what movie to watch was a grueling process. "Richard, *Goodfellas* isn't APPROPRIATE; it's TOO VIOLENT. YOU HAVE NO BOUNDARIES!" my mother would scream. "Oh, but *MISERY* is a good choice?!" he would retort. "YOU'RE CRAZY!" At the age of five, I would sit with my arms folded, watching the verbal assault, wondering if *maybe* there was a way to hurry this up so we could all get on with our lives. After the adults finally landed on *Misery,* an R-rated film in which Kathy Bates traps and abuses an injured and recovering James Caan, my parents would then proceed to viciously attack each other in the car about how late we were going to be. "CAROL, why can't you be on time for anything?" "FUCK YOU, RICHARD! FUCK YOU! I'M NEVER LATE; YOU'RE *SUCH* A LIAR!" my mom would volley back. I would sit in the backseat attempting to melt away.

By the time we'd make it to the movie theater, fifteen to twenty minutes late, we would shimmy into our seats in front of the other *Misery* enthusiasts. I would sit between my parents as a buffer zone/holder of the popcorn, which had *also,* of course, been a fight to select. My dad would shout at my mom, "YOU DON'T NEED BUTTER ADDED TO THE POP-CORN, *CAROL;* YOU'RE ALREADY FAT!" Unbuttered it would be. Once we were settled, my mom would whip out her Toshiba laptop, which in the 1990s was the size of a large brief-case, and begin to do work. What work did she need to do during the movie she had selected and brought her family to, you ask? No clue. But as the people around hissed that the screen was too bright and the typing obnoxious, she would loudly whisper back, "I'm a *doctor;* I have important *work* to do."

I never really thought of myself as a "child" to my parents. I thought of myself more as their disempowered supervisor, a put-upon boss in charge of underqualified nepotism hires. I couldn't fire them, so I had to find work-arounds. Sometimes, after school, I would be dropped off at my mom's gynecology office. Instead of coloring or doing whatever it is children at the age of eight do (I would not know), I would arrive ready to take control. I'd kick the receptionist out of her swivel chair and answer the phones. I would take appointments, console women who were nervous about their upcoming surgeries, run circles around the staff demanding that they "work harder and better." I would admonish anyone who seemed like they weren't pulling their own weight. "That was a pretty long cigarette break, Kathleen. And while we're at it . . . smoking isn't exactly healthy. You should think about what *that* choice looks like for this office." I thought I was in control. I thought it was my job to fix my parents' lives, which, even to an eight-year-old, were clearly unraveling.

But the truth was, I wasn't doing so hot myself. I was constantly inundated with messages that something was "wrong" with me. For instance, my mother relentlessly told me I was dyslexic. "There's just something not right in your brain, or you're just lazy. I'm not sure, but it's awful and a huge problem and you're going to have to repeat the third grade," she would tell me. These words would not be followed by caring action or investigation or perhaps even a visit to the doctor to find out if indeed I was dyslexic. Instead, the accusations were just left there for me to absorb as unassailable fact. While I was never actually held back in school, I believed my mom that there was something intrinsically wrong with me, and I lived my life on edge that other people would find out and, somehow, I'd be punished for it. *Would this be the year I'd be condemned, kicked out of school? Would this be the spelling lesson in which it'd finally be revealed how stupid I was?*

All of the disorder I felt in my own life, I enacted on anything smaller than me. I was mean to Diana and cruel toward pets, and for as long as I could remember, I had been in therapy for "acting out." By the age of ten, I had become so used to the school intercom blaring the words "Tara Schuster, please come to the front office" that I began to have a sixth sense for when I might be called to confess my sins. On these visits, I would be met by a school counselor or social worker who would ask me questions about my family. In a small, private room, they would ask in a hushed, super-serious tone, "So, how *are* things with your mom and dad?" People could see the chaos of our home, I guess, and they would leave anonymous tips for Child Protective Services to investigate. "Are you eating enough?" *Yes, I have a stash of candy under my bed if you wanna take a look.* "Does anyone hit or physically assault anyone in your house?" *Not that I know of, but I mostly lock myself in my room and turn on the TV to max volume to drown out the screaming.* "Do your parents fight more than average?" *Well, what's average? They just fight all the time.* I hated these meetings. They felt like a condemnation, further evidence that there was something fundamentally unacceptable about me. The social worker's questions danced around the core of the problem: My parents simply did not know, or have the capacity to learn, how to take care of children. Sure, we ate, but were we nurtured? It was more like we were fed a steady diet of neglect, instability, and shouting. It never once occurred to me that the social worker might be able to help me, or that maybe things actually *were* bad at home. This was just my life: surviving my time in my falling-apart, death-ridden house and evading questions from the authorities at school.

By the time I was ten, my dad ran a "family" restaurant, which he was embarrassed to have his actual family visit. I can't blame him. The place was country music–themed, and when you entered, it was through the gaping mouth of a two-story, neon Wurlitzer jukebox. This led directly into a grand, if artificial, "country desert" scene with a cornflower-blue, fiber-optic star-studded night sky. One evening, as we were walking in through the front hall, my mom *almost* slipped and fell on the freshly mopped floor. "I COULD HAVE DIED!" she wailed. Though she had not actually fallen, she proceeded to lie down on the ground and refuse to move until help arrived. She screamed to anyone who would listen that she had a lawsuit against "RICH-ARD SCHUSTER, THE OWNER OF THIS UNSAFE PLACE!"

After my mom's tantrum passed, we sat down to eat a dinner of ribs. My parents were fighting so loudly that the poor waiters didn't know what to do. *Yes,* they wanted to serve their boss cheese bread and show him how attentive they were, but, *no,* they did not want to be anywhere near our table of doom. While my parents screamed about how "broke" they were and how "crazy" the other was, the resident balloon artist of the restaurant approached our table. I think he sensed something was awry and thought that, through his elastic craft, he could make a difference. Maybe, through balloon animals, he could show us the meaning of family? He began to design two balloon crowns, each with a white swan sitting on top. The swans were kissing, and their interlocked orange beaks connected the hats together. These were balloon hats of unity and love. "Go ahead, put them on," he said, motioning to my parents. They refused. "That hat is stupid," my mom scoffed. My dad just looked away, not wanting to be seen. I begged them to put on the hats; I began to cry, "PLEASE, PLEASE JUST PUT ON THE HATS. YOU LOVE EACH OTHER!" I was having a full-blown meltdown, willing love into existence, and in an attempt to calm me, my parents dutifully, unhappily put on the hats. With the swan crowns atop their heads, my mom looked at my dad and loudly whispered, "I want a divorce, *Richard.*"

Here Are Some More Jokes

Again, I have no jokes. I *KNOW*. I shouldn't be deflecting.
That all sounded pretty bleak, but that's exactly why I'm here:
to report to you from the other side. If I could go from a neglected little girl to a miserable, self-destructive, drunk-dialing-
her-therapist twentysomething to a well-adjusted, HAPPY (a
word I never dreamed would apply to me), stable, enjoying-
her-life, successful adult, well, then most anyone can. You, in
particular, most def can. What you are about to read is a guide
to healing your traumas, big and small, in the pursuit of creating a life you will adore and be proud of. You don't need to
have had a mess-wreck-disaster childhood like mine for these
tools to work for you. These lessons in self-care will be useful
even if you had super-stellar parents who nurtured the shit out
of you. This book is for anyone who simply needs to take better
care of themselves—anyone who wants to lead a life they
choose, embrace, and *fucking love*. It is my wish that the following stories will offer you a practical, reassuring, relatable, hopefully funny, sometimes sad guide to ultimately learning to love
yourself in a non-throw-up-in-your-mouth-it's-so-cheesy way.
I call this kind of self-care "re-parenting,"* a process in which
you figure out what nurturing you still need and then give it
to yourself. Even those of us who are all grown up still have
room to become the people we *want* to be.

The afternoon after my twenty-fifth birthday I knew I had
to change my life. My past had shaped me into this mess in
Spanx with no standards and no core. I was super good at surviving but super terrible at living. I wanted a life that I could

---

* Many years later, I googled "re-parenting" and found out this term also refers to a
specific therapeutic practice. I know approximately zero about that. When I talk about "re-
parenting" in this book, I'm referring to the hacked-together way I comforted and cared for
myself over the course of many years.

enjoy. I wanted a life where I felt good and like I was *enough*. But, sitting on my bed that day with dried puke in my hair, that goal felt far beyond my reach.

How could I change? I couldn't even change a vacuum filter without complaining about it for two years before sucking it up and dealing with the dusty disaster that had accumulated.* I didn't have the funds for an *Eat Pray Love*–style journey of healing and self-discovery. I also—again—didn't have THE WORST childhood in the world and I kinda felt like a fraud for being such a mess. But I decided it was time to stop comparing my pain to others', time to quit telling myself that I *shouldn't* feel this way, and time to start focusing on how I actually *did* feel, because that was real. I hated my life and wanted a better one. But how would I figure myself out? What values did I believe in? What were my principles? What were vegetables?

Sitting in bed, I took out a notepad and wrote down the things I *did* know:

1. I knew I didn't have great parents. Not the kind who nurture you and teach you how to lead a stable life. No new parents were coming to the rescue either. I was not the secret daughter of a royal family (truly a bummer). I had no adult role models on which I could rely or mentors to guide me. If I sincerely wanted a different life, I would have to learn to take care of myself. I would have to take full responsibility for my life and well-being.

2. I knew my damage wasn't something I could ignore and just move past. I couldn't avoid it any longer. I wanted to know what my wounds were and apply a salve of glitter, kindness, and forgiveness to them one by

---

*   I recently bought a vacuum cleaner that has NO filter to avoid this grimy situation.

one. I had recently heard the saying "Sunlight is the best disinfectant," and that's exactly what I wanted for my past emotional injuries. I would have to re-parent myself and give myself the support I never had. I just needed to start trying *any* advice, anything I read or heard or even *imagined* might work. I decided I would take notes in a Google Doc so I could track my own progress. Maybe by writing it all down, I'd be able to see what direction I was heading in. Maybe not. I didn't have any answers—yet—but at least I could start asking questions.

3. I knew I would like some poached eggs and avocado toast with a side of industrial-strength ibuprofen, please and thank you.

In these stories you will find honest, tested, not-impossibly-difficult ways to re-parent and care for yourself. I'm not interested in giving you theoretical, "out there" advice from a place on high. I've been at the ground floor with you, and this is my offering. I went through hell, took notes, learned my lessons, and, now, it is my deepest wish that the tools I developed will work for you. At a minimum, I think you will laugh. With me. Hopefully not at me.

I'm really happy to be with you right now.

I think the way you are doing your hair today is lovely. I mean, I always like the way you do it, but today, it's next level.

LOVE AND KISSES AND LOTS OF GLITTER,

TARA

A.K.A. T$ (GO AHEAD AND CALL ME THAT)

I

THE
MIND RITUALS

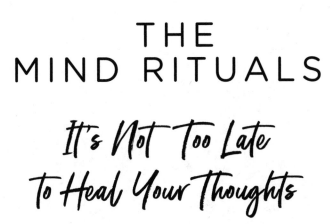

*It's Not Too Late
to Heal Your Thoughts*

Be the Best at the Worst
Start Where You Are

AT COMEDY CENTRAL, WHERE I have worked for the past ten years, we have an intern lunch during which our group of hardworking, sweet, so-clueless-I-have-become-embarrassed-that-I-was-ever-that-young interns can ask us executives for advice. The questions are usually the same.

Q: **How do you deal with being a woman in Hollywood?**
A: Um . . . Do you have ten hours to talk and *not* in this room full of my dude colleagues?

Q: **How do you make a "good" TV show?**
A: No idea. All I do is find the most talented people I can, say a prayer, and get out of the way. Anyone who tells you differently, or that they have some secret sauce, is probably an egomaniac.

Q: **How did you get your first big break?**
A: I was at my own intern lunch at *The Daily Show with Jon Stewart* when a fellow intern asked that very same question. I had never worked in television before, and I

was in awe of the rigor of that show. Jon* was there every day, the entire day, overseeing *everything*. And the people around him were just *so smart*. They were the adults you wanted to be: single-minded in their dedication to their work, rushing about in a manner that screamed *importance,* and totally uninterested in us, the lowly interns. When we finally had our official time to sit with Jon, another intern asked him what his first "big break" was. Jon very quickly, very firmly responded: "There are no big breaks. There are only a series of tiny, little breaks. The key is to work your hardest and do your best at every little break." Jon Stewart is/was/will forever be my hero, and so I took his words, swallowed them, and tried to make them part of me.

That entire semester at *The Daily Show* I made it my mission to be the best at the worst of jobs, with the hope that I might find my own little break. When I noticed that a correspondent wanted oatmeal every day but by the time he got into the office it had all been eaten,† I saved him packets and put them on his desk with a bowl and a spoon. When I saw that the permanent staff was genuinely annoyed by the interns who constantly did "bits," trying to out-funny one another in a misguided attempt to "get dis-covered," I decided to be quiet and polite. My greatest contribution, however, was cleaning the capsule coffee machine.

Every afternoon after rehearsal, Jon would make himself an iced coffee in a little kitchen nook outside the studio door. I noticed that the machine was often dirty, out of water, or—even worse—broken, and I imagined how an-

---

*   I do not know Jon Stewart as "Jon." That would be insane.

†   Probably by we, the servile, free-food-greedy interns. I gained at least fifteen pounds in bagel weight during this internship.

noyed that must make Jon. Here he was trying to get one of the funniest, most important shows on the air, and he couldn't even get a mediocre capsule coffee? Not on my watch! I saw my first little break.

I treated that machine like a precious object, cleaning it, refilling it, pulling it apart, putting it back together, making sure it was perfect. I read online how to fix the machine and practiced at home by buying a similar model. I spent a good part of my day making sure the thing was in order so there would never be a time when Jon couldn't have a little coffee. It didn't occur to me then that I was being pretty intense-bordering-on-psychotic about the machine; instead, I saw this as my way to make a contribution to a show I loved. If I wasn't going to be a writer on the show, if I was just a lowly intern, at least I could be the lowly intern who could be called upon at any point to fix the single most important item in any creative environment: the coffee machine. I don't know if it was cleaning the coffee machine or my polite quietness that impressed the producers, but at the end of the semester, they helped me get an entry-level job at Comedy Central. The rest of my career sprung directly from that decision to be the best at something that seemed like the worst.

Today, I tell young people who ask for professional advice to be the best at the worst. Take whatever weird little opportunity you have and maximize the fuck out of it. In a best-case scenario, someone cool will notice. In a worst-case scenario, *you* will notice and feel pride knowing you are doing a good job, even if the task sucks. Simply put: Start where you are without worrying too much about how far you have to go.

After my twenty-fifth birthday, on my floral duvet, I decided to start where I was. I knew that when it came to healing my own mind, I would have to apply the same persistence, care, and attention I brought to that coffee machine. I would have to show up, figure out what was wrong with the water tank, and work like hell to fix it. I would have to be vigilant and patient, knowing that for no reason at all, sometimes the machine would have a total meltdown and refuse to work, and I'd be left with an ominous red light staring me in the face. While I didn't have an owner's manual to my own mind, I did have a quote from Jay-Z to guide me: "Only thing to stop me is me, and I'ma stop when the hook start." I ardently believe in the first part; I don't totally know what he means about the hook starting.

Start where you are. Wherever you are. Be the best at the worst.

Writing It Down
Saved My Life
Connect To Your Innermost Self

BY TWENTY-FIVE, I *KNEW* I was damaged, but I wasn't totally sure *how*. Just what exactly was my problem? That shameful drunk-dial to my therapist was just one of many "not okay," "Are you even being a real fucking person right now?" ways I had acted recently. Many days at work, where I was kicking ass at my entry-level job, I would find myself uncontrollably weeping in my cubicle. I would be in the middle of logging stand-up videos when I would feel tears well up from an inexplicable pit of sadness within me. I would look at my snotty, sobbing reflection in the computer monitor and think, *What are you doing?* The walls of my cubicle insulated me from outsiders just long enough for me to make my way to the personal call room and have a proper cry.

These meltdowns followed me through the office and into the streets of Manhattan, where I often played the role of "girl mysteriously crying on your stoop." I also played the part of "girl encumbered by too many bags about to burst into tears because the train is slightly delayed/there is a long line to buy a sandwich/any little thing has gone wrong." I was raw with feelings of extreme unease that manifested into a persistent, slightly dizzy feeling, like I was living outside my body. Was I sick? I seemed to have a permanent headache that throbbed at the base of my cervical spine, then crawled up my neck, wrapped itself around my skull, and finally settled its claws into two painful points above my ears. I had no clue what to do about all of the tears, the sadness, the headaches, the physical and mental pain. I didn't understand any of it or where it was coming from.

Growing up, fantasizing and creating new stories for myself had been my refuge from the anarchy of my life. From as early as I can remember, I would perform little plays or look for ways to act the part of someone else. When my parents would take me out on their date nights, I would quickly flee our table in order to play the role of "adult friend" to the diners around us. Eight years old and pulsating with tenacity, I would compliment women, telling them, "You are very pretty!" I would ask men, "Are you a sexist, misogynist pig?" I had heard from my mom that this was a *very* big deal and I wanted to catch any "sexists" and "misogynists" in my midst. The adult couples would politely indulge me as I asked questions like "Do you have enough sex?" or "How do you keep your love life fresh?" The grown-ups would usually burst into surprised laughter before giving me a very PG answer ("Relationships are work") and looking for my parents. As soon as I got home, I would write down the stories I had heard from the adult world and then perform them in front of my mirror.

I became so enamored with interrogating grown-ups and telling their stories that my mom briefly set up a cable-access television show for me. *Girl Talk* was filmed in an exam room of her medical office. A pink construction-paper mural covered in puffy paint designs of flowers and hearts hid a gynecological exam chair. On the show, I would interview such luminaries as my mom's personal trainer, Kim, a bodybuilder with a short blond ponytail and greased-up, Day-Glo orange limbs. I would catch any patient in the hall and ask/demand that she be a guest on my "very important, very popular, very funny television show."* A stunning number of people agreed. My mother canceled my show, not due to poor ratings (because we didn't have any ratings) but because she needed her exam room back. *That's Hollywood, kiddo.*

With my show canceled, I began keeping my own journal. It was full of the musings of a child prodigy: "Jamie Belsky-Briley is 11 out of 10 HOT"; "I would marry Luke Perry, eff Jason Priestley, and kill Ian Ziering (duh)"; "I'm scared to leave my room because my parents are screaming and I don't want to see them but I ALSO really want to GET OUT OF MY ROOM because mom said the world is full of rapists and murderers who want to kidnap me and I think one is plotting to break in through my bedroom window! How do I escape?" My journal was a safe place where I could be vulnerable and write about how my world *felt:* violent, tumultuous, confusing, and dangerous.

My diary was something I kept only for me and hid in my candy stockpile under my bed. One day, a family friend walked into my room as I was writing in it. She was a self-described "Wiccan witch" who once "cursed" my father, but I, for some reason, trusted her as the only "normal" adult I knew. (Kind of shows you the lack of reasonable grown-ups I had to choose from, huh?) "What do you have there?" she asked. I confessed that I was keeping a journal where I was tracking everything going wrong around me. My parents were just beginning their divorce, and somehow, just by writing in my little purple-and-green-paisley-cloth-covered diary, I felt some relief. "That's

---

*   I am fairly confident only three episodes ever aired. Do you have any idea how I might retrieve these?

great you're keeping a journal, honey, can I see it?" The request felt a little odd, but so was *everything* else going on in that house. I agreed. As she skimmed through the pages, reading my secrets, my lies, my truths, my whole body throbbed with one thought: *NO, NO, NO, IT'S MINE.*

She took my journal straight to my mother, who then told me she was going to ENTER IT INTO MY PARENTS' DIVORCE PROCEEDINGS as evidence that I was a liar. Here, my mother insisted, was proof that I, a twelve-year-old, was not a credible witness, and that if I were to testify in the divorce, whatever I said should be discounted. My innermost thoughts had been used to shame me, and I still feel a sharp pang of grief and betrayal when I think about this. After that incident, even though I had loved making my own stories, even though I had found a respite in journaling, I decided it was too dangerous for me and I stopped writing altogether. What if someone exposed my thoughts again?

But after the night of my disgraceful twenty-fifth birthday, when I was attempting to pick up the pieces of my life, I went to drinks (Good call, right? Keep drinking? *Oy*) with my best friend* Isabelle to ask what she thought was wrong with me. She had been present for so much of my recent out-of-control behavior, had been by my side on so many nights as I bawled over glasses of wine in various bars, and so I thought maybe she would have some insights into what was going awry. "I'm not really sure; you never share what's going on with you or your family. It's almost like you're hiding it." "DUH, ISABELLE," I wanted to shout. Didn't she know it wasn't safe to share *any-*

---

*   You're going to notice that I call a whole hell of a lot of people my "best friend," and for an enthusiastic, sentimental mush-ball like me, I absolutely believe I have multiple best friends. It's more of a category to distinguish a deep, loving bond than it is about an individual. Once a "best friend," always a "best friend," even if I haven't spoken to you in many years.

thing about my past? I just smiled at her and replied, "Yeah, it's boring to talk about old history."

"Well, if you can't talk to me about it, I think you should read *The Artist's Way* by Julia Cameron. It's like a twelve-step program toward recovering your inner child. You do exercises to uncover and heal your traumas and learn prayers toward a more abundant universe."

"Recovering your *inner child?*" I scoffed. "Prayers toward the *universe?* Does it come with Tibetan prayer beads and my own guru too?" I snidely asked.

"I mean, yeah, it's a little cheesy, but wouldn't you rather be a little cheesy than crying and not sleeping and just feeling like shit all of the time?"

I reluctantly bought and then flipped through the pages of *The Artist's Way,* and among the exercises, I came upon a tool for creativity called "The Morning Pages." Every morning, before you've had time to think, before you hit up Instagram, before you check out how many likes your photo of a perfectly carved pumpkin has received on Facebook, you word-vomit your thoughts onto three pages of paper. Every morning. THREE pages. Single spaced. You simply scribble down whatever flows out of you, without editing, without thinking, without worrying. This seemed similar to journaling and therefore off-limits/dumb/dangerous to me, but it *wasn't* journaling; it was "The Morning Pages." *Huge* difference. The book explained how this practice was a way to get in touch with your core feelings by forcing you, in writing, to become aware of and engaged with the innermost self.

My first thought was *Who has the time, every day, to write THREE pages?* It seemed like a pretty overwhelming burden. But, again, I was at a point in my life where, *on a good day,* I was openly sobbing on the subway. Okay. I would try it, but I would keep the notebook hidden away in my nightstand, under magazines and my television remote control. No one would find it there.

In the beginning, my Morning Pages were unbearably boring. They mostly listed complaints: "Why can't you get up half an hour earlier? If only you woke up at 8:30, then you wouldn't be rushing to do these stupid pages before work!!" Or I listed errands I had to run: "YOU MUST BUY TOILET PAPER INSTEAD OF USING PAPER TOWELS FROM THE KITCHEN!!! YOU DESERVE TOILET PAPER." As I continued to write, however, sharp fears began to emerge: "You will fail." "You have no good ideas." "If you aren't professionally successful yet, you never will be." It was as if some force within me was moving my pen across the page, exposing worries I hadn't yet been aware of. "You will never find someone who loves you and you will be alone forever. You don't deserve love." *Yikes.* I hadn't been writing in my journal for more than a week and I was already confronted with the deep-seated and inescapable dreads of that neglected little girl at my core. The one who grew up in a house where things came to die, the one who was never comforted or taught how to take care of herself. As I wrote, it felt like I was receiving DMs from my soul. Secret, semi-sneaky messages from my most vulnerable center, nudging me toward the places I needed to heal. This was my little survivor voice, a soft cry from deep within me, someone who knew exactly where I needed to comfort myself. I thought it was going to be difficult to unpack all of my trauma, but here were all of my scariest thoughts, top of mind and easy to excavate.

One morning, totally unexpectedly, I wrote about my childhood dog, Giya, whom I hadn't consciously thought about in years. She was a black standard poodle, almost the size of a small pony. Giya was smart, she was kind, her fur was cut into poofs at her paws and tail that I would run my fingers through, wondering how a dog could have hair like spun silk. At the age of eleven, I thought she was the height of sophistication and elegance. My parents had fought viciously about buying her. "CAROL, you'll never take care of a dog; you barely take care of yourself!" my dad had screamed. "FUCK YOU, *RICHARD*, I can buy a dog if I want!" my mom had shot back in her usual chill manner. My mom brought home our dog without my dad's approval and introduced my sister and me to Giya. Since my mom had bought Giya *just before* their divorce, the dog, like Diana and me, was predictably, sadly, unforgivably forsaken. One day she ran away and, rather than look for her, my parents just shrugged their shoulders and said it wasn't worth the search. I remember thinking, *If I were to go missing, would anyone look for me?*

I canvassed the neighborhood with my babysitter, knocking on doors and asking if anyone had seen Giya. When we reached Mrs. Miller's house, I peeked in her front windows and saw *my dog* running to the front door to say hello. *YAY! We had found Giya and could bring her home!* Mrs. Miller, however, had other plans. "You don't deserve this dog. Your family doesn't take care of her, so I will," she simply explained. I had no recourse, no adult who could intervene to save the dog. So I left her there.

For years, when I was asked if I ever had a dog growing up, I deflected and "joked" about how mine had been "kidnapped" when I was young. But as I wrote about it in my journal, I found that this wasn't some hilarious detail from my "odd" childhood. It was something that deeply bothered me. I had never mourned the loss of Giya, so in my notebook, I let myself admit that it still upset me. I wrote about how scary and disorienting it was that, at the time, no adult had stepped in to help me. With my pen, I touched the sadness and the anger of my eleven-year-old self, the self that was confused, already heartbroken from life, scared, and probably wearing an ill-advised crop top. Since Giya, I had developed a fear of dogs in general, and I never felt like I could talk to anyone about this. It almost seems like a sin *not* to love dogs today. Since I was expressing all of this on paper, however, I risked nobody's judgment. I let myself get curious about why this was coming up for me now. Did I feel jealous of Giya in some way? That she had made her way to a loving home? Or, could *this* be why I had developed a fear of dogs, because I was too afraid that if I ever loved a dog again, I would lose it? I decided I would try to make a playdate with a Cavalier King Charles spaniel that belonged to a friend of mine. For some reason, that dog didn't scare me, and I felt like that might be a good baby step. It felt *so good* to finally have that fear out of my head and on paper. No longer was this some issue stewing in the back of my mind. I could deal with it because I was aware of it. I'm telling you, there is nothing so awful that you can't confront it if it's written in a notebook with a golden spine and a peony-decorated front cover.

Inspired by Tara Brach's meditation, "The R-A-I-N of Self-Compassion,"* I've built a tool for you to effectively excavate past wounds in a way that isn't totally draining-and-soul-crushing-and-why-oh-why-am-I-even-doing-this-to-myself?

1. **Admit the thought or feeling** you're having, no matter how dark, petty, or seemingly insignificant. Permit the feeling or thought to exist even if it's something as small as "An ex reached out today and it made me feel uncomfortable thinking about all the *what-ifs*," or as

---

* In the most soothing, wise, and loving voice, the brilliant Tara Brach teaches self-compassion through guided meditations. In "The R-A-I-N of Self-Compassion" you Recognize, Allow, Investigate, and Nurture any challenging feelings. This is an incredible (easy to remember) tool for self-care and I *highly recommend* that you subscribe to her podcast. Her voice makes you feel like you just put on your favorite comfy sweater. Nothing bad can happen to you while you listen to Tara Brach.

large as "It's always bothered me that my dad isn't much of a hugger. I haven't ever really talked about this, but I always wanted to be held."

2. **Touch all of the feels** associated with that thought. This is the time to vent to your heart's content. For example, "It's not fair that my ex reached out after he promised to give me some distance. Was the douchebag really trying to 'wish me well'? HE SUCKS! I'm still furious about how he broke up with me." Or maybe it's "I wish I had been hugged. I still feel sad that I wasn't. I feel angry too! Parents should hug their kids!" Give in to how you *actually feel*. Don't resist or deny your feelings; allow them to exist. Resistance adds kerosene to our flaming emotions. Pause and put the butane down.

3. **Get curious** about why this is coming up for you now: "Maybe I'm feeling heightened emotions because my BFF Sarah is moving in with her boyfriend. . . . I'm happy for her, but I feel a little hollow space inside of me when I think about how in love they seem to be, how they *laugh* so much, and how *not* in love I am right now." Or maybe it's "I realize I'm having trouble being intimate altogether and wonder if it has something to do with my childhood." Keep questioning yourself. Sometimes it can take a while to get answers. But you are getting into the practice of becoming self-aware. You have to know the wound to heal the wound! An easy question that always works—though you might have to ask it a few times—is "Why am I feeling this way?"

4. **Commit to a healing action.** A real one. It doesn't have to be big. If your ex reached out and it upset you,

maybe you get to put on your favorite moisturizing Sephora face mask while you remind yourself that he's the kind of guy who likes to stir shit up. Maybe you take yourself on a romantic date at the new hip place down the street with great bar seating. If your dad didn't hug you and it's bothering you now, maybe it's time to go get a massage or ask your BFF for a big old hug.

5. **Finish your emotional mining with this affirmation: "I am lucky to deal with this issue now instead of letting it fester. The shimmering, platinum lining is:"** and then fill in *why* it's a good thing, a great thing, a fucking *miracle* that you are dealing with this right now. That which you do not deal with deals with you. Always.

In addition to working out your past traumas (small and large), I've found that journaling can give you *physical* relief and peace. I know this because when I *don't* write in the morning, I feel tense and can be savage and mean. I become the bitch in line at Starbucks who is sneering and rolling her eyes while you take too long to order your drink. *It's Starbucks. How do you not know what you want to order?* When you journal, you don't have to carry your fears and anxieties with you all day and inadvertently unleash them on innocent bystanders. THANK GOD!

Keeping a diary is not only a way to deal with your "issues," however; it's also a practice that makes space for your dreams and wishes. STAY WITH ME, DEAREST READER; THIS WON'T BE *THAT* CHEESY! Somewhere along the way, I had given up on the idea that I could have a remarkable, joyous life. I was stuck in a rat-race mind-set, cluttered with anxious thoughts like *You are a failure on all levels* and *You will never find romantic love* and *How are you so lazy that you haven't picked up your dry cleaning for* three *weeks?!* Those thoughts took up almost ALL of my mental space. But by putting my worries on the page, *now* I had room for dreams, too, and a place to pay attention to them. "Maybe I could work with great artists," I wrote one day. "In my fantasy career, I would be writing and creating. Is there a job where I can be Tina Fey? Well, you know, not HER, but you get it," I wrote. "In my ideal life, I am living in Los Angeles with a home office and desk that looks out over my own backyard." I wanted to move to LA? And have a *yard*? Since when?

Until I started journaling, I didn't realize that I had put such a low ceiling on what I thought my life could be. The daily writing gave me a broom to poke and lift up the roof I had built over my mind. Journaling gets you in touch with what I like to call your "Oprah Mind." A mind that is expansive, abundant, and full of possibility. Your Oprah Mind will win an Oscar, write a book, write ten books. It will make the ballsy move of ending a hugely successful TV show to start a TV *network* if it damn well pleases. This mind is as boundless as the night's sky. Do you think Oprah spends all day consumed by her worries? Hell no. She has an empire to run and new ventures to imagine and put into action. She dreams and thinks BIG, and *that's* what I want for both you and me.

I don't often look back at what I've written, actually, but when I do, it's become easier to see my patterns. If I complain, in writing, for six months that I want to get up earlier in the morning but am failing to do so, then I know it's time to find a solution. What about banning all screens after 9:30 P.M. and placing my phone on the opposite side of my bedroom so I'm not tempted to stay up late scrolling through Instagram? If I read that I have felt lonely in the company of my boyfriend for the past year, then I am oh-so-sorry but it's probably time for that relationship to end. I can't trick myself into thinking it's working. It's harder to believe my convenient lies when I see the truth written down, over and over again.

A journal is not a place to record the daily events of your life. It's not a place to describe the sushi you had for dinner last night (although, if it's really good sushi, go ahead and do that). It's a place where you can get in touch with your core, with what you *believe*. Some of us have very limiting beliefs but are totally unaware that we've set such a low bar for ourselves. Journaling is the gift that gives us a chance to uncover what *is true*. Because a belief and the truth are two very different things. You might *believe* you are not capable of having your biggest, glitteriest dreams become reality. But I know that's not the *truth*. The truth is that you can heal your past traumas, you can build the life you want for yourself, but you're going to have to do the work.

The work here begins by writing down and exploring what bothers you, what you dream about, and what you will *now* make true. Out of your head and onto the page, you have a chance to tackle your worries, to give voice to your dreams, to see if there are patterns holding you back. You might have been born into a set of circumstances that were less than ideal. You might be currently living in circumstances that are a *hell of a lot less* than ideal. But only you can decide if those things define you. Is it time to change your story? Have you always let negative people suck you dry of your energy as you tried, in vain, to bolster *them*? Are you tired of that yet? Have you always felt embarrassed that you didn't come from a "good family"? Maybe it's time to question if telling yourself that story is doing anything for you. What about instead, "Yeah, I might not have come from a perfect home, but, really, who even does, and I'm grateful for *almost* everything I've learned on this path. I have the chance to build my own family." If there's something about

yourself that you want to change, then the first step is to identify it and then write how your story might play out differently.
Get to writing, because I love you very much, but I'm sorry to
say that we don't magically grow into new people.

One of my favorite quotes in the entire world is from Nora
Ephron. In her commencement address to the Wellesley College Class of 1996 (which I highly recommend you watch on
YouTube *immediately*), she urged the graduates to "above all, be
the heroine of your life, not the victim." There is no better
place to live those words than in a journal. You have the ability
to *literally* write your own story, to slay your worries, to un-
bridle your dreams. You can be the version of yourself who
wears a dress made of all the night's stars like it ain't no thing,
who floats above the petty little annoyances of life and looks
back down on Earth with clear, peaceful perspective. You can't
control the narrative of the outside world, but you can control
the story you are telling yourself in your journal. I suggest you
make it a good one.

A List of Ways to NOT Avoid Journaling in the Morning

1. If you are avoiding writing because you have a new person sleeping over at your place, get out of bed, grab your
   notebook, and go into the kitchen. Make some coffee
   and write while doing it. Three pages of single-spaced
   writing takes about twenty minutes. When you return,
   two coffees in hand, they will be none the wiser and
   impressed that you were so thoughtful! GO, YOU!

2. If you are avoiding journaling because you are sleeping
   over at a new person's place, that is stupid. Sorry, but it
   is. Tell them you have Pilates, spinning, or brunch with
   your sister, and get to your notebook! Or bring it with

you and tell the person the truth: You are a goddamn adult with a goddamn ritual. If the person is weirded out by this: NEXT.

3. If you are avoiding journaling because you DON'T HAVE TIME, none of us has time. Beyoncé has no time. She has three children but still manages to be *Beyoncé*. You can find the time. Set your alarm to wake up ten minutes earlier tomorrow. Try to do that for the rest of the week. Then next week set it for *twenty* minutes earlier. Start small. You can do it. I know you can! I forced myself, ten minutes at a time, to carve out an hour of alone time in the morning. It took me months (maybe more like a year if I'm being totally honest) to make it stick, but now I have an hour to journal, light a candle, hang out, and day-dream every morning. It's fantastic and gives me something to look forward to when my alarm goes off.

4. If you are avoiding journaling because it's "dumb" or "self-centered" or because only "broken narcissists" keep journals, let me tell you this: Mark Twain kept a journal. Frida Kahlo kept a diary full of illustrations and her thoughts. Charlotte Brontë kept a diary, and Leonardo da Vinci kept around fifty notebooks. Ida B. Wells crusaded for civil rights in America and still found time to keep a diary. Albert Einstein, Marie Curie, Susan Sontag—they all kept journals. Do you think you're above Mark Twain, Frida Kahlo, Charlotte Brontë, and Leonardo da Vinci, Ida B. Wells, Albert Einstein, Marie Curie, and Susan Sontag? No? Then get to writing.

5. If you are avoiding journaling because you think you will fail and it seems hard and you would rather not

start something you might mess up, know this: It's okay to fail. I write my pages most mornings, but I skipped them yesterday because of item two above (sleeping over at someone's house). I forgot to bring my journal with me, and when the boy offered to take me to breakfast (*yay!*), I caved and went with him. And ya know what? That's fine. I did feel a little uneasy for the rest of the day, but I understood why. When I opened my nightstand this morning and saw my new journal, light blue and with navy ribbons, I felt a deep rush of happiness. My notebook waits for me.

Writing Prompts to Jump-Start Your Inner DM

Sometimes, getting started journaling seems really daunting. Where does one even begin? You begin exactly where you are, my dear. Here are some prompts to use as jumper cables for your writing. Let's go!

1. **"Today, here is what I feel in my heart . . ."** Keep writing until you've emptied out all of the things you are currently feeling.

2. **"Today, here are ten things I like about myself . . ."** If this is incredibly difficult to do, you still MUST do it. You must COMPLETE the list. When you complete it, please send it to me. I know how hard it is to write down what you actually value about yourself, and I'm proud/happy/excited to read what you wrote!

3. **"Today, I am grateful for this very small thing that happened yesterday . . ."** Let it be something slight but nice. Did you see some great flowers? Did someone from your past email to say hi? Appreciate a

little thing. If you can't think of something, your home-work is to find one little thing to relish later today. Yes, I just assigned you homework. Deal with it.

4. **"Dearest Journal, I have a question I have been mulling over in my brain and I thought you might have an answer . . ."** Write down just the question today, and then tomorrow be prepared to be amazed when you can answer it more easily. Your "journal" (i.e., innermost self) might have answers you don't.

5. **"Here is what I want people to say about me when I'm not around . . ."** How do you want to be known and perceived? This is a useful tool for uncovering the kind of person you are working toward being. What accomplishments would they laud? What characteristics would they love about you?

6. **"If nothing else mattered—not money, not other people's expectations, not kids, not jobs, nothing—my dream day would look like . . ."** Be super specific! What do you DO in your dream day? Do you eat a chocolate croissant looking out over the Seine? Do you run a business where you've hired all of your friends and you sit at the head of a reclaimed-wood boardroom table? Visualize every aspect of that day because THAT is the day we are working toward. I wonder, are there little elements of it you can achieve now? Go get a croissant; tell them to add it to my tab.

7. **"Today, I set an intention to act with . . ."** Write out how you will carry yourself today. Do you want to work on focusing on one task at a time? Do you feel

like you've been a little mean to your roommate lately (Why can't she load the dishwasher correctly?! Is she trying to drive me crazy?!) and so you want to act with more affection (OMG STOP, Tara! Who cares about the dirty dishes! She's your best friend; she deserves kindness, not you being so nitpicky!)? Check in with yourself throughout the day and see how it worked out.

8. **"There is something I've ALWAYS wanted to deal with, but I haven't for some reason. Here goes . . ."** It's amazing, but most of the time we actually know what we most need to tackle. We just need to commit to it.

If you find yourself writing, "I don't have a boyfriend," "I don't have the job I want," "I don't have a flat stomach," write instead about what you DO have. "I have awesome friends," "I have a candle that makes me happy," "I have money in the bank and food on my table." It will make you feel better and reframe your perspective to notice what you do have. Every. Single. Time.

~~When Life Hands You a Lemon, Stick a Pen in It and Turn It into a Bong~~
Nah, Don't Self-Medicate

JOURNALING WAS MY FIRST STEP toward self-care, but it would not have been effective without the help of another important decision. A decision I really, *really* did not want to make.

Now would be a great time to tell you that by the age of twenty-five, I was miserably, hopelessly, frustratingly dependent on weed. I had been using it since high school as a way to blunt, dull, and totally ignore both my childhood and the constant nervousness I felt swirling in my stomach and brain. Weed had put up a smoke screen that hid my problems from my awareness and made it possible for me to keep moving forward. That strategy had helped me survive, in a way. But weed had so effectively helped me to dissociate from my memories that eventually I dissociated from *myself*. It was hard to tell how I truly felt about anything.

One morning, a few months into my journaling practice, I sat at the micro-table in the kitchen-slash-study-slash-dining-room of my closet-like apartment, writing about my anxiety about not having the "right" job. I was a production assistant at

the time, barely hanging on to the bottom rung of the entertainment ladder. I wasn't bothered by the idea that I needed to
work my way up; I knew I had to pay my dues. Instead, what
made me so anxious was that I didn't know *what* I was working
my way up to. What ladder was I supposed to climb? What
should be my dream job? What would be fulfilling? My friends
all seemed further along than me, working in jobs that had
foreseeable futures or studying in grad schools for careers that
would set them down a predictable path. "If I don't have it
figured out by now, I never will," I hopelessly scrawled. I had
been in therapy for *years,* on and off for most of my life, but I
couldn't seem to make much progress in terms of my destructive behavior. When faced with anxiety, I had no power to stop
myself from diving nose-first into a spiral of weed and doom.

Instinctively, I got out of my chair to grab my weed and
smoke all my worries away. But I froze mid-movement, seized
by a thought: If I smoked away this feeling, if I didn't allow it
to exist, if I didn't wrestle with my anxiety, then I would never
truly *know* myself. What was more terrifying: having to deal
with my feelings or never getting to meet my true self?

I had been accidentally introduced to weed by my father in
high school, when my parents' divorce was in year three. There
was screaming. So. Much. Screaming. On the phone at each
other and in cruel emails in SCREAMING CAPS, and if my
parents couldn't get ahold of each other, they would scream at
my sister and me. "YOUR *MOTHER** IS FUCKING CRAZY
AND DRIVING US BROKE WITH HER LAWYERS."
"YOUR *FATHER* DOESN'T CARE ABOUT YOU AND
HAS STOLEN ALL OF OUR MONEY." My dad once
shrieked so hard that he clenched down on his jaw and one of

---

*   My parents have a lovely way of making the words "mother" and "father" sound like
insults.

his teeth exploded. He had to get a rod inserted into his gums and have a new replacement tooth built from scratch. When I think about that screaming now, I can feel the tension in my muscle memory. My ears get hot and tingly and strain to close up like little folded sheets.

Around this time (the screaming time), I noticed that my dad must be smoking what I had heard about in so many Snoop Dogg songs at bar/bat mitzvahs: marijuana. After school, in my dad's bachelor pad on Mount Olympus,* I would smell something skunky. I'd walk into my dad's room to kiss him good night and would have to listen to a lecture about how the movie *Moulin Rouge* was "the purest expression of love." I was fairly confident it was just an *okay* film. In the long forgotten year of 2002, weed was not the ubiquitous, socially acceptable pastime it is now in California. I felt ashamed that my dad was doing "drugs." Moreover, as far as I was concerned, my dad was my *only* parent at that point, and so it terrified me when he was high. I should explain.

By this time in my parents' divorce, my mom and dad, exhausted from fighting, split my sister and me up. Yes, you heard that right: My parents split up their children, *Parent Trap*–style (but with no fun pranks, sing-alongs, or unrealistically blissful reconciliations in the end). Diana stayed with my mom, and I went to live with my dad. That way there didn't have to be any pickups or drop-offs. That way my parents hardly had to see or speak to each other. No one ever asked my sister and me if we were cool with this plan. SPOILER: WE WERE NOT. We were angry, confused, and fucking sad that we wouldn't be able to see each other regularly. My parents didn't consider how my

---

*   This is a real-life housing development based on the Greek gods, built by real-life adults. I lived on Electra Drive. Just off Hercules Drive. No joke.

sister and I would maintain a relationship. My parents didn't consider anything at all.

My connection with my mom, which had always been tenuous, was also quickly deteriorating. Throughout my childhood, she had been a constant source of criticism, but now that I was out of her house, she took it upon herself to leave voicemails that erased all doubt of what she thought of me. "Hi, Tara, it's your mother. You are a pathological liar and greedy and only care about money. Call me when you get a chance. I love you." *Message deleted.* "Hi, Tara, you are bad and evil and just like your father who is scum and I won't let you see your sister and destroy *her* unless you get your nails done with *me* first. Call me if you want to get a pedicure." *Message deleted.* Here is what you need to know: I believed my dad was the only reliable parent I had. So I didn't judge him for being high; instead, I dreaded that in a fucked-up state, he would not be able to rescue me from the various disasters I always assumed were right around the corner.

While my dad was smoking a lot of herb to escape his reality, I was working my ass off in high school so that I might eventually flee mine. I wanted out of Los Angeles. I wanted out of my family. I wanted to be rescued by college. In a new place, with new friends and new supportive adults (the wise professors I would surely meet), I would be saved and then this whole so-sad-it's-almost-funny-but-it's-not-actually-funny-I've-just-learned-to-laugh-at-horrible-things childhood would be behind me.

I set my sights on Brown University, which had the distinction of both being geographically as far removed from Los Angeles as possible *and* having no math requirement. I hate math. I knew Brown was a hard school to get into, and so, like my hero Jay-Z, I became committed to the game of winning—

high school, that is. I would hustle for these grades, son. I took all of the AP classes, I participated in all of the extracurriculars, I did all of your basic "I want to go to a good school" things, but I also put my own brand of swagger on it. I was in our honors theater company. I wrote sketches for our school assemblies. At lunch, I was either running my school's literary magazine, leading a panel discussion on a new schoolwide honor code, or fomenting a revolution by founding a protest movement to bring Coca-Cola back to the cafeteria after a vegan mom insisted that soda was *the major* evil of our day. I was friends with the teachers. I went to their homes for dinner. No adult was pushing me to do *any* of this. In fact, I don't think my dad ever asked to *see* my grades. But I felt like I needed to do all of the things, right now, or I would not survive.

My dad's smoking at home was a nightly thorn in my side, and so I asked my school's "human development" teacher for advice. Mrs. Kelley's job was to guide our malleable child minds into fully developed adult minds. It was essentially sex-ed meets group therapy: She would tell us to use condoms, and the class would complain about how Madeline Beck was the biggest bitch in high school. I explained my situation: My dad smoked weed at home constantly and it made me uncomfortable. Not only did it make me worry about my own safety, but I just didn't like to see my dad act so out of it. Again: *Moulin Rouge* is just an *okay* movie and I was tired of being told otherwise. Mrs. Kelley laughed. "I bet he doesn't even *know* that *you* know." *Oh,* I thought, *maybe this just was a miscommunication? Maybe my dad just thought I was too young to know what was going on???* "All you need to do is tell him how you are feeling. He'll respect you."

With Mrs. Kelley's advice in mind, one day at home, post-studying, I walked into the living room to find my dad watching the evening news. He paused it and asked what was on my mind. "Hmm. Well, this is hard to bring up, but it's important to me. Dad, I love you, but when you smoke weed in the house it makes me uncomfortable. Would you maybe consider smoking less? Or not in the house? Or just not when I'm here?" GOOD LORD each one of those words felt like carrying a boulder up a hill. Difficult to push out and hard to balance. As I waited for his reaction, I felt like my chest was going to explode with anticipation. Finally, he looked me in the eye and replied, "Tara, don't make me choose between the weed and you."

That was the precise moment I decided to start smoking. *Fuck it,* I thought. *Why not try weed?* If it was helping my dad, then maybe it would help me. And it would be so easy! There was a free and—I assumed—good supply in the house. I went straight into my dad's closet, opened a little wooden box with gold hinges, and found a stash of vacuum-packed herbs with names like "OG Kush" and "Purple Haze." I pilfered as much as I wanted. I didn't think he would notice if a little MJ went missing from his hefty reserve.

My first time smoking was a revelation. Alone in my room, holding a cheap glass pipe to my lips, I watched the smoke billow out of my mouth. It unclenched my mind and eased my anxieties as I listened to the Beastie Boys on a loop. I breathed in the weed and exhaled my worries about college, my fear of impending disaster, and my sadness about my family. I could now listen to my mom's voicemails and laugh. "Hi, Tara. You're a liar who needs psychiatric help because you're sick like your father. Call me when you have a chance. It's your mother." *HA. How funny was that?! Like, what a NOT MOM message. HAHAHA.* Weed let me laugh off things that were truly not funny.

I was hustling as hard as I could to get into a good college, but I was also trying just as hard to obliterate myself, and, oddly enough, it worked. By the time I graduated high school, I was given the "Bruce Belt Silver Bowl Award" for the student who "most raised the bar for academic and intellectual integrity and achievement." I packed up my trophy bowl and my weed bowl and headed to Brown, where I continued to smoke away my reality. How does the saying go? "When life hands you a lemon, stick a pen in it and turn it into a bong."

To be very clear, weed never once made me more creative. Weed never helped me unlock some secret part of myself I couldn't otherwise unleash. Weed obscured the parts of myself I wasn't ready to meet and allowed me to dissociate from my moods. By the time I turned twenty-five, weed had successfully helped me outrun my childhood, but the person I met at the end of the race was a burned-out hull who didn't know herself. My smoking had gotten so habitual that if I wrote down an uncomfortable thought in my journal, if I had a cold, if my electric bill was more expensive than I had anticipated, I felt a reflexive, gravitational pull toward my pipe. It was the way I dealt with everything. But if I was going to actually understand and untangle the clusterfuck that currently was my mind, then I knew I would have to be *not-high* long enough to at least feel my own feelings.

I sat at my "kitchen table" (honestly, it was more of a cabinet with a drop leaf you could swing out to turn it into a semi-straight surface) paralyzed with indecision. Smoking would be *such* an easy way to escape this moment. But what kind of life was I leading if I was perpetually fleeing from it? I walked into my bedroom-slash-living-room-slash-TV-room, reached into my nightstand, and pulled out my pipe and weed. I took the pipe and threw it into my kitchen trash. I emptied Greek yogurt on top of it so I wouldn't be tempted to fish it out of the garbage. That would be a humiliation even I could not endure.

Then I went into the bathroom, chucked my weed into the toilet, and, as quickly as I could, I flushed. On Post-it Notes I wrote, "Weed no longer works for you, I'm so sorry," and stuck them around my apartment.

Today, there is no world in which I would consider touching weed. I can't have half of your marshmallow edible, even tho it's supz high quality and artisanal and I am sure it's just as fun as you say it is. I can't smoke with you before a movie date, because if I do, my body will reject the THC and I will projectile vomit onto your living room wall. That's a true story. That's exactly what happened the last time I smoked. ON A FIRST DATE. I simply can't mess with weed, and I don't want to either. I now prefer my own company to the numbed-out way I used to feel.

So let me ask you this, as delicately as I can: *What's your weed?* You might not be as dependent on something as I was, but still, is there a substance or behavior you run to when you want to feel safe and warm and comfortable but you know, deep down, isn't so good for you? I'm not talking about the little treats we indulge in; I'm not asking about the special cupcake you get whenever you're at that particularly excellent bakery on the other side of town. I'm talking about the four middling cupcakes you buy at the supermarket after a breakup and eat in one sitting. I'm talking about the glass of rosé at home alone after a hard day's work that becomes two, then three, then, *why not,* the whole bottle. I'm asking about the time when, after a nasty fight with your boyfriend, you watched four hours of reality television until your mind was numb. I'm asking about when you catch yourself saying, "I had a hard day, I *need* this," or "I had a hard day, I *deserve* this." Chances are, if you are justifying something you are doing as a means to "deal" with your day, then it's probably not a great idea. Listen to how silly this sounds: "My meeting was awful today, I *need* to breathe oxygen." "I got into a major fight with my boyfriend, I *deserve* a glass of water." We don't justify the healthy things.

The problem with self-medicating is that it doesn't work. I am so, so, so sorry to tell you this. I wish it did. The cupcakes don't treat the heartache; the wine doesn't make your boss any less of a screamer; the reality television is just making us all dumber, I'm pretty sure; and the weed doesn't make your childhood better. These actions might blunt the pain you feel in this moment, but they can't possibly heal the root causes of your uneasiness.

Please don't feel bad or criticize yourself if you know *exactly* what I'm talking about. It takes a lot of courage just to recognize when we are self-medicating. It means we are willing to look at our lives and see them for what they actually are. Not the pretend, made-for-Instagram life in which having a bottle of wine to dull our evening is cute and glamorous (#RoséAllDay), but the real life in which we know that we are pouring the wine into some deep, empty part of us that needs to be filled.

The author, and one of my personal heroes, Cheryl Strayed describes these dark places within us as "wounds." Traumas that are deeply suppressed, hard to see, incredibly tender to the touch, difficult to heal, but always present. I now visualize them as actual lesions on my soul: big, bloody gashes that need nurturing (*and not weed, Tara!*) in order to heal. These ancient wounds, the ones that cut us most deeply and lurk deep within us, if brought to the light, examined, and healed correctly, can be the source of profound revelation instead of throbbing, seemingly inexplicable pain. What important lesson or wisdom have you learned that *didn't* come from something harrowing? If you're anything like me, the answer is, "Eh . . . not much." Somehow, by seeing these wounds as something physical, I'm less tempted to try to treat them with things I know won't work. It's time to allow those wounds to exist without trying to serve them a pint of ice cream. Both you and I know that the only thing you can expect is a melted, sticky mess of an emotional state. It's time to stop self-medicating and start allowing yourself to feel your feelings—even the most awful ones. I know it sucks, but I'm right here with you (hi!). I get how incredibly difficult giving up a crutch can be, but unless you have a broken leg, that crutch is only getting in your way.

I'm proud of you already. As I said, it takes courage to face something we are doing that we know ain't great. I have some ideas on how you can put the pipe/wineglass/spoon down.

A List of Ways to Stop Doing That Destructive Thing You Do

1. **Figure out your crutch.** Get honest with yourself: What's the thing you know you don't want to be involved with as much as you are? What's the *very first* thing that comes to mind? Is it making out with random folks in bars? Is it eating ice cream straight from the pint on a day you wanted to be "healthy"? Is it drinking so much that you have to stock emergency Trader Joe's pizzas in the freezer to soak up the massive amounts of booze you know you will consume this weekend? I have done all of these things to "feel better," so no shade, no judgment. Write it down.

2. Okay, can't be honest? **Recognize the thing your friends tease you about the most.** Write it down, circle it, and just think about it for a minute. I'm not saying your friends are right, but if more than one of them has joked that you are so addicted to work that

"your schedule is allergic to friendship," you might want to consider that most jokes hold some truth. If your friends tease that you "have an alcohol problem" and tell you they are "proud you didn't fall down drunk last night," I would suggest that's probably not much of a JKJKJK situation.

3. **Write down your crutch and why it doesn't work for you on a Post-it Note and stick it to your bathroom mirror.** Examples: "Weed makes me feel bad." "Staying at work too long exhausts me." "Too much chardonnay makes me cry." Read and reread this note until it sinks in. This could take weeks. Months. But it's hard to ignore something you have to read every time you look in the mirror, and, eventually, you'll *feel* this truth.

4. **Baby-step away from the crutch by making a deal with yourself that you can keep.** There should be a real reward involved. *If I don't smoke weed this week, I get to take a bubble bath on Sunday. If I leave the office by six P.M. at least three times this week, then I get to buy myself a delicious-smelling candle. If I take a break from drinking at home this week, then I get to go for a thirty-dollar Thai massage.*

5. **Consider how the deal worked out.** Did you keep it? If you did, how do you feel? And if you didn't, then it's time to make a new deal. One that you're more likely to keep. But DO NOT beat yourself up. Giving up any habit is difficult and takes time! The good news is you are replacing your bad habit with a good one— a habit of self-care. You'll like it more! I swear.

6. **Be patient. Srsly.** If you've successfully identified your distracting crutch, then you have already done something radically brave: You have been honest about a weakness that does not serve you. That's SO FUCK-ING HARD. I would like to high-five you, then hug you, then give you a kiss on the forehead.

Is that too much? I'm just proud of you, that's all.

When I Get Anxious, I Get Moving
Exercise Is for the Brain

AS SOON AS I STOPPED smoking weed, three super-cool things happened: 1) Without the numbing qualities of the drug, I found out I had an awesome case of physical anxiety that was so bad I could not sleep at night or fully function during the day; 2) A breakup I had numbly experienced months ago—pre–birthday disaster night—decided to rear its ugly head; 3) My long-blunted, now-uncovered anxiety fed on said breakup, making me an insecure, nervous mess. Now, to be clear, it was a good thing that I got dumped. Keats and I had a massively unhealthy relationship. And it pains me to say this, because I like to be right, BUT: A lot of it was my fault. I had dated Keats in college and "decided" to move in with him after graduation. To use the term "decided" here is a bit of revisionist history. It was more like I was so upset with the prospect of graduating that I collapsed into Keats and he carried me away to his apartment in New York City.

Leaving college was a grueling process. I had spent so much effort to get there, and now, just because it had been four years, I had to leave? OH, HELL NO. I clung to the walls of my room, telling anyone who would listen how "unfair" it was that they were "kicking me out." When Keats proposed that I move in with him in New York, I was too distraught to think about other options. "I'll take care of you, my little demon lover," he devotedly reassured me. Keats was a theater kid in the most intense definition of the word: He spoke with drama, often invoking Shakespeare to prove his grandiose points; he wore long black overcoats with scarves that made him look like a modern Oscar Wilde; and his father was an artisan loot maker (yes, that is a real thing), and Keats couldn't understand why anyone would take a job that did not serve Art with a capital A. Our whole relationship revolved around me being this emotionally splintered mess whom Keats, with melodramatic flourish, would Frankenstein back together. I would then push him as far away as possible in an attempt to show him (and possibly myself) that I was unlovable. I WAS SUPER COOL AND KIND. Could he forgive me for shouting at him in Grand Central Station, "I AM THE BEST YOU CAN DO!"? And for telling him that he would "never leave me"? *Ugh.* Could he forgive me for making out with a skinny hipster boy we both knew from college AT A PARTY WHERE KEATS WAS ONE ROOM AWAY? *Jeeeez. I really wish I hadn't done that.* Could he forgive me for smoking weed in the bathroom while his parents were visiting? *Insert emoji of a girl with her palm on forehead.* But he did forgive me! He most certainly shouldn't have, but there was something in it for Keats, as there is in all codependent nightmare situations: He considered me his property.

Just how much was he in control of me? Let me show you. In college, my roommate Fisch would often sheepishly come into my room to inform me that "Keats is lurking outside on the quad. . . . He's got on that coat and he's just staring into your room. It's beyond creepy." I thought it was kind of nice. Someone was paying attention to me! He was jealous of *anyone* who talked to me. After we moved to New York, when Diana came to visit us in our apartment, he locked himself in a closet and cried. "If your sister is here, when will WE be together?" *Well, we live together, so . . . all of the time?* I was "in between opportunities" at the moment, looking for my first adult job after college, and he was actually *hurt* that I would consider something full-time. (I graduated at the height of the 2008 recession and was finding it really difficult to get *any* consistent work.) Why, he whined, would I stoop to an entry-level job when I could sit at home all day and watch *The Wire* with him? When I explained to him that I needed money, that I didn't have a trust fund to live off of like he did, that the only reason I could be with him in New York at all was that he offered me a free place to live, through tears and a flushed face, he choked out, "WHAT ARE YOUR PRIORITIES EVEN?" When I finally landed my first job, one that came with something called "insurance," he didn't congratulate me, he didn't celebrate me. He felt hurt that he would have to share me with work.

We both knew the relationship had to end, but when it did, I was shocked that he cut off all contact with me. Some people imagine getting married to the person they love, but I imagined having a tortured, turbulent "will-they-won't-they" with him, forever. I fantasized that we would break up, I would move a few blocks away, and we would alternatively cry at coffee shops together, make out against city walls, and tell our friends that "love is just so complicated. You get it, right?" But he didn't want to see me. He didn't want to talk to me. He certainly didn't want to make out with me. He wanted exactly none of my noise.

Without weed to dull my restlessness and without Keats to soothe said restlessness, I began to experience my anxiety, fully, for the first time. I felt a constant knot in my chest. It lived above my left breast, on a shelf next to my heart. I would knead it all day, hoping I could work it out. This searing pain of angst would radiate into my armpit, and now I was the girl rubbing her left breast and armpit on the corner of West Tenth Street and Sixth Avenue. *Cute.* I would wake up in my apartment with a mystery migraine at the back of my head, biting down so strongly that little black dots would fly into my vision. The clenching then radiated pain through my skull, and I was finally able to understand how my dad had exploded his own tooth. Keats had abandoned me. Just like my parents had abandoned me. Just like college had abandoned me.

Nothing could get the anxiety of desertion out of my mind. Not going to my friends Alexandra and Alice's apartment to work on a play we were writing (I usually love playwriting!). Not a vacation to London with a friend who happened to have a free place to stay (I usually love travel! Esp *free* travel!). Nope. My eyes were red and puffy from constant tears. I stopped washing my hair. Who could wash their hair at a time like this? I looked like a crazy person. I *was* a crazy person. This lasted for four months.

I wrote out in my journal possible solutions: "Double down on therapy. Pills. ~~Weed.~~ Move away to a town where someone will love me (what town???). ~~Weed.~~" More therapy seemed like the easiest option, and so I began to see Dr. Goldstein twice a week. Could I afford this? Absolutely not. Was I a wreck most of the day and so nothing else mattered but getting better? Absolutely yes. But luckily, I had chosen Dr. Goldstein because she was the only therapist who accepted my new health insurance, so all I had to take care of was the co-pay. (P.S. I *highly* recommend finding a therapist who will either accept your insurance or, if you don't have insurance, offer a sliding scale where you pay based on what you can.) I made myself a deal: I would eat and drink out less so I could pay for regular therapy.

Dr. Goldstein suggested wearing rubber bands on my wrists so that when the obsessive thoughts looped in my head, I could snap the bands against my skin and say, "Let go. Let go." Somehow, the pain would change the neural pathways in my brain and help reprogram my thinking. Instead of thinking, *I am abandoned,* my brain would say, *Ouch! That thought doesn't pay off.* As weird a solution as that sounded, it did help. The little, harsh snaps gave me momentary breaks from my panic, but by the end of a month, my wrists looked like I was into some serious S&M play.

I rewrote my list of possible cures for anxiety: "Weed." *Ugh, no weed, Tara.* "Get drunk? Phone a friend?" Maybe there was someone in my life who was dealing with anxiety in a healthier way? I decided to ask the calmest person I knew what she did to keep an even keel. Julia was one of my best friends and roommates from Brown, and she had witnessed both the "Keats is lurking outside of the dorm" and my "college is dumping me" periods. Even though I don't think she was particularly happy to leave school, she never looked panicked or worried or like she might jump out of a window. I knew she had gone through her fair share of tough times, but she's one of those people who exude composure, even mid-crisis. I wanted that.

"So Jules," I asked, "what's your deal? Why do you never look like you're going to have a full-blown panic attack? Are you just good at faking looking normal? WHAT IS YOUR SECRET?" She laughed. "Sometimes I'm stressed, *obviously,* but to get through it, I usually go for a run."

That was her *secret? She went on a run?* Bullshit. My anxiety was SO important! My turbulent state SO DEEP. A silly little *run* wouldn't help me! I pressed her. "I don't know anything about running or sports; I'm a theater kid! I've never moved, aside from pacing across a stage." Afraid of sports? The first person to leave when a small table needs to be moved? Suspicious of my own body and unwilling to look in the mirror when naked? Yes, yes, yes, of course, to all of those things. I am an "indoor kid" to the core. In high school, the only C I ever got was in a class called Cardio Fitness. Coach Flores wrote on my report card that I "hid between treadmills" and took "excessive water breaks to avoid actually working out." And she was right! I DIDN'T WANT TO WORK OUT.

I explained to Julia that I had very practical reasons why running would not work for me. "My boobs hurt too much when I run. When they bounce, it's actually painful *and* makes me feel stupid." She replied that there were such things as "sports bras." "Yeah, but the one time I ever jogged, my ankles bugged me. I think I have bad ankles." She cheerily explained, "There's a great shoe store close to your apartment that videotapes your stride to figure out how to correct it. They will find the perfect sneakers for you!" Julia even pointed out that I lived right next to the Hudson River, which would make for a beautiful running backdrop. To every single one of my paper-thin excuses, Julia had an easy solution. *Fucking Julia.*

To be real with you, I think I was *scared* of working out. As a young kid, I was chubby and embarrassed of my little potbelly. In middle school, I lived in perma-dread of the annual Presidential Physical Fitness Test. (Did you have this at your school? Was it nationwide?) It was a series of tests meant to gauge our fitness level through arbitrary assessments that we students never trained for. For me, it was a much-feared, shameful time of year when I would be forced to demonstrate all of the things I could *not* do in front of *all* of my classmates. Pull-ups? High jumps? Sit on the ground, place a weird metal box on top of me, and lamely push a slider over my legs with my fingertips to show how close I could get my fingers to my toes? Spoiler: I could not touch my toes EVER. The worst by far, however, was the dreaded mile run. I remember running the mile when I was ten years old on my middle school's black asphalt parking lot. My parents hadn't remembered to send a "sports" outfit with me to school, so, as the California sun beat down on us, I ran in my tights, gabardine uniform, and saddle shoes. *Saddle shoes.* I came in dead last. The kind of last where all of the other students had filed back into the classroom while Coach Rodriguez disappointedly looked at his stopwatch, wondering if he should just let me quit or if I needed to finish. It was humiliating for both of us.

Over time, I had turned that fear of failing into a kind of pride. It wasn't that I *couldn't* work out, it was that I was sooo above it. Wasn't there something cool about the fact that I had never physically exerted myself? I would *boast* to people that I "never worked out a day in my life." I mean, who even had time to work out?! Well . . . Julia did. Julia, whom I respected, admired, and wanted to emulate. She had played soccer all through high school and college. And she was the calmest person I knew. Julia had a conceivable solution for my anxiety where I had none. UGH. Okay. Fine. I would try her advice. But I wasn't going to like it. AND it wasn't going to work.

I bought a stupid purple sports bra that gave me a uniboob. I went to the store that videotapes your stride and bought even stupider orange-and-white sneakers, the bulky kind dads wear to embarrass their kids. With the recent failure of my relationship burning in my mind, I incredulously started with small goals I knew I *could* achieve. Run for one Feist* song. Run from one stop sign to the next stop sign. Run for ten minutes

---

* This is how much I didn't know about running: I ran to lovely, but SLOW, heartbreaking acoustic songs. LOVE Feist, but maybe not the best "pump-up" running jams?

without a break. *Oh boy, that's too hard.* Okay, run for five minutes without a break. My lungs stung, my thighs felt like they were on fire, and I would sometimes think, *I can't do this.* But just as I had learned to do in my journaling, I decided to flip the story. I began to repeat, "Yes, I *can* do this," even when I thought I could not. "Yes, I *can* run from one pier to the next." "Yes, I *can* finish this godforsaken run." I repeated this phrase to myself so many times that it started to become true: I *could* complete the modest goals I had set for myself. To be clear, I *hated* the actual running. I would give up *the second* I reached whatever small target I had set for myself. But where I used to feel dread pushing down on my chest like a stack of well-laid bricks, I now began to feel room to breathe.

As I built up my slight successes, I began to like the fact that if I ran for a little longer, my hair would get damp and I could taste salt on my lips, that my cheeks would turn red and I would feel hot inside. I liked that if I ran from my apartment, down along the river, and then back, my clothes would be completely wet with sweat and I would have to peel them off as they clung to my skin. I liked throwing my sweaty knot of spandex into the hamper and hearing a thud. I couldn't believe I had made my clothes heavy with sweat! Kinda gross, but also pretty fucking cool.

Running blasted through that anxiety knot in my chest. The more I moved, the more I was able to shake loose the mean little bullet of worry that had lodged itself in my heart. There was something cathartic about the motion of pushing myself forward. The movement itself broke up the harsh thought loops in my head. My journal from the time is full of revelations like "Whoa, who knew working out was a *thing*?" and "Thank goodness I am exercising, it feels really good." As I ran, I stopped keeping tally of how many days I cried or felt panic; instead, I was able to count days unmarred with anxiety. "Day TEN, count them—TEN!—of no crushing anxiety!!! No tears!"The running gave me physically good feelings, but, more important, it gave me a larger sense of triumph.

Working out for me is now nonnegotiable. It is my preventive measure against the anxiety that lurks in my mind. I *must* throw myself out of bed in the morning and make it to the gym because I will *always, always* feel better for it. When I go on a trip, be it vacation or business, I *always* wear my running shoes on the plane so I have no excuse not to work out when I land. If I'm having a super-busy/stressful week at work, even more reason to deliberately schedule a half hour to sweat in the morning. Hungover, tired, just not in the mood? I don't give myself an out. The simple reason is that I have never once shown up to the gym and regretted it. When I tell people this, I usually hear something about how "disciplined" I must be. To be clear, I am not disciplined. I just ate a three-day-old black-and-white cookie because I found it in my living room. Working out sucks. Getting breathless hurts. But exercise gets me out of my spinning head. It's a moving meditation that forces me to feel my body, be present, and focus on a goal: Just get the running done.

You were right, Julia. *Fucking Julia.*

What's *Your* Running?

> *Do you have a physical way to ease your mind? Something that makes you a little sweaty and is difficult enough to complete that you simply can't think about whatever is pre-occupying your attention? If running isn't your thing, might I suggest some alternatives that are not terrible? Well. I mean, all working out is a little terrible, but I can actually PROMISE YOU that exercise, done with regularity, WILL MAKE YOU HAPPIER. It's nuts how effective it is. But you have to stick with it!*

1. **Try a class you enjoy at your gym/YMCA/the park next to your apartment where other people will suffer with you.** It's easier to do something wretched like squats in a group setting. Misery loves company. Spin! Pilates! Barre! A group class, taught by an instructor, forces you to listen and follow along, two things that make thinking/obsessing/worrying very difficult. Take every class you hear about until you find one you *kinda* like. You can stick with something you *kinda* like.

2. **Find an Internet video you can do at home.** My friend Fisch, who just had her first baby, found a *superhot* Australian woman online who makes YouTube exercise videos that are fun and require NO equipment. Fisch has no excuse not to work out if she can do it in her house, to the soothing, peppy words of an Aussie as her daughter naps/plays/raises hell in her playpen.

3. **Take a long-ass walk during your lunch break.** If you are strapped for time, use your lunch break to take a walk. Get away from your office, set a timer, and don't come back to work until your walk is over. Cram a sandwich in your face when your walk is complete. Thirty minutes is a good amount of time. Too hot outside and don't want to get sweaty? Why not walk up and down the stairs *inside* your air-conditioned building? Snowing outside? I've spent a lot of time in Wisconsin; I know there are whole caves-slash-cities within your buildings. No excuses. You can always figure out how to take a walk.

4. **Sweat with friends.** Instead of brunch, what about a hike with your friends? Or how about trying that new group class taught by the cut Australian dudes you heard

about? (*What is going on with me and Australians rn?*) Going with your friends makes you accountable to other people, and if you *like* your friends, it will be guaranteed fun even if it's super hard. You can also commiserate with them at the end of the class.

5. **Ask an athlete.** We all have friends who are pros at working out and actually know something about how the human body works. Find your friend who played soccer in college, ask your colleague who's on the company volleyball team, seek out the person in your life who knows about exercise, and see if they'll teach you. Ask them to show you some routines that you can do at the gym or by yourself. They will LOVE to do this, because everyone loves feeling like an expert.

No matter what you choose, make sure you can actually do it, regularly. Please do not go from "never working out" to "I signed up for a marathon." That *rarely,* if ever, works and ultimately makes you feel disappointed in yourself. Instead, choose something small that you can do with consistency. You can take a walk in your neighborhood three times this week. You can do four ten-minute Internet workout videos at home. *Yes, you can.* Mark in your calendar the three days this week you will work out and make AN ACTUAL PLAN for *how* you will do this. Whatever special considerations you need to make, do them now. No, I'm not kidding. Make the plan now. I'm waiting.

And, again, I can't be clearer with you: It WILL work. If you work out regularly, you WILL be happier. So stop complaining, trust me, and *try.* What's the worst-case scenario? You get mad at me for making you work out? I can take it.

I Tell Myself I Am Grateful for Everything, Even When I Am Grateful for Nothing

Fake Gratitude Until You Feel Gratitude

I WAS INCORPORATING NEW PRACTICES into my life. I was journaling, I was not getting so high that I'd forget who I was, and, by some miracle, I was using my human body to exercise regularly (which was still SO WEIRD to me). Over the course of six months, I was starting to feel better—or at least not like a total disaster. Around that time, my BFF Isabelle—the same Isabelle who suggested I start writing in a journal—invited me on vacation with her family in Maine.

Maine? I dragged my feet. Isabelle's family are WASPs of the highest order. They came to America on the *ARBELLA*. What's the *Arbella,* you ask? Oh, it was just the boat John Winthrop took to America in the same fleet as THE *MAYFLOWER*. Her family are libertarians with a zealot's faith in the virtues of capitalism, and they talk an awful lot about skiing. I am a Jew who is so liberal I've fallen off the political spectrum, and the one time I went skiing, *as an adult,* I cried on the bunny slope before declaring that I was more of an "après skier." Would I enjoy being in the Sauron's Eye of White Anglo-Saxon America? The truth was I loved Isabelle's family. Though we could not be politically further apart, they are kind and smart and inclusive, and they had welcomed me to their house in New York City every Sunday night for dinner. If I was looking for ways to change my life, why not start with some new scenery and a free getaway?

On the drive up to their "compound" on Deer Isle, I envisioned something Kennedyesque. I imagined we would pull up to a white mansion with a red door. I fantasized about American flags errrwhere, and that in Maine, I would say phrases like "Be a good chap, old boy!" before taking a sip of a cool Pimm's Cup. But instead of Cape Cod chic, we arrived to a puritanical, clapboard shantytown. The little homes of the "compound" had walls so thin you could hear through them, and there was absolutely no heating for the forty-degrees-at-night "summer." I covered myself in mounds of wool blankets to stay not-freezing. Apparently, this was wealthy WASP culture: austerity, lobster boils, and drunken sailing accidents.

I was excited to visit a place I had never been before, but I was also distracted by my anxiety about a new boy I had just begun dating. Matt was a literal rocket scientist with whom I was obsessed for two reasons: One, he looked alarmingly similar to my most recent ex, Keats (you know Keats, the dude who cried when my sister came to visit?). And two, Matt was pretty "meh" about me. That really got under my skin. When I would tell him, "I like you," he would smile weakly and evade saying anything back. His ambiguity about me fueled my desperate desire to prove that I was a catch. I know this makes zero sense, but I thought that if I could get Matt to like me and validate me, maybe somehow that would trigger the universe to show Keats that *he also* liked me. Then *both* men would be in pursuit of me and I would have a difficult but delicious choice to make between the two of them. Yeah, my logic was not flawed *at all*.

On my first day in Maine, Isabelle's cousin Eliza arrived. She is the reason the term "birdlike" was invented: She's blond with the most delicate features. She is also one of those annoying people who, after going to Harvard, became a professional ballerina and then one day just *decided* to become a lawyer. Add to that the fact that she's effortlessly kind . . . it's pretty obnoxious, TBH. Isabelle, Eliza, and I took a walk around the village as I explained why I was stressing. As we passed the "knot-makers" shop (because that's a thing in Maine), I told them, "I just can't get Keats and Matt out of my head. And none of these thoughts are *nice* thoughts. It's not about how I miss them or how great they are, it's all about how much they don't like me and how there's just something wrong with me. I'm *so* down on myself, and it's exhausting." Eliza, with her perfect, beaklike smile, chirped, "Well, have you heard of positive psychology?" No, Eliza. I had not.

She explained that positive psychology is the idea that you can train your mind to not only feel stable but also to flourish. "Positive psychology is all about making yourself actively happier." That sounded interesting (if corny). "I don't know a ton about it, but I know a big part of it is about finding gratitude in your life." What did she mean by "gratitude"? I was pretty sure I had never used that term, earnestly, in reference to anything. I know that's hard to believe, but the practice of gratitude was just not something I had learned at home, and I certainly hadn't cultivated it on my own. I grew up in a house where I listened to my mom constantly lodge accusations that "everyone, *EVERYONE* is out to get us. You have to outsmart and fight them!" Eliza explained that "apparently people who are grateful are just happier overall." That sounded suspicious.

"But what if you have nothing to be grateful for?" I probed. "Maybe you have more to be grateful for than you think! Why don't you start writing a daily gratitude list and see what happens?" Eliza cheerily suggested. "Why don't you go fuck yourself and see what happens?" I wanted to retort.

Maybe a daily gratitude list could work for already-happy people like Eliza, who were ballerinas-turned-lawyers and had houses in Maine, but it would never work for me. A gratitude list would not benefit a person who was currently driving herself crazy by obsessively thinking about two boys who didn't love her. I had a visceral "you-don't-understand-me-or-reality-you're-so-privileged" reaction. SO MANY FUCKS BOILED UP IN MY BLOOD. "Fuck her, fuck everyone, I have nothing to be grateful for!" I wanted to scream.

But. Ugh. I had asked her for advice. And I *did* want to change my life. Was I really going to turn down one of the first solutions I had been offered? Partially to prove my point that Eliza was wrong and partially because I was at a low point where I was willing to try anything, I decided to test her ridiculous idea. "Thanks for the tip, Eliza. I'll try it!" I seethed through a smile. I made an agreement with myself: I'd write a morning gratitude list every day for one month, and when it didn't work, I could say something condescending to Eliza and feel self-righteous. Deal? Deal.

My lists from that time include such illuminating thoughts as "This is such a waste of time" and "You're not grateful for any of this, liar." And I wasn't. Genuinely, I felt no gratitude. But I forced myself to write things down. I started with the most simple, physical things I appreciated:

1. Espresso.

2. My bedsheets feeling cold when I get into them at night.

3. Wet hair on my back when it's hot outside.

4. A new A.P.C. candle that is particularly delightful even tho a coked-up dude in a leather jacket gave it to me after hitting on me all night.

As I kept writing the lists, surprising things emerged:

1. Strangers smiling at me.

2. When someone opens a door for me.

3. When I open a door for someone else.

4. My lovely little studio apartment, which is my safe haven.

5. My friends and their love.

6. My family. As flawed as they are, at least I was born.

7. My health.

OH YEAH. My health! What a privilege, what *luck* that I had health to take for granted.

As the list writing went on, I began to realize that I did indeed have a lot to be grateful for. That didn't mean I also didn't have trauma in my life. It certainly didn't mean that I had worked out all of my issues from childhood and now everything was "perf, thanks, *byeee*." The trauma and the gratitude were able to live in the same space, together. Little by little, I pulled the golden thread of gratitude out from the blanket of pain I usually wrapped myself in. At the end of the month, the only thing I could tell Eliza was that I was grateful for her advice. *Fucking Eliza.*

I have now been writing a daily gratitude list for nine years. Every morning, as a part of my journaling, I write down ten things I am grateful for. If I can't come up with something, I fake it, write down something silly, and don't worry too much about it. It adds up: Over time, the practice of writing 32,850 things I am grateful for has made me aware of just how lucky I am. Did this practice alone lead me to enjoy my life and believe that I am loveable? Nope. If it did, there would be no more book for you to read! But gratitude helps you to, once again, see that you have a choice in what story you tell yourself.

You can tell yourself you are worthless and ugly because some guy hasn't texted you back. You can tell yourself that because you haven't gotten the next promotion, you're falling behind professionally. Or. You can remind yourself that you are grateful for the love of your friends. You can tell yourself you are happy to have a steady job. You can be pumped as hell about the most perfectly sweet and plump blueberries you bought at the farmers market. Life is not always a list of problems to be solved; sometimes it's actually made up of fun and ease and beauty and laughter. By keeping a gratitude list, you can look at your inventory of blessings and recognize that there is much more love, so much more good, so many more AMAZING niceties in your life than you ever realized. Gratitude flips the narrative of "I am not enough" or "I don't *have* enough" and shows you, on paper, how much good you really do have in and around you.

I'm pretty sure I just faked gratitude until I became truly grateful. That's great news for you. If I could go from being cynical about gratitude to reluctantly trying it to sticking with it even when it didn't feel genuine to being a true believer, a happier person who thinks gratitude is one of the most powerful tools for self-care, then YOU CAN TOO. I'M TELLING YOU.

What are you grateful for *today*? I would love to know. Write it with me, right now. I'm sharing my gratitude list from all those years ago, back in Maine, so you can see that your list doesn't have to be life-altering and full of revelations and perfect. Just start with ten little things today. And maybe another ten tomorrow? And maybe the day after tomorrow? And if it doesn't work, and it's not worth your time, we can both blame Eliza. *Fucking Eliza.*

8.10.2011

Today I Am Grateful For:

1. Getting back home to CLEAN SHEETS on my bed. THE LUXURY.

2. The opportunity to visit a new place: Maine! I've been there now!

3. Isabelle, her family, their friendship.

4. My little family of friends and lovers.

5. Music: The Velvet Underground. When do I *not* want to listen to The Velvet Underground? They are the best.

6. The full-on, in-your-face humidity of summer in the city. I love how everyone looks like a hot mess and no one cares. Humidity is the great equalizer.

7. Seeing the sun through the leaves outside my window.

8. Coming to realize that no one else can solve my problems. It's not something someone else can give to me. I have to give it to myself. I'm glad to know this.

9. Books. Their smell. Their weight. Reading.

10. A tall glass of cool water sitting on my nightstand.

T$'s Guide to Thank-You Cards

The Best Selfish Thing You Can Do

I WRITE THANK-YOU NOTES LIKE my dang life depends on it. Because it does.

When I feel hopeless or depressed or like an anxiety ball of bad vibes, I write a thank-you card to someone, anyone. Bad night's sleep that has me cranky in the morning? Time to write a thank-you card for a piece of advice I was given last week. Conversation with my dad gone awry and now I'm feeling demoralized? Time to write a thank-you card to my cousin for hosting Thanksgiving dinner. Coffee with my ex-boyfriend that made me question my sanity? Well, first off, I shouldn't hang out with people who make me doubt myself. *No more spending time with Matt.* But, second, time to write a thank-you note to my friends Annie and Monika for a *truly lovely* dinner during which they fed me both pizza and confidence. There is something about sending that love and acknowledgment into the universe (yes, I just earnestly said *universe,* bear with me) that immediately makes me feel better about my life. I write thank-you cards for *me.* Is that selfish? Probably. But it's the best selfish thing I do.

My parents never taught me that thank-you cards were a

thing. If you knew me from the age of one to twenty-five, I'm so, so sorry that you never received a single token of my appreciation. I picked up the practice after receiving some particularly lovely thank-you notes from my friend Isabelle. *Jeez, I guess I have a lot to thank Isabelle for.* Her snail-mail letters were always so thoughtful, full of memories and inside jokes, written on stationery that was just *so her*. Each card just *felt* like Isabelle, covered in Indian block print designs she adored, and whenever her thank-you notes would arrive in the mail, I'd get giddy. Here was someone I loved who was taking the time to send something thoughtful and personal to me. It felt smooshy and warm and great. I decided to cop her style.

Since it was new to me, and a habit I wanted to make stick, I worked out a formula I would like to share with you. If you are ever stuck on how to write the perfect note, please read the recipe below. Use it until you find your own secret proprietary blend™.

My Surefire, Crowd-Pleasing Thank-You Card Recipe

1. Select a card that is very *you*. My cards are floral and bright. Most come in gold envelopes, and I seal each with a glitter heart sticker or a piece of sparkly washi tape. If you see great cards in a store, buy them on the spot! It's okay to hoard thank-you cards.

2. Begin with your salutation, e.g., "To my dearest Isabelle."

3. Next, write about something you enjoy about the person or about an experience you had together that you are thankful for. You want something that is specific to the receiver and could in no way be mistaken for a stock phrase. "I had such a fantastic time with you at dinner.

It's always a treat to laugh with you and get your opinions on writing, politics, and what kind of handbag I should consider." But don't say "thank you" yet! We're getting to that. This third step is all about re-creating and memorializing a special moment you shared.

4. Now we are at the actual *thanks* part. Find something to directly thank your subject for: "Thank you for making it to SoHo, five months pregnant. Five months! I can't believe it! I appreciate that you came out to see me even though your ankles were killing you." *Or* if you are thanking someone for something tangible, a gift let's say: "Thank you for the gorgeous floral notebooks. You know how much I love writing. And notebooks. And florals. You basically nailed it."

5. Now tell her how you really, really feel. Be vulnerable. "You are a part of my heart, and every time I see you, I feel immediately at peace and ease. There's something about you that makes me feel safe."

6. Now let's lighten it up, shall we?! "I look forward to all of the swanky nights we'll be having forever, because you are a forever friend. #Blessed #SorryNotSorry #WhyDo-PeopleUseHashTags #TheyAreNotLanguage"

7. Sign it like you mean it: "All of my love, T$"

Use this template to get started. And just get started *now*. I once worried that I was writing too many thank-you cards and that people would be annoyed with me. Let me tell you this: No one has ever complained about getting too many thank-you notes from someone if the sentiment is authentic. I now keep blank cards with me wherever I go, much like one might keep emergency Xanax. You never know when you are going to need the sweet relief of gratitude.

Do you have any thank-you cards you've been meaning to write? Maybe it's for something that happened a long time ago? Maybe there is a professor you've always meant to tell how important they were in your life? Maybe it's simply for a great dinner party two months ago? Don't overthink the timing. It's never too late to be grateful.

So I guess this would be a good time to take my own advice and tell you:

Dearest reader,

It's been a total delight to meet you. I savor this moment we are having together. It's kinda *the best*. Thank you for reading. Seriously. It was my dream to share this book with *you,* and now that we are doing it, it's more magical, more important, more life-affirming than I ever thought possible. But let's not get too gushy; we still have plenty of time together left. Thank the good Lord.

MUCH LOVE,

T$

The Frenemy Within
Stop Insulting Yourself

DO YOU EVER FEEL LIKE self-critical thoughts have hijacked your body? You'll be at home, say, watching *Shark Tank* on the couch while eating take-out Indian food, when a mean, Gollum-like presence will crawl out from somewhere deep inside of you and sidle up next to you on the sofa. She'll whisper in your ear, "Chris doesn't want to date you because you aren't good enough to love." She'll knowingly explain, "Your boss actually thinks you're a fraud and bad at your job." She'll criticize what you're eating. "Do you really need to be stuffing your face with rice and naan? *Two* carbs?" Now, instead of enjoying a nice night at home, your mind is spiraling. You get misty-eyed, you begin to wring your hands in angst, you have no idea how to stop any of this. All you wanted to do was watch *Shark Tank*. What the fuck happened?

My Frenemy Within is what happened. She is *such* a bitch. She's super mean and always looking for ways to bring me down, yet I keep inviting her to my dinner parties. I continue to share my artisanal charcuterie boards and chardonnay with her. She's at my table doing shots and generally being exasperating while I'm explaining/apologizing to friends that "she's an old pal; it's hard to cut her out entirely. . . . She's the type of person I wouldn't be friends with if I met her today, but we have so much history . . . ya know?" She lives within in my heart and feeds on my self-esteem.

I first discovered her while writing in my journal. She was the voice continually slamming me like a never-ending diss track. Even if I was feeling proud of myself and wrote down something I was grateful for, like "YAY! I finally, finally got my promotion!" she would scream back on the page, "Yeah, but it's just because you tricked them. I know you. You're no good." *Damn,* girl. Give me a break! Where did this super-intense critic bitch voice come from?

Well. I think she had been with me from the get-go. Growing up, as you know, I was often told there was something wrong with me. One of my earliest memories is of literal sock-puppet therapy. I could not have been older than five. I'm not sure if it was my preschool or my parents that sent me, but I remember being in a small cinder-block office as a man in a fishing vest, with a beard like Raffi's, spoke to me through a dirty tube sock on his arm named Mr. Fuzz. "Why don't you tell Mr. Fuzz how you're feeling?" the poor man's Raffi probed. "Yes! How are youuuuu doing today, Tara?" Mr. Fuzz implored in a singsong voice. I looked Mr. Fuzz straight in the googly eyes and refused to speak. He was not someone with whom I wanted to socialize, much less divulge my secrets. *Get it together, Mr. Fuzz,* I thought. *Respect yourself enough to take a bath and not live in a filing cabinet.*

My mom told me in grade school that I was bad at math and bad at spelling in the same way one might tell someone they have an inoperable brain tumor. There was simply nothing to be done. "It's terrible; you're dyslexic and you're going to be held back for remedial math this year," she would mourn. "How are you going to win the Nobel Prize in science now?" I was eight. I wasn't sure what the Nobel Prize was, but apparently I wasn't going to get it, and I felt like a terrible failure. And there was no follow-up message implying that I could be redeemed. No "Math is practice, you'll get there" or maybe even "This isn't the *worst* thing in the world." It was a judgment that I was innately doomed in a very serious, unfixable way. To this day I do not know if I am dyslexic. I don't remember a doctor telling me I was, but my mom said it with such conviction, so consistently, for years and years, that I just internalized it as truth. I know for sure that I am very terrible at spelling. Is that the same thing?

I was told my body was wrong too. By the time I was nine, my mom would pin me to the gray carpet of her bathroom floor and wax my upper lip, my eyebrows, anything on my face that wasn't "right." She would prod and poke at my skin, and as I cried for her to stop, the tears and hot wax mixing, I would think that I was a failure for having this body. My mom would dye my hair, paint my nails, pop any blemish on my skin. "You love having your hair dyed," she'd tell me. Truly, I did not. It stung and smelled terrible and I kinda liked my naturally super-dark hair. I didn't think I needed to change, but I guess I was wrong if my own mother thought so. In her bathroom, there was a wall of mirrors and a giant skylight that illuminated everything. It's perfect lighting if you want to check your makeup, but it's damningly bright if you would prefer not to face your appearance. After one of her inspections, I would stand in front of the mirror while hot waves of shame swept across my body, tingling on my neck and resting heavy on my shoulders. I was all *wrong*.

This is where my Frenemy Within was born. On that bathroom floor, she curled up next to me. She is my oldest friend, the one who has been with me through it all, yet instead of supporting me, the way your oldest BFF might, she is always out for blood. It was easy to recognize her in my journal because my frenemy's indictments were so much more vicious, so much more wounding and irrational than mine. It really was the voice of a different person, a voice that didn't come from me. *I* certainly do not have the energy to be at war with myself. Usually, I barely have the energy to do my laundry. But *she* has nothing better going on and makes it her full-time job to be nasty.

After seeing her unfairly monopolize the pages of my journal, I decided it was time to confront the bitch. Rather than avoid her or suppress her like I might have done in the past, I decided to be fully present with her spite. Maybe I would find a way to deal with her if I understood what she was thinking? I wrote down a complete inventory of all the things she alleged:

A List of Judgments from Your Frenemy Within

1. You are a fraud, and if you haven't accomplished your goals yet, you never will. It's too late. You're too old.

2. You have the wrong job and you will never have the right one.

3. You didn't buy Jana a wedding present. It's been eight months! Who is so lazy and disorganized that they can't buy a wedding present?

4. Your college boyfriend is getting married (thanks, Facebook, for that discovery). You really fucked that up with Ben. He was the best person you ever dated and now he's in love with someone else.

5. Your body looks like a soup dumpling.

I looked at the list and laughed. JEEZ. *So harsh*. I would *never* say such unkind things to someone else. But here I was, talking this way about myself. Instead of dismissing this inner critic as "stupid," I wondered what would happen if I treated my frenemy the same way I behaved toward friends with whom I have a conflict. Now, having grown up in a screamy environment, I don't deal well with verbal confrontations. If you raise your voice to me, I will shut down. So I tend to write out my feelings when I need to express them. My sister has received plenty of letters and texts describing my feels (sorry, Diana). My boss has also received plenty of emails detailing my grievances (sorry, Boss). My letters help me say what I mean without going off topic, without chickening out, without breaking into tears. (Well . . . sometimes I still break into tears. It can't be helped; I'm a total crier.) So I wondered: *What would happen if I wrote a cease-and-desist letter to my Frenemy Within and really took that bitch to task?*

Dear Frenemy Within,

I want to let you know that I have received and reviewed your complaints.

I understand you think I am a fraud and will never accomplish my goals. I just want to say that I *have* accomplished *many* of my goals and am on the road to accomplishing more. There is no evidence to the contrary. Also: What does being "too late" and "too old" even mean? The need to SHINE THE BRIGHTEST, BE THE YOUNGEST, RIGHT NOW is just an ego thing, a short-term distraction. I'm playing a long game, baby. I want more success, yes, but I *have* success and not all of it has to happen at once. In fact, I hope it doesn't. I don't want to flame out. I am a smart, capable person doing the best I can. That is the opposite of a fraud.

I understand you think I have the "wrong" job. I want to let you know that I actually enjoy what I do. I love the people I work with and the stability of working in a large company. I am also on the path to finding the sweet spot between a job that is creative and one that is business-oriented. This doesn't happen overnight! I'm putting in the work and doing an excellent job, as demonstrated by my promotion, *bitch*.

I understand you found out via Facebook that one of my college boyfriends is newly engaged and you are worried I fucked up. You think he *might* have been "the one," and you think it's my fault we are not together now. First off: Why are you stalking my FB, *loser*? Don't you have anything better to do? Second: I want to remind you that while falling in love with Ben was *wonderful,* after a year and a half, *I* ended it because Ben and I were not compatible. I never came during sex AND he had terrible anxiety, which, I'll remind you, was no match for *my* terrible anxiety. It's great he's getting married—especially great that it's not to me!

I understand that you think I am a flake and a fraud for not getting a gift in time for Jana's wedding. I want to remind you that Jana is my friend, and she is not thinking about this at all rn, because she is busy living her life. Also: I *will* get her a gift. You know I will. I always do.

To the charge that my body looks like a soup dumpling . . . Yes, actually. I'll take that. I look like a perfectly crafted, beautifully detailed, handmade, most delicious treat that everyone wants to eat because they know just how good it is inside. I am the hottest app at the party.

In conclusion, Frenemy, I want to thank you for taking the time to register your complaints, and now I dismiss you and all of your charges and wrap myself in a cashmere blanket of self-compassion. As usual, you are very wrong. Kindly cease and desist from trying to tear me down. You can't.

XO
T$

I took the letter, sealed it in glittery gold tape, and pinned it to my Idea Board in my home office, right next to a picture of Coco Chanel. Coco didn't suffer fools, and neither should I.

Writing a letter to my Frenemy Within is a tool that quickly sucks the wind out of my fires of self-hate. First, it lightens the mood. It's silly to write a "letter to self," so it makes me laugh. Laughter is the enemy of self-loathing because laughing means you are removed enough from your total self-absorption to actually be able to find something funny. It allows you to be self-aware, and self-awareness is *always* part of the cure. Second, every time I defend myself in writing, my brain and my right hand unite in self-defense. The reflex of defending myself gets in my muscle memory. And it feels exhilaratingly powerful.

I've chosen to stop insulting myself. The simple reason is that nothing good comes from it. You are not more successful when you allow your fault-finding, vindictive inner bitch out to play. Instead, you are insecure, doubtful, and questioning your own worth. You feel wobbly and you accomplish less. If being thoroughly critical of yourself worked, if it got results, I would keep doing it. *Trust me*. I am a results-oriented person. But the simple truth is: Being mean to yourself is counterproductive, feels awful, and takes way more energy than being kind. Why would you do that?

Do you have a Frenemy Within? Someone who knows *exactly* how to twist the knife of criticism into your guts? Is she named Karen? I want you to identify that voice as something separate from yourself. That's not *you* speaking. That's your inner assassin. You are lovely and wonderful and taking care of yourself. You are, in fact, a ninja of self-care, dressed in an all-black, dope-as-hell ensemble, showing up quietly when it's least expected in order to subdue your inner assassin. Think of it this way: You wouldn't let someone else speak to you like this, you wouldn't let someone try to shoot down your self-esteem, so why-oh-why would you let someone *in your own head* be this cruel?

The next time you hear that voice, instead of ignoring it—or, much worse, *believing* it—try writing down the accusations you hear. Then, for each argument your inner critic makes, I want you to write out *exactly* why she is wrong. Be specific. "No, I'm not a bad person because I forgot to buy almond milk. It was a simple mistake, and the only consequence was I drank my coffee black, NBD." Get aggressive. Write in your own words how much she sucks and then dismiss her. "I get that you have no life and just want to tear me down, but not today, sweetheart. Today, all I can say is 'BYEEE, bitch, be gone!'" Sign, seal, and pin this letter somewhere you can see it. Let it be a reminder that you are worth defending and you are strong enough to do it yourself. If you need a little more help, tape a picture of someone you admire right next to the letter. Someone fierce who will team up with you to fight your Frenemy Within. For me, as you know, it's Coco Chanel. For you, it might be Rihanna, Tarana Burke, Trevor Noah, or Sully Sullenberger. If Sully can land a plane on the Hudson River, he will for sure help guard you against your Frenemy Within.

This entire week, keep a beautiful little notebook on you, and *every time* you hear a criticism of yourself, write it down and fight it. *Every* time? Yup. Every damn time. *You are bad for not having a boyfriend.* Reject it! *You are irresponsible and a flake for being late to work.* Knife it! It takes vigilance and practice to defeat a well-trained confidence killer. But I know you have this. I know you are *worth* defending and that you have the power, right now, to beat this mighty foe. I'll be the one cheering you on and chanting your name in the middle of the street as you brawl. I won't mean to embarrass you or cause a scene; I'll just be so happy that you did the damn thing, I won't be able to keep it to myself.

You've got this. I know you do.

I feel kinda bad for your Frenemy Within. She's not going to know what hit her.

Who Even Are You?
Chart Your Own Course

THERE IS ANOTHER WAY I'VE learned to attack the Frenemy Within, but I'm so shy about it that I wrestled with whether to even tell you. It makes me feel dumb and faux spiritual and like one of those people who has a vision board. Ick. Blech. Gross. Ew. But guys . . . I HAVE A VISION BOARD! I JUST CALL IT MY "IDEA BOARD" BECAUSE I DON'T WANT TO SEEM LAME, BUT IT'S COVERED IN ALL KINDS OF CLICHÉ SHIT. I am *totally* one of those people who believes in vision boards! But I'm not here to talk about that. If you want to find out about vision boards, just google it. I'm going to talk about another tool that helped change my life (it *is* kind of like a vision board, tho).

Attacking my Frenemy Within was going great. That bitch was super dead at least three times a week. But in the place of the negative self-chatter, I wasn't exactly sure what to put. What would I say to myself all day if it wasn't "You suck"? That sounds ridiculous, but when you've spent more than twenty years with "You suck" playing as the soundtrack to your life, it can be jarring to suddenly have silence.

I wondered if I could learn to approve of myself, just as I was? Could that be my new refrain? You know that scene in

*Bridget Jones's Diary** where Colin Firth says to Renée Zellweger (a.k.a. Bridget Jones), "I like you very much, *just* as you are"? I wanted to be able to say *that* to myself. What did I embrace and love and hold dear about myself?

Around the time I was thinking about this question, I went to the High Holy Holidays at a new temple in my neighborhood. I had grown up Jewish-*ish*. The kind of Jewish where I intermittently went to Hebrew school but was more concerned with getting Hanukkah gelt (chocolate in gold foil) than I was with understanding the actual holiday. Something about a temple and then a lamp and then some oil for some candles but then it wasn't *enough* oil but then it lasted so . . . *celebrate?* Dope story, Jews. But as I started to get better at taking care of myself, I found that I was oddly curious to learn more about Judaism.

I had decided to go to the temple down the street both because it was in walking distance and because it had a reputation for being liberal and inclusive and having a baller female rabbi who also had a TED Talk. As someone who was/is always looking for people to learn from, this seemed like as decent an opportunity as any. I came for Yom Kippur (the Jewish Day of Atonement) services. It's maybe the most depressing holiday. Ever. You don't eat all day, but you *do* reflect on all of the things you've done wrong in the previous year. Super-light stuff. I kicked myself for choosing *this* holiday to get "pumped on religion." Why hadn't I picked Rosh Hashanah, the Jewish New Year? On Rosh Hashanah, you sing a song about eating apples dipped in honey (which symbolizes a sweet new year), and then you get to *eat* said apples dipped in honey! Again, on Yom Kippur, you don't eat at all!

---

* We agree this is one of the finest pieces of artwork *ever* made by human hand, right? Sorta like the movie equivalent of Michelangelo's *David?*

I arrived at synagogue in my usual black High Holy Holiday/ funeral clothes, ready to be fucking depressed and probably bored. I was immediately taken aback, though, when I saw that *everyone* around me was wearing white clothing and seemed ... happy? As I stood in the parking lot, surrounded by a sea of white flowing dresses and suits, I felt immediately out of place. I asked a woman standing in line next to me what was going on. "Oh, the white? I think it's supposed to stand for spiritual purity and renewal," she said as she eyed my black-on-black ensemble. "I just like that it's less depressing than all black."

Self-consciously, I entered the temple and picked up my prayer book. But it looked different from the prayer books I remembered from years ago. On the cobalt-blue cover, in big bold black letters, it read, *A Way In: A Map to the High Holy Holidays*. As I leafed through the booklet, I realized this *wasn't* the prayer book; it was a *guide* to understanding the prayer book, an actual map of the prayers and the different rituals of the day. In clear-as-could-be, well-drawn graphics, it charted out how the ten days of the High Holy Holidays (there were ten?! I thought there were only two!) could change your ways. Each page was a part of a larger blueprint that clearly explained what it all meant. I was used to prayer books that I not only didn't understand, but that I didn't care about at all. Here, I read that "the High Holy Days are a big communal kick in the pants: a reminder to use the time we have to reflect on who we have become and who we could be." *Damn.* I was going to get sucked in to this service.

After the service, as I walked home from temple, one of the questions from the guide stuck in my head like a lean, bespec- tacled, mysterious boy at a coffee shop whom I wanted to find the courage to introduce myself to: "Who even are you?" (I know, pretty edgy-bordering-on-confrontational for a house of worship.) I wanted to be able to answer that question just as simply as it was asked. Suddenly, I had a flash of inspiration. Could I map *myself* out the same way that the rabbi's guide had mapped out Yom Kippur? Maybe, to better understand myself, I could create a blueprint for what mattered most in my life? Back in my little home office, I took out index cards, a Sharpie, and my favorite hot-pink tape and decided to try. I used questions from the prayer book to guide me as I started to build a physical map of myself on the back of a door. I have continued to work on this map over the course of years, asking myself questions I've read in books, including advice from people I've met and songs that I think are particularly soulful.

My door has three panels on it. On the bottommost panel, I have written about where my self-esteem comes from. It's not from clothes, it's not from promotions, it's not from the one time, ten years ago, when John Mayer said "hi" to me at a Yankees game. On three index cards, I have written: "Writing," "Exercise," and "Being a Good Friend." That's it. These are the three things that, when done regularly, make me feel calm and optimistic and like I am *enough*. Notice how success isn't one of the things from which I derive my self-esteem? It doesn't matter how the writing *performs,* it doesn't matter if I lose weight by running, it wouldn't matter if you asked me to be your bridesmaid as a show of your affection. It only matters that I *do* the things that make me feel good and respect myself.

On the next panel, I have written out my principles. How did I figure out my principles? Well, I happened to be invited to an ashram in India, where a wise old man told me ...JKJKJK. I sat at my computer in my pj's for a day and googled, "What are principles?" and "What principles should I have?" Then I journaled about what I read. I asked unsuspecting friends on text chains what their principles were. Through my research, I found that a principle is something foundational, a code of conduct by which you live your life.

On index cards, I have written out my six core principles, and underneath each word, I've come up with an example of how I express that principle IRL. Gratitude, authenticity, enjoyment, integrity, awareness/presence, and kindness are my main principles. If my principle is to live a life of gratitude, then I demonstrate that by "giving thanks to others, to the universe, out loud, in cards, whenever I can express it." If my principle is integrity, then "I act in a way that makes me proud. I don't do things that would embarrass me if others knew about them. Less gossip, less words that could harm, plz." (I didn't say my door map is particularly eloquent.)

On the third panel, the one close to the top of the doorframe, I have written out the "Things About Myself I Want to Be True." Things I want to be remembered for. When I'm dead and buried, these are things I want people to eulogize about me. "Oh yeah, Tara? She was a gem. When you were with her, she made you feel seen and important." "She was a good friend who both loved others unconditionally and was loved unconditionally." I mean, I guess it's a little morbid to use what I want people to say at my memorial service as a guide to who I want to be *today,* but I also think it's an incredibly useful tool that reminds me that what I want to be true of myself in the future is my responsibility to *make* true now. This list is all about the kind of long-lasting impact I want to have on the world. Here I have written on one card, "Generous, kind, grounded." On another, "She knew and spoke with great people, great minds." On one that is tacked on with floral tape, I have, "Stylish, chic, kinda French." Not everything has to be so serious.

And on the very tippity-top of the door, I have the affirmation "I can be who I want to be. I AM who I want to be."

If you have trouble approving of yourself, I highly encourage you to create a map of who you are. So many of us are taught principles both explicitly ("Do unto others as you would have them do unto you") and implicitly (It's okay for Mom and Dad to scream at each other, ergo, it's fine for you to scream at others) at an early age, but we never take time to make sure that these foundational truths are what *we want* in our lives. Creating a map of yourself forces you to make decisions about who you are, and these decisions can and *will* make you proud. Forget what your mom thought was important for you. To hell with what your first boss said you *should* be. Get really clear on being the person YOU approve of and want to be.

You don't need to be this *exact* person today, but it's powerful to merely envision who you will become. The very act of going through the exercise makes you realize what you stand for. And if you don't stand for anything yet? Well, this is a great time to make those choices. Did you see *Hamilton*? DON'T GET MAD AT ME IF YOU THINK IT WAS OVERRATED. I HAPPEN TO LOVE IT. There is an *excellent* line where Alexander Hamilton challenges Aaron Burr (who seems to have v. shape-shifting, wishy-washy principles): "If you stand for nothing, Burr, what'll you fall for?" BOOM! DID YOU JUST GET THE *TINGLES*? Let's choose our principles consciously so we are standing on the solid moral ground of our own choosing. Or at least so we don't end up like Aaron Burr, vilified in one of the most successful musicals of all time. Sucks to be Burr.

You don't have to take up a door in your home like I did; you could just as easily do it in a notebook, but I would tape that sucker up! I find that seeing myself reflected in a physical way is helpful when I feel like I might cry because YET ANOTHER BOYFRIEND SITUATION HAS BURNED TO THE GROUND, WTF. Or when I'm disappointed that I lost out on an opportunity at work. Or when I feel sad because there is no more of my favorite TV show to watch. I can look at my door while dancing to the hottest, newest Ariana Grande track in my home office and feel good about the person I have become and the person I am working toward being.

To get started, you might try taping positive affirmations to the door as well. "I am allowed to nurture myself," "I am talented," "I am loveable," "I am brilliant and prolific," and "I am confident, enthusiastic, and expansive" have all served me well.* Say these affirmations every time you look at the door. Say these affirmations every time you fight your Frenemy Within. Say them when you go on a run or when you're trying to drag yourself out of bed in the morning after staying up way too late doing karaoke in a tiny little private room in Koreatown. *I'm sooo tired this morning, was it worth it? HELL YES. If one of my principles is enjoyment, then I enjoyed the fuck out of my night.* Say these affirmations all of the time because they help you learn how to approve of yourself and that's key here.

I now fully approve of myself. For the most part.

After the Yom Kippur service, I received an email from the temple explaining how the prayer guides were NOT meant to be taken home. Printing them was costly, and those who had taken them should return them. *Oh dang. I already fucked up religiously,* I thought. I emailed my apology and explanation that I was so taken by the book, by the cobalt-blue cover, by THE MAP, etc., that I *thought* we were meant to take them home, but I would be *happy* to send a check or return the book??? The temple never emailed me back . . . so . . . don't you think that's *possibly* a sign? That I was meant to hang on to it??? I'm just going to assume there was some divine intervention involved. . . .

I approve of myself, even if I do sometimes accidentally steal Jewish literature.

---

* These are all either from Julia Cameron's *The Artist's Way* or are the spiritual grandchildren of her excellent positive affirmations.

Hype Men, Road Warriors, and Those You Must Avoid

Know Your Team

I USED TO MAKE A terrible mistake. One of the ways I used to be cruelest to myself was when I shared information, secrets, or dreams with people who would treat my confidences with zero care. When I had an idea I was excited about, something I thought was just *so* great, I instinctively told the person who would be the least supportive and most destructive. My gut was appallingly bad on this one! And appallingly consistent.

Having grown up in a house of constant criticism, I didn't trust compliments. When I heard feedback that was flattering, it went in one ear and out the other into a holding dumpster, where I quickly set fire to the praise. All that would be left were the ashes of the compliment, which I'd then bury at sea so I'd never have to recognize anything "nice" about myself. If, however, someone made a dig at me, or even lightly criticized me, I would take those words as *absolute truth,* build them into an ever-present blinking neon sign in my mind, and do everything in my power to either change according to the expressed opinion *or* prove the person wrong in such a grand fashion that EVERYONE, the whole damn world, would see how mistaken this person was. This way of living was not exhausting at all.

I saw this clearly for the first time in college when I took an introduction to playwriting class. I adored my hippie grad-student teacher, Kate. She had thick blond hair streaked with glitter extensions and a beautiful gap-toothed smile. She is the reason the term "earth mother" was invented, and I mean that in the nicest possible way. On the first day of class, she sat on the floor, cross-legged, and invited us all to gather around in a "circle of trust." She explained, "Down here we can talk about what pains us, what is struggling to be born through our writing." This could have come off as hackneyed, but on her, it was pure magic because it was totally authentic. She really was creating an environment where it was safe to experiment with writing.

Midway through the semester, she pulled me aside, looked me in the eye, put a hand on my shoulder, and spoke into my soul: "You've got a voice, girl. Raw talent. You have to keep developing it." Her compliment had me shook. I could only kiiinda listen. Kate had made the fatal flaw of showing any enthusiasm for my work, and I could neither accept nor internalize it. *Yeah, yeah, yeah,* I thought. The fact that she thought I was in any way capable was proof that *she* didn't know what she was talking about. Instead of receiving her kindness and continuing with the work, I decided that I was wasting my time in a beginner class and needed to be in the hardest, showiest class possible RIGHT NOW. There, I would really be put to the test and, *then,* when I had succeeded, I would prove to EVERY-ONE (Kate included) that I was a worthy writer. I needed to be at the finish line of writing, with a gold medal, *ASAP.* When you grow up in a house where the literal foundation might slip out from underneath you at any moment, I think you end up in a real hurry to achieve before it's too late. I dismissed Kate's gentle, tender, nourishing encouragements and leaped into an advanced class.

Advanced playwriting was taught by a v. v. v. fancy, v. v. v. accomplished, v. v. v. hip professor. She was also v. v. v. cold. I don't think all teachers need to be "warm"—I get that my professors weren't replacements for my mom and dad (wouldn't that have been nice tho?!)—but what I needed, what would have actually been helpful to me, was someone encouraging, someone supportive. The very thing I had just walked away from in Kate with the sparkly hair. Professor Laurie, on the other hand, was a cool customer. I would visit her office hours constantly, hoping to get a little feedback from her on my work. She'd speak in riddles about "the plasticity of the page," the "mis-en-scene" of a "theatRE," and something called "onto-logical double vision." I hadn't taken all of the prerequisite courses and had no real background in theater other than per-forming in high school plays, so I was out of my depth fo sho. Mostly, though, we would discuss her own life. "You know, I never finished my thesis novel when I was in college," she would lament. "It's my biggest regret that I didn't pursue my own art." She would follow her list of disappointments with tales of her *fabulous* life in San Francisco where she was SO SUCCESSFUL as a director. Um, what did this have to do with my play? And, actually, could we talk about structure? How *do* you write a play? It's hard for me! Could we talk about *that*? By the time I got the courage to ask more direct ques-tions, her office hours would be over. I would shut the door, close to tears, wondering where I had gone wrong. I wanted her to like me. I wanted her to think I was worth her time and attention. I wanted, at the very least, to understand what the fuck she was talking about.

I invited Laurie to opening night at the student theater of a comedy I had written and directed about the life and times of Anna Nicole Smith. It was a mash-up of a nineteenth-century French melodrama and a reality television show. You're going to have to trust me that it was hilarious and made sense. I was super proud of the production, and when Professor Laurie accepted my invite, my heart sang and ran up the walls of the classroom, parkour-style. I had written the play on my own, outside of class, and this would be my opportunity to show her how talented I was.

On opening night, I saved her the best seat in the house. I wrapped her chair in masking tape and put her name in glitter letters: "RESERVED FOR PROF LAURIE." I anxiously awaited her arrival as the theater filled in. Kate entered and gave me a big, loving hug. "This is fantastic, honey! I'm so proud that you put this all together!" she told me in her patchouli-scented embrace. *Yeah, yeah, yeah. Where was Laurie?*

I scanned the seating. Maybe she had missed her seat of honor and was scooched up on one of the benches? As the minutes ticked toward the curtain opening, I asked the stage manager to hold off on opening the show. "Tara, you have a packed house; it's time to get going," she snapped back. (Stage managers are not to be fucked with, BTW.) "But I have an important person coming. . . . Can you give me, like, *three* more minutes?" Maybe Laurie went to the wrong theater? OR! Maybe she had been in a car accident and was emerging from her mangled Subaru??? As I spun possible scenarios, the stage manager, without telling me, started the show.

I scrambled to my position at the back of the theater, past the rows of the audience, still scanning the crowd for signs of Laurie. I was surprised to see so many good friends who had turned out and also many faces of people I didn't know at all. I wondered how they all had heard about the play. Maybe blanketing the entire campus in posters for weeks had worked? In the back of the house, opposite the set I had stayed up late with the cast building, I stuck my fidgeting hands into the pockets of my silver minidress. It was the dress I wore whenever I had something to celebrate. It made me look like a sparkly ziplock bag of tinsel. I should have been ecstatic. I had a sold-out show and the theater was packed to the walls with supporters, but I could have burst with how disappointed I felt.

Laurie never showed.

I felt my chin tremble in a way that lets me know I'm about to cry in a particularly ugly, sobby way. I might have fallen apart in my self-pity party had I not been rudely interrupted by the strangest, loudest, most wonderful sound: LAUGHTER. What began as a rumble in the audience when Anna found herself strewed upon the shores of Hollywood, California, unprepared for a life in television, grew into a roar so deafening the actors had to pause their lines to wait out the noise. I could hear Kate's distinct "HAAAAH," which sounded like a comic book bubble come to life. Laughter, for me, is the highest form of praise. For a drama to work, the audience doesn't need to cry. But for comedy to work? The audience can't just be amused; they can't think, *Oh, how interesting.* No, their bodies have to actually emit laughter. Standing there, alone in the back of the theater, I breathed in the sound and let the tears recede back into my eyes. It was time to enjoy the show.

What I learned from Kate and Professor Laurie is that there's no point in seeking false idols. Do not look for the approval of someone you *think* will make you approve of yourself. Approve of yourself first, *just as you are* (see the last chapter, and *Bridget Jones*), and if you need support from others, trust the people who are in your corner. These are not always the people you desperately *want* in your corner. These are not always the people you *wish* treated your ideas with care. These are not the people about whom you think, *Well,* maybe *they'll come through this time. Fingers crossed!* These are the people who *actually* show up for you. Being able to identify your tribe of well-wishers is an incredibly powerful tool. You will learn to stop vying for the attention of people who, frankly, don't deserve your time, and you will start embracing the cheerleaders who are already around you. This has been a tough lesson for me to learn (and relearn), so here's what I do to make it stick: In my little home office, I keep the names of the people I can trust taped to the walls.

I have my "Hype Men" list. These are people I go to when I need love, care, and encouragement, not criticism. They handle my new ideas like delicate birds' nests that need protection and reinforcement rather than new construction. If they do have feedback, it's always given in a constructive way. Not in a shitty "It's okay, BUT . . ." kind of way. BTW, when you hear, "It's okay, BUT . . ." that should set off alarm bells in your head! Hype Men won't "but" you to death. They won't find the holes before they've admired what you've already built. If a Hype Man gives me a particularly reassuring piece of encouragement, I write it down or print it out and tape it to my wall, so when I doubt myself, I can remember that this person I deeply respect has no reservations about me. I'll just trust in them and their knowledge. Try it! Print out emails that praise you. Write down when someone you trust says something kind about you. Pin these words of reinforcement somewhere you can easily, and regularly, see. My Hype Men list is written on pink paper and affixed to my office wall in gold-and-white-striped tape.

I have my "Road Warriors" list. These are people of all ages who have been in similar career situations to my own. These are people I turn to when I need advice or am seeking feedback. They tend to be people who don't tell me what to do, but instead ask me excellent questions that help guide me. They have shown me, over the course of many years, that they want the best for me and would never undermine me. I will not hesitate to ask for their help. If you need to find more Road Warriors in your life, more people who you think "get" you and might offer great advice, why not email someone whom you look up to and ask them to coffee? I've found that the more successful a person is, the more likely they are to enjoy teaching those who are still on the road. They are confident enough in what they have accomplished to want to give back to others. PLUS, people *love* to talk about themselves. Ask a potential Road Warrior for their story and see how their eyes light up at the idea that someone is interested in them. My Road Warriors list lives right next to my Hype Men list, written on crisp white paper, the borders covered in floral washi tape.

And then I have my "ABSOLUTELY NOT/ARE YOU CRAZY?" list. These are people who might be wonderful, they might even love me, they might be my *actual* family, but, historically, they will say something snide or dismissive about my ideas and I just can't go there anymore. These are people who have said to me, "That's a terrible idea!" or "You can't do that." They make me feel small and stupid and might even tempt me to give up on a dream before it's had time to incubate. This list is outlined in glittery gold tape. I want this list to stand out for my protection! My Hype Men, Road Warriors, and ABSOLUTELY NOT/ARE YOU CRAZY? lists all live together on the painted pink wall of my home office, right to the side of my computer screen. That way, at a glance, I know whom to go to.

Who is on your Hype Men list? What about your Road Warriors list? And who is on your ABSOLUTELY NOT/ARE YOU CRAZY? list? Do you know? The power in keeping these lists is twofold. First, it helps you identify what kind of support you need. Let's say you have an idea for an Etsy Beef Jerky company. *Great idea.* Do you need encouragement, or do you need feedback? Do you need someone to treat you gently, or someone to offer guidance on how best to display your precious dried meat? If you need inspiration to get started, go to your Hype Men. If you are looking for feedback on the packaging, go to your Road Warriors. If you don't want to feel bad about yourself, stay the fuck away from your ABSOLUTELY NOT list. It's the same for relationships. If you just started dating a new dude, do you want to tell your best friend, who will be excited for you, or do you want to tell your mom, who disapproves of everyone you date? Your mom loves you, but maybe she's not the best one to tell in the beginning. Keeping these lists helps you identify what you need from the people in your orbit.

The second excellent consequence of these lists is that you can *quickly* know whom to go to before your mind plays tricks on you. When I have a new idea for an essay, I can immediately scan my office wall and find the *exact* right person to talk to. I don't even have time to think, *Maybe I can win the support of swanky Caitlyn, who knows all the "important" people but who seems apathetic toward me.* NOPE! I'll call a Hype Man to get a little motivation. I approve of myself and I have so many awesome people in my corner already. I'm all good.

And if you're having trouble identifying your Hype Men or Road Warriors, look harder. I swear they are around you. If you're anything like me, it's easy to ignore the kind Kates of the world because we don't want to believe that we might *actually* be talented, smart, and capable. That thought is scary because, *then,* instead of struggling and spending energy thinking, *Ugh, if only I didn't suck,* we would actually have to *do* something with ourselves. We would have to start our Etsy Beef Jerky company, we would have to leave our shitty job where toxic Larry keeps pushing a promotion further and further into the future, we would have to put ourselves out on a limb and TRY. But if we have the talent and ability, why *wouldn't* we be able to succeed? Write down who has shown up for you again and again.

Speaking of which, can you please sign me up for *your* Hype Men list? I don't think your ideas are crazy or out-there; I think they are *excellent*. I think it's dope as hell that you took a Reiki class, started throwing pots on a wheel, and got your scuba certification. I think you are so skillful that you absolutely *must* see where this all takes you. Henry David Thoreau once wrote, "Go confidently in the direction of your dreams! Live the life you've imagined." I think he wrote that for *you* in particular. Keep walking down the path you see for yourself. As you continue, you will find new trails open up to you. Trails you would have *never* discovered, adventures you would have never taken had you stayed indoors thinking of what you *couldn't do*. Lace up your sneakers, put one foot in front of the other, and walk down the path you see in your dreams. You've got this, my love! And the view? The view is going to be stellar.

Am I hyping you up yet? See. It works.

Buy the Fucking Lilies
Don't Cheap Out on Yourself

FULL DISCLOSURE TO YOU, DEAREST FRIEND:

Talking about money feels super weird and almost taboo to me, yet money plays an inordinately important role in all of our lives. I have never had real conversations with my friends about it. In fact, I'm scared to write about it, so here are my caveats:

Please do not judge me; I don't have a great sense of how much anyone makes. How much does a doctor make, for example? Or a teacher? I feel like teachers should make *all* of the money, given that they are legit responsible for instructing humans about how to function in a civil society, but when was the last time you saw a blinged-out kindergarten teacher? There should be more teachers dripping in diamonds, in Escalades with chromed-out rims. What does a car mechanic make? Or the person scooping ice cream at the latest artisanal creamery? Or, actually, what's *my* total salary when you take out the taxes and include all of the "benefits"? What *are* my "benefits"? My company's website is too complicated to understand (why so many drop-down menus?!). For many years, I willfully ignored my own paycheck. I'm a pretty frugal person (I will ask for a discount anywhere, for anything; sorry, friend who is waiting with me in line at Lululemon—shit's about to go *down*), so I knew I didn't spend more than I made, but that was *all* I knew, and all I wanted to know. When I went to Bank of America's website to pay my bills, I did so as quickly as possible, never pausing to think about the bigger picture of my finances. Before I started paying attention, I hadn't looked at my (meager) 401(k) in three years.

This was definitely an "ignorance is bliss" approach, and I fully recognize that it was a great privilege. I wasn't poor, but I wasn't incredibly wealthy either. I would never pretend that I have financially struggled, but I have skipped a few meals to save a little cash. I have worried about having enough money to pay my rent. I'm fine right now, stable even,* but as I took on this project of self-care, I saw that my relationship with money was like my newly discovered, late-in-life allergy to *all grass*. I kinda knew it existed since I had been legitimately afraid of grass since I was a kid, but on the real, I only dealt with my hypersensitivity when I broke into painful welts and hives that urgently needed attention. Mostly, I just wished I could find a good cream to make it all go away.

As a kid, I was subject to several homespun boom and bust economies. My parents' finances were always in one extreme state or another, and their prosperity, or lack thereof, dictated the overall health and emotional stability of our family. At times, my parents were flush. My dad would take his friends and our family out to dinner and pick up the bill as a point of pride. "We'll have the check flambé!" he would joke to our waiter before dismissing everyone else's credit cards with a wave of the hand and a firm "I've got this." He always had the latest gadgets: the first mobile car phone, the first at-home fax machine, a SEGA Dreamcast videogame console that was so new it came directly from Japan. It predated the American variety, so, of course, it did not include directions in English. This

---

*   *Knocks on wood so as not to tempt fate.*

meant we couldn't use it, understand it, or buy any games for it. It sat, brand-new, in a pile of technology none of us knew what to do with, along with our laser disc player, fruit dehydrator, and in-home tanning bed. Our living room was full of so much idle stuff—so many bulky big-screen TVs and racks of clothing with price tags still affixed—that it looked more like a shitty warehouse than a place where a family might live. For my parents, money was synonymous with happiness. The way you knew you were thriving was if you had lots of STUFF. It didn't matter if you wanted or needed the STUFF, or if the STUFF was suffocating your life, the point of money, the point of having a job, the point of living at all was that it allowed you to have big-screen TVs in every room of your house.

My parents' affluence was belied by the fact that they were often deeply in debt. Our kitchen had stacks of unpaid bills that mounted like an impending, yet totally disregarded, hurricane. Everyone knew a Category 5 storm was on the horizon, but no one heeded the evacuation orders. One of my strongest early memories is of witnessing my first car repossession. At the age of ten, I was standing on the fire escape behind my mom's Beverly Hills office—the office that I often heard my parents scream about being "on the verge of foreclosure." I was standing in the sun, looking down onto the black asphalt parking lot bordered by magenta bougainvillea. As I held on to the metal railing, my jaw dropped as I saw a man jump into my mom's convertible. He appeared to be hot-wiring it, just like in the movies. I screamed in terror, "MOOOOOM! ROBBER! THIEF!" The door behind me flung open as my mom rushed out to see what was happening. "HEY! That's my car! I'm a *doctor!*" my mom protested. The "thief" hollered back, "I'm from Mercedes-Benz credit, bitch!" and sped away. My mom self-righteously explained to me, "Mercedes is unfair and evil and out to get me! I HAVE the money. I called them to tell them that! I just forgot to pay the bill because I'm busy *saving lives*. What do *they* do except make cars for rich scum? It's disgusting." Wait, she was not-busy enough to call them and say she had the money but *too* busy to actually pay it? Hmm. I felt embarrassed, not so much because we couldn't afford what we had, but because our affairs seemed so chaotic.

In the money or out of it, one thing was always true: My parents never took care of the basics. Even as we went on lavish vacations to Hawaii, doctor's visits were not a given. In the fourth grade, I remember Beth Glazer complaining about how she had to go to the dentist for her regular checkup. "I'm so scared! My mom made an appointment with Dr. Wong!" she fretted. I felt a pang of jealousy deep in my stomach. My parents almost never "made an appointment" for me. I knew getting your teeth cleaned wasn't a "fun" thing, but I envied that Beth even knew the name of her dentist. I had never been to the same person more than once, if I went at all. I am assuming this was because we either had unpaid bills we were dodging or because consistency was simply not valued in our home. I fantasized about how nice it must feel to see "Dr. Wong," to have her crack cheesy jokes with me, to sit in a big plastic exam chair and dread having my teeth cleaned by someone I knew. I would have loved to fear the dentist.

Despite the fact that my parents were *clearly* not meant to be together, their marriage lasted as long as they were somewhat well-off. When my mom and dad both lost their jobs (at the same time! *FUN!*), there was nothing holding their marriage or our family together. Money was the glue, and we had run dry. To my dad's credit, he valued my education enough to work his ass off to keep me in private school, where at least some adults were paying attention to me, but he complained incessantly about the cost. "Your school is putting me in deep credit card debt. I don't know how we'll ever get out of it.

We're doomed." Was I the cause of all of my parents' money problems? Was I guilty of ruining their finances and thus their lives? Would my dad be better off without me weighing him down into debt? I felt like a total burden on my family.

Looking back, what is clear is that my parents never thought about money as something that could provide the basics and give them stability. Money was the icing on life, something decadent and sweet and showy. Who needed the actual cake, who needed a foundation, when you could have so much whipped sugar?

By twenty-five, I had heard and participated in so much financial fright that I had the hopeless sense that I would never escape my parents' cycle of budgeting disasters. I felt so tied to their mistakes, so woven into their fates, that I couldn't see that I was an adult capable of making my own choices. Instead, money took me on an erratic, emotional roller-coaster ride. I sat in the caboose, strapped in with no access to the brakes.

Should I buy the nicer toilet paper? IDK. Was I really worth three-ply? And if I started buying three-ply now, would that send me down a path of financial excess and later ruin? I was in my mid-twenties, had gone to college, and was working an "adult" office job, but I would freeze when confronted by the most basic purchases. What about pants? My entire wardrobe of pants was made up of three pairs of itchy stretch jeans that had holes in the crotchal region. This forced me to walk strategically so as not to expose myself at work. Was I allowed to buy new jeans yet? Or should I wait until the jeans were completely threadbare and falling off my legs? And what about the co-pay to see my lady-parts doctor? Yes, I was already paying for insurance, but wasn't *that* enough? Did I really need to go in and pay additional money for the actual checkup? Maybe that was unnecessary? I both believed that I wasn't worth the very basics and that the very basics weren't worth very much.

Don't get me wrong; I wasn't totally prudent either. I crowded with my lady friends into various bathrooms in the Meatpacking District, inhaling way-too-expensive, way-too-terrible coke out of minuscule plastic baggies. I enjoyed many costly, boozy brunches. But that was all money spent to show off my worth to others, not on things I needed to care for myself. And when I did indulge in those flippant extravagances of a twentysomething in New York City, I would then have a panic attack thinking about how one decision could wreck my entire financial future. Those mimosas would not only force me into a four P.M. fever-dream nap, but they'd also send me down the path to bankruptcy, I'd tell myself.

I would stand in the flower section of Trader Joe's debating whether I was worth seven-dollar lilies. Lilies are my favorite flowers (aside from peonies, *of course*). I love how they open up with the most wonderful burst of perfume. Lilies give any room instant elegance and calming vibes. I would see the lilies, fall in love, put the flowers in my cart, circle the entire store, decide the lilies were too good for me, put the flowers back in their bucket of water, continue shopping for my weird three-dollar microwavable Indian dinners, only to return to the flowers and, finally, angrily, fearfully, grab them and run for the register. Then I would wait in line for what felt like a lifetime, dwelling on my decision before asking the person in front of me to hold my place, taking the lilies out of my cart, and ditching them on a shelf between the kale and pita chips.

After extensive thought, agonizing in various stores about every single purchase, and a couple of decades of constant money stress, here is what I know:

1. **Buy the fucking lilies.** You are worth seven-dollar lilies. You are worth *the thing* that instantly makes your life better. I've heard people talk about their favorite

exercise class this way. I've heard people talk about an order of guacamole with their tacos this way. I've heard people talk about the ten-dollar, ten-minute massage at the nail salon this way. That small, pleasurable thing that makes you feel like you are treating yourself—do not deprive yourself of this. Buy the fucking lilies, take the class, order the guac, get the massage.

2. **Make the appointment.** The basics *are* the luxuries. You don't *have* to go to the doctor for your yearly exam, you *get* to. How lucky are you?! What a comfort to know that the basics are covered. Get the three-ply toilet paper, own a pair of pants without holes, buy socks that don't make you embarrassed to take off your shoes in the security line at the airport. The essentials can give you a sense of gratification far greater than any trip to Hawaii. Luxuriate in the indulgence of a drawer full of socks without holes. Take pride in the new toothbrush that isn't gross. Treat the basics as the luxuries they are.

3. **No stretching allowed.** This is not yoga. *You* are the one who decides your own money stress. Don't buy, lease, or agree to money things that will "stretch" your income. Sure, your BFF might be having a destination bachelorette party, destination bridal shower, *and* destination wedding, but that doesn't mean you *need* to go to all three. Especially if it will lead you into financial instability. If you strain toward something you can't really afford, is that even enjoyable? Why do it? No financial downward dog, please.

4. **No debt until something terrible happens.** Don't willingly go into debt for something that is not totally

necessary. Some unforeseen calamity might befall you and throw you into the red, that's life, but in the meantime, there's no need to deficit-spend your way into a "bigger life" to "keep up" with friends (see rule number three). The stress of debt is not worth having a remodeled kitchen, taking a blowout weekend in Vegas, or going to nine weddings next summer. It's okay if you can't afford these "fun" things. IT'S EVEN OKAY TO TELL YOUR FRIENDS, "I love you very much, but, I'm sorry, I can't go to your wedding because I can't afford the flight, hotel, and gift." THEY WILL UNDERSTAND. And if they don't? It's time to reevaluate that friendship. Student debt is an entirely different category. I am still paying off college, which I do not regret AT ALL, but I skipped grad school because, for me, the stress of debt was not worth the education I would have received. I found other ways to learn, and I'm glad I made that choice. It was the right one for me, but maybe it's different for you.

5. **Become aware of how you use money.** This seems so obvious, but few of us do it! Don't ignore what you do with your paycheck just because you're getting by, like I did! First, become conscious of *how* you put your money to use. Use an online budgeting tool (I like Mint) to track every dollar you spend. Not your style? For the next week, keep a notebook with you and write down *every single* thing you spend money on. *It's annoying as hell,* but this is only one week of your life and it will give you an accurate picture of how you are spending. Now ask yourself, is this what I *want* and *need* to be spending money on? Did I really *want* or *need* to somehow spend forty dollars at CVS on gum, cotton balls,

random nail polish, and some makeup that I'm fairly confident doesn't match my skin color? Or, looking back, would I rather have saved that money and put it toward my future dream trip to Europe? Did I really *want* to spend fifteen dollars over the course of the week on matcha lattes? FUCK YES, I DID! They make this shitty assignment at work tolerable. It's okay to spend money on small things that make you happy (see rule number one), BUT IT'S NOT OKAY TO SPEND MONEY UNCONSCIOUSLY ON THINGS THAT BRING YOU ZERO JOY AND DON'T COVER THE BASICS. Put that CVS-brand makeup back!

6. **Have a friggin' budget.** Now that you are aware of how you are spending, create a monthly budget. Your budget should start with the unavoidable costs: housing, transportation, bills (utilities, phone, student loans, etc.). PROTIP: Keep one doctor/dentist/eye exam place-holder in every month's budget so you never have an excuse not to go. Now look at your unavoidable costs and see if you are comfortable with them. Is your car too expensive? Are you stretching your paycheck to cover the rent on the super-cool place that's *super* out of your budget? If you answered yes, then it's time to do something about it. Maybe it's time to get a car that's a little less expensive? Time to look for a cheaper place? If you have money left over after you've covered the basics, BUDGET NOW for what you want to do with that extra money. Don't just let it slip out on frivolous things! How much do you save every month? How much will you allow yourself for a treat? I set aside forty dollars each month to get a pedicure and a back rub.

How much do you *decide* to spend on restaurants? You don't need to think, *Oh boo-hoo, I don't know if I can eat out tomorrow night.* Instead, you will *know: Oh yay! I have fifty dollars left in my restaurant budget. I can totes go out!* Or maybe it's *Ya know what, I've hit my limit for the month but there's always next month.* I'm telling you, deciding now what you will do with your money will give you more control over your life.

7. **Making more money is not a reason to spend more money.** In fact, it's a reason to save for a possible future calamity. More money and more stuff will never make you happy, I'm *so* sorry to say. It would be great if you could buy your way into feeling good, but it's just not possible, my dear.

8. **It's okay to talk about money.** *BUT choose wisely with whom you do this!* I didn't learn how to budget in school, or from my parents; I cobbled together a budget on my own, out of total necessity. You know what would have made my life easier? Talking to my friends about it—asking what they were spending on rent, what they were saving every month. I think that women in particular often avoid talking about money, but this just puts all of us in a weaker position because we have little practice discussing finances. Nowhere is this more true than when it comes to talking about salaries. Instead of feeling competitive or secretive about this information, HELP YOUR FELLOW WOMEN OUT and talk about what you are making. TELL THE WOMAN who is negotiating for her salary what you get paid if you think it will help her. BUT HERE IS A MAJOR CA-

VEAT: Only do this with people you trust and who are in a similar situation to your own. Do not tell Susan, who undercuts you in meetings, what your salary is. Do not ask Becca, who is living off a trust fund and whose parents bought her a house, what she is saving. Becca is never going to see a financial rainy day, so let's not ask her for the weather forecast.

9. **Forgive yourself for how you feel about money.** I know people who are outrageously rich and feel guilty that they don't understand how their trust funds work. They feel inadequate and undeserving. I have seen some of these people deny themselves the basics as a punishment for their good fortune. I know people who have had severe misfortune in their lives and feel like total failures for being in debt, despite the fact that it was unavoidable. It's okay. We ALL feel weird about money. The best way to feel un-weird about it is to become aware of the role it is playing in your life and to forgive, forgive, *forgive* yourself for any shame, any fuckups, any times you have stumbled. If you need to, every day this week write in your journal five times, "I forgive myself for feeling weird about money." Do this until it feels real.

Above all else: You are worth the lilies. The small, attainable luxury of lilies is not something to stress about, it is not something to deny yourself, it is something to make plans for and embrace. Small things that make you happy ARE a part of taking care of yourself. If you can't put your money where your mouth is and say, "I am worth the lilies" or "I am worth six-dollar beef jerky" or "I am worth the almond butter that makes me actually *look forward* to the morning," then why are you working so hard at your job anyway? Seven-dollar lilies won't ruin you and they won't make you poor; they will make you stronger. You are stronger when you treat yourself well. What are *your* lilies? Please go buy them today. If you feel weird about it at all, just blame me and then enjoy the fuck out of your flowers.

I've come a long way, but I still have trouble shaking off the way I used to think. Currently, I can't bring myself to buy a printer. I'm writing a book . . . I'd love to see my words on actual paper. But a *printer*? Can't I just print things at work in a clandestine manner or at Kinko's? And aren't printers hundreds of dollars? I don't know because I am too afraid to look up how much a decent printer costs.

If I Don't Take Monday Nights Off, We'll Have a Murder-Suicide Situation

Make Time for YOU

WE HAVE TALKED A LOT about self-care, so much so that it might not be obvious that I have a full-time corporate job. Five days a week, I'm in the office working for "the man." I am not my own boss, I am not independently wealthy, and I certainly *do not* choose my own hours. I don't have the luxury of sitting at home all day, glowing in the flicker of a grapefruit-scented candle, listening to soothing piano music as I consider how best to take care of myself. That's just on Saturday mornings. On the regular, I am rushing to get to work after journaling and the gym, my hair usually soaking wet and in a low bun because I never have time to dry it, and then I am scrambling through an overwhelming day of meetings. By the time four P.M. rolls by, I'm floored by how quickly the day went and how little I actually accomplished. I spend the next few hours working like a maniac to make up for lost ground before fighting traffic to get home and collapse into my bed. Hollywood is just as glamorous as it seems, baby.

My problem is that I overplan. With work, I feel like I have to suck the marrow out of every single opportunity: Why not say yes to every comedy show I have the pleasure of being invited to? Why not fill every breakfast, lunch, and dinner with meetings with incredible artists, writers, and directors? I'M SO LUCKY *RIGHT NOW* to be invited to *anything* at all. What if I get fired tomorrow? Wouldn't I be so upset that I didn't take advantage of *everything*??? And when it comes to personal commitments, I feel compelled to see my friend family as often as possible. Maintaining and prioritizing my friendships are where I derive my self-esteem from, after all! What if they move or I move or someone gets sick? With so many commitments, I walk through my days with an air of "I am very busy, I have no time to chitchat, let's not smile at one another." Then I feel guilty when I haven't checked off everything on my to-do list at the end of the day. I often give myself zero credit for what I *have* done and gobs of self-criticism for what I *haven't* done.

The problem with this scarcity-focused way of living, however, is that when I say yes to others, when I say yes to plans, I inadvertently say no to *me*. If I say yes to booking every single night of the week with interesting, incredible people, then I am also saying *no* to time in the week where I can hang out with another pretty cool person I know: myself. And, as the week goes on, being so busy just drains me. I'm spread so thin that I'm barely present. You might be having dinner with me, we might be splitting the pasta carbonara and talking about your breakup, but my mind is miles away, fantasizing about what it would be like to just sit on my bed, alone, in my navy-and-white polka-dot pj's, wearing one of those Korean facial sheet masks and reading a book by candlelight. (Whoa, that sounds so nice I'd like to do it rn.)

My cure for my own proclivity to overplan my life so I have no "free time" is to take Monday nights off. Every Monday night, in my calendar, I have blocked off as "BUSY WITH

ME." These nights are time when I allow myself to enjoy my own company. These nights are time when I can explore something I am deeply interested in and passionate about, like what is happening on *The Real Housewives of Beverly Hills,* for example. I can do NOTHING on Monday night and that's totally allowed because this is MY night. There is no checklist to go through. There is nothing I need to achieve. The only thing to do on a Monday night is enjoy the night. And if a work thing comes up or a friend is in town and I really can't take Monday off? Then I block off Tuesday or Wednesday or any other night of the week that works. The point is that I make sure to schedule time each week that is purely for me.

No matter what you are busy with, whether it be your job, your dating life, or taking care of children or aging parents, I think we all suffer from this societal pressure to always be occupied. "Busy" is worn as a badge of honor these days; the busier we are, the more important we feel. But busy doesn't mean important. Busy just means you are preoccupied. And often it means you're distracted. It doesn't mean you are esteemed, fun, smart, worthy, valued, loved, appreciated, excited, or happy. Busy likely means you are not paying attention to the current moment but instead are hustling around in a fog of things you "have" to do. Busy isn't special. We are *all* busy. So why label yourself something so *common?* You're better than that.

It's easy to give in to other people's requests for your attention. It's easy to say yes to your boss, to your parents, to your friends, to things that sound cool or are legitimately important, but it's oh-so-hard to say, "No, I need time to myself." It's difficult *not* to be busy. But we must learn to spoil ourselves with the most luxurious, sacred, scarce treat of all: time. Time to do nothing. Time to read. Time to take a long walk just cuz. I love you very much, but *no one* is asking you to run yourself ragged. There is no special prize at the end of life for "the busiest." I would not be pumped if my tombstone read, "Here lies Tara. She was *super busy*," with a portrait of me with a cellphone to my ear and an outstretched hand signaling "not right now" etched into marble.

So I ask you this: If you find that you're constantly describing yourself as "so busy I'm exhausted," why not try to take a Monday night off? Or a Wednesday night? And if you can't take a *whole* night? What about a lunch break that's just for you? What about an hour at seven A.M. before anyone else in your apartment is awake? What about an hour after work when you take a walk in that neighborhood you always meant to check out? The idea is to pick a time this week that is just for you and guard it as the precious commodity it is. See if you can be present with enjoying your own company.

If you're feeling at all guilty about taking time for yourself or think that it won't have a major impact on your life, let me tell you that none other than Mahatma Gandhi took one day off a week for prayer and meditation. Tara Brach (nice first name, BTW!) is one of my favorite thinkers/spiritual gurus/gangsters of self-care, and she tells the story of how even though good old Gandhi was *actually* busy fighting for Indian independence and *literally* changing the world, he recognized that he needed alone time to make sure that his "actions [came] from the deepest, most awake part of [his] Being." Fucking *Gandhi* understood that alone time replenishes the soul. I know that your life is *very full* and you have *a lot going on,* but you don't have more on your plate than *Gandhi* did, my love.

And if, by chance, you *are* the modern Gandhi, that is dope as hell. HI! WE REALLY NEED YOU RN! Please, please take a page out of his book and appreciate that there is something sacred and pure in setting aside time for yourself.

I think you're going to like it.

And if you don't?

Blame Gandhi; it's his advice, not mine.

The Well

Find What Inspires You and Cling to It for Dear Life

DO YOU EVER GET BOGGED down? Do you ever get so in your own head about your problems and worries that they are *all* you think about? Do you ever get to a place where it's hard to see what's good in life because you are preoccupied with all of the things you haven't yet accomplished, with all of the issues you need to "fix" about yourself, with the fact that if you were more responsible you would have emailed your aunt back last week instead of letting the message decompose in your inbox and now it feels like an awkward amount of time has passed and it's too rude to reply and maybe the best solution is just to pretend you never saw the email? It's either that or you can never speak to your aunt again. *No?* No one else is considering cutting people they love out of their lives because they just *can't deal* with how long it takes to respond to emails? It can't be only me who sometimes feels weighed down by the minutiae of living.

When I used to feel this way, I didn't know what to do. I would try to aim all of my self-care tools at my worry, hoping that they could dissolve my angst like a fire hose spraying a stack of sugar cubes. Sometimes that would work, but when I *really* felt depleted, I needed something stronger, something more encouraging, something that could physically lift me out of the muck of my own making. I asked my friends if they had advice for what to do. I read memoirs from adults I admired (Steve Martin, Cheryl Strayed, Maya Angelou) to see what they did when they felt their energy sapped by life. I came upon a common idea that each of us has a creative "well" that must be kept full. I've read about this so-called "well" in hokey self-help books; I've read about it in Ernest Hemingway's *A Moveable Feast*. Which, for the record, is in *no way* a self-help book. It might be the opposite, actually. Old Hem meditates that he "always [had] to stop [writing] when there was still something there in the deep part of the well, and let it refill at night from the springs that fed it." The well is something bottomless within us that, while nourishing, must also itself be nourished. It's the place where our creativity and happiness spring from. Hemingway used reading and spending time in Parisian cafés to feed his inspiration as he pounded down tumblers of whiskey and pounded out novels. I knew I had a well to fill, but what exactly was it? And how do you feed a well that lives inside of you but you can't see?

Up to this point, I had spent so much of my life denying pleasure and chasing things that would predictably make me feel like I wanted to crawl into a dark, dank hole and stop living my life altogether that I actually needed a little help figuring out what inspired me. So I hopped on a Google Hangout with my best friend Fisch, who was living in Tokyo at the time, to see what she thought lifted my spirits. "This is an easy one; you love to travel. That's what makes you excited and happy." "Fisch, that's so *silly*. Travel? Isn't there something small or not so wasteful that I like to do?" Didn't Fisch know that travel was an indulgent privilege for the wealthy or for people from "good" families like hers? In Fisch's parents' house, the walls are lined with photo collages of her clan in far-off lands. The "Africa collage" lives in a frame her mom hand-beaded in the aesthetic style of the Samburu tribe. *That's* who travel was for. People who had the money to go on safari and the time to make crafts. Not me. "Tara, you're being ridiculous. You asked me what inspires you. Why does it have to be practical? Why aren't you allowed to have things that are silly that you like? And travel isn't even silly!" Fisch's question cut me to the quick. Why *wasn't* I allowed to travel? Who decided it was too good for me? Oh yeah, *I* had. "Why don't you come visit me in Tokyo?" she suggested. "I have an apartment, so it would be free for you to stay. Plus, I feel like I've gotten to know the city. I'll be your personal tour guide!" At first, I was hit with a wave of *No, no, the ticket is too expensive! If you do that, it will lead to financial ruin!* But I knew enough about myself at this point to know that if I'm really uneasy about something, if the very thought of exploring something makes my skin crawl, it's probably the *very* thing I need to investigate. I looked at ticket prices, found one I could afford, and booked my flight that night, before I had time to back down.

I went to Tokyo with the intention of being the kind of person who goes to Tokyo. I didn't *totally* believe I had permission to travel to such an exotic place, so I faked being the kind of person who travels for fun. What kind of clothing would that person bring on a trip? Clothes they loved, things they thought they looked dope as hell in and not ratty T-shirts they didn't care about. I packed my bag as if I were an international jet-setter and *not* someone who was barely comfortable on an airplane. I figured this kind of person would know a lot about Japan, so I read a Haruki Murakami novel and a book on the history of Tokyo. And would that kind of person let a little jet lag get her down? Hell no. She would kick it into high gear the moment she landed.

With this new version of me in mind, I said yes to unfamiliar things, even if they made me deeply uncomfortable. I ate fresh eel. How fresh? It was alive and swimming in a glass just moments before I devoured it. On a solo day trip to Kyoto, I wandered through a bamboo forest in the rain and heard the chanting of Buddhist monks. Their voices vibrated through my soul in a way that I can *still* feel. I had a one-night stand with a tall guy with great glasses who studied medieval Buddhism, and when my phone died the next morning, I navigated the Tokyo subway system and figured out how to get back home on my own. In Japan, I faked being the kind of person who could enjoy her life, until, late one night, as I sang *terrible* karaoke in a bar with local friends we had made, I realized I *was* a person who could enjoy her life. And I was enjoying the fuck out of belting out "Purple Rain."

I have come to understand that travel is not a fancy luxury beyond my means. Travel is an important part of appreciating my life. It's deeply pleasurable, it expands my understanding of the world, and more than anything else, it gives me *perspective*. It gives me freedom from the everyday concerns that can weigh me down in my "normal" life. These trips don't have to be as adventurous as going to Tokyo for two weeks. Anything can be "travel" for me if my attitude is that I am on a voyage. A drive down to the beach, two hours in a beautiful public library, skipping breakfast on a work trip so I can explore the Detroit Institute of Arts. All of these count. One of my favorite trips I take each year is a solo day excursion to Ojai, California. It's a small town an hour and a half from Los Angeles, and I drive there early in the morning to go to the farmers market. Then I loaf around the town and soak up the magical golden lighting of the valley. I watch the sun set on Meditation Mount, the sky painted with insane swaths of pink and orange. Then I walk to my favorite little bar, listen to jazz on vinyl, and drink sake. It's not a big deal to go to Ojai—it costs the price of a half a tank of gasoline—but I go there with *intention;* I make it a big deal. My outlook toward the journey turns a small day trip into a life-giving adventure.

What feeds your well? What's the thing you love to do that makes your heart glad? Is it flower arranging? Is it people-watching at a café? Is it reading a book in a park without knowing what time it is? Is it going back to that dance class you used to love but for some reason stopped taking? What makes you so happy that it gives you rest and ease and feels so damn good that it sets your soul on fire with inspiration? These things that inspire us are often the easiest to lose sight of. We give them up because there is just so much "to do" in a day. We are "very busy," after all. But you do not gain strength from denying yourself pleasure and being *so serious* about your life. That's how you become brittle and drained. Instead, keep your well full, and be astonished at the power, the motivation, the brilliance that you will inevitably find in the rest of your life.

I am writing to you at the end of my day from a hotel room in New York City. I am on a work trip, but at lunchtime, instead of hastily eating my sandwich over a garbage can like I normally do (my sandwiches are in a conspiracy against me; they *always* fall apart . . . it's just easier to let gravity do the cleanup), I decided to take a walk through the West Village. I strolled down the cobblestone streets with no direction in mind and eventually found myself in Washington Square Park. In the background, a jazz trio played as I watched old men joke with one another during a game of chess. I kept walking and looked through the triumphal Washington Square Arch and onto the giant cement water fountain, which inexplicably turned on with gushing streams of water at that *exact* moment. The water jetted up into the sky like a tree coming into im-

mediate existence. A little girl next to me screamed out in gleeful amazement. I felt my whole damn body smile. How much
better was this moment than my sad garbage-can sandwich?
For the rest of the day, I was buzzing with inspired energy.

What can you do today that inspires you?

A Permission Slip
to Light Up Your Soul with Inspiration

I know how hard it can be to "allow" yourself to enjoy something, so if you are having trouble, please let me give you permission.

> *I, Tara Schuster, being of sound mind, hereby give you permission to find and pursue something that makes you excited, happy, and interested in your life. Here are a few prompts to help you find your inspiration:*

1. **What's something you used to *love* doing when you were a kid but long ago decided was too silly for an adult?** For me, it was making collages with lots of glue and glitter, like a toddler who has gone manic on Pixy Stix candy. _____
   _____
   _____

2. **What's something you've always *wanted* to do but haven't made the time for?** For me, it's jumping on a giant trampoline. It seems too dumb to carve out time for, but I REALLY want to do it._____
   _____
   _____

3. **What's something outrageous and crazy and fun that you want to do but the circumstances of your life make it seem impossible?** For me, it would be living alone in Europe for a year and traveling around

with one perfectly packed suitcase, talking to interesting people._____

_____

_____

I now give you permission to do ALL of the above activities and *any* others you've formerly deprived yourself of. You *must* pursue them. Even if it's just a little at a time. Sure, you might not be able to do all of number three tomorrow, but what is *one thing* you CAN do today that brings you closer to that version of yourself? For me, it would be having an espresso at a café, possibly while silently judging what other people are wearing. Write that thing here: _____. It is your sacred duty to do that this week. You are building toward a shinier, more glorious and bountiful life, and it's your obligation to keep yourself refreshed and happy, to feed your well. This week, you will carve out the time, you will make the necessary arrangements, you will make it your job to inspire yourself. You will not flake out. I know you, and you are no flake.

Signed,   Countersigned,

Tara Schuster

Tara Schuster   Your Name

Imagine a tinfoil golden heart here. That's my seal.

What's your seal?

Breathe In, Baby, Breathe In

Life Is Not a Series of Crises To Be Endured. Life Is To Be Enjoyed.

DEAREST READER,

Hi. Hello. How's it going? Where are you reading this from? I am writing to you from a hotel room, where I asked the front desk to change the stylish but super-uncomfortable desk chair to a legit computer chair. You know, one of those big, bulky office deals on wheels? Someone in the hotel's accounting office is letting me borrow it. God bless the good people in accounting. I did this because I wanted to be in a comfortable position to write to you today. I have something extremely important I must tell you.

All of the tools you've read about—the journaling, replacing self-medicating with exercise, developing a gratitude practice, writing thank-you notes, battling the Frenemy Within, mapping myself, figuring out whom I can *actually* trust, BUYING THE FUCKING LILIES, guarding my free time, and finding inspiration—did not heal me overnight. I did not wake up after the morning of my twenty-fifth birthday with all of the answers. Instead, I built these rituals one by one, taking each day at a time. I did so with urgency and great attention because I knew I wanted a better life.

Before I began my path to re-parenting and healing my wounds, it never occurred to me that you *could* enjoy your life. Having grown up in chaos, I naturally and easily built disorder into my adult life. I was *so good* at it, you guys. I thought that *was* life: a series of problems to be tackled until you lived another day, only to face a new disaster. Divorce, fights, your parents losing their jobs, fights with your boyfriend, *you* possibly losing your job, being too high, not knowing yourself—*those* were the things my life was made up of. In that place of turmoil, I only had the wherewithal to survive to the next day. I was barely present for a life that I felt was happening *to* me.

About a year and a half into developing my self-care regimen, I came home from a run, just beating the snow that was now falling from the sky. In my sweaty spandex, I sat at my little desk, lit a delicious candle that smelled like a spicy campfire, and began to journal. On my run, a phrase had popped into my head that I kept repeating: *I can be a remarkable person.* I wanted to know what that meant. Was I an egomaniac for thinking something like that? *No, Frenemy Within, it's okay to think expansively about myself.* By this point, this was by far the grandest thought I had had to date. "That thought is so big and scary," I wrote. "Why am I having it? I think being a remarkable person might mean giving back to the world. I think it means living your life in a way that when you leave the Earth, it is better off from having you in it. I think it means meeting smart, interesting people and being held in their esteem." Hmm. Could I achieve those things? I wasn't totally sure, but it was fun just thinking about the ways I could have a positive influence on the world.

That's when it hit me: I was enjoying myself.

I WAS ENJOYING MYSELF.

I adored the way I felt sweaty in my workout clothes but the surface of my skin was cold from the winter air. I LOVED how my apartment was so small that one little candle made the entire place smell like the perfect winter fire. I was grateful that I had that tiny studio to myself. The whole place was decorated in a way that was so very *me* because I knew who I was and what I liked. I cherished the little nook where I kept my desk, the wall above it now covered in pictures of Nora Ephron, Coco Chanel, and Paris. At the top of the wall, I had taped a quote from Cheryl Strayed: "Write like a motherfucker." I had taken the time to write that phrase on thick cream-colored paper in calligraphy with one of those pens that you dip into an actual inkwell. I did that just for fun. Wait, I was doing things *just for fun*? I wasn't living crisis to crisis? Nope, I wasn't. I loved my life. I LOVED MY LIFE. WHAT THE FUCK?

As I continued to write, this phrase came out of my pen: "Life is not a series of crises to be endured. Life is to be enjoyed."* This felt so true, so urgent, so unexpected, so *electric* to be coming from *me* that my arms instantly broke out with goose bumps of joy. Writers talk about that one time something *just came to them* and *this* is my *that*. If you take ANYTHING away from this book, please let it be these lines above. Please say it to yourself one million times. *Life is not a series of crises to be endured. Life is to be enjoyed.* Please remember it when times are tough, but also when times are excellent.

That day, sitting in my sweaty workout clothes, it finally hit me that life is not something you have to "get through." Life is not a list of problems to be solved. Sure, there are issues along the way to deal with, but part of learning to savor your life is learning to see the process of figuring things out as pleasurable. It's *gratifying* to figure out how to treat your messiest, most vul-

---

* My copy editor points out that Gordon B. Hinckley, a religious leader, said something very similar, before my time. He said, "Life is to be enjoyed, not just endured." I guess great minds think alike? And I happen to think like the former president of The Church of Jesus Christ of Latter-day Saints?

nerable traumas. Don't get it twisted, though. It may not always be *fun*. Working through the things that make your stomach churn with anxiety isn't like going to your favorite concert. You won't be wearing a floral headdress and dancing. Or maybe you will be, in which case, *rock on*. But my point is that there is profound satisfaction in really working on the tough shit.

My unbridled optimistic view that I can and *will* enjoy my life, even when it's difficult, is not some "cute" or "naive" thought. It is a powerful, pragmatic tool to help me not just *survive,* but to thrive, to fully *live* my life to the hilt. Do you know where the phrase "to the hilt" comes from? The hilt is the visible part of a sword, the handle, the only thing you can see once you've plunged your sword *all the way* into something. I am living my life like a goddamn warrior.

I don't believe in a singular God, but I do believe in whatever wild energy made this universe. (It's fucking crazy and magical and awe-inspiring that we are here *at all*.) I have faith that whatever made us up doesn't think my life should suck. He/She/They *want* me to lead a remarkable life. If they didn't, then why would they tell me, "Life is not a series of crises to be endured. Life is to be enjoyed"? Why take the time to give me a secret message if I didn't have the power to follow through?

And really, I ask you, what is the alternative? Are you going to sit at home wallowing in your trauma? The dog died (or got kidnapped, in my case). You were laid off. Your boss is a lunatic and you are constantly stressed out by his unreasonable demands. Someone important to you is no longer with you. You don't feel like you do enough, have enough, or *are* enough. If these are the things you find yourself thinking on the regular, then I am going to tell you something you need to hear: You are the one hanging on to what's *wrong.* It's not that the painful stuff doesn't exist; rather, two things can be true at the same time. You can be torn apart by the divorce of your parents *and* you can be grateful for how it taught you, by opposite example, to find a life filled with stability and joy. You can be stricken with grief that you never had the relationship with your mom you deserved *and* you can appreciate that it pushed you to find other mentors who opened up your world. You can HATE your day job, absolutely dread going in, *and* you can be thrilled that you are taking singing lessons that make you feel more alive. The sooner you can get comfortable with the ambiguity of two things being true at the same time, the sooner you will enjoy all parts of your life, even the not-so-great ones, because you know that's not the *whole* story.

Your whole story is so much richer than any one trauma or obstacle. With practice, you can learn to acknowledge and care for the "not-so-great" while also holding up what is absolutely stellar. You can dive deep down to the ocean floor of your feelings, find your unknown issues, drag them up to the surface, hold them to the healing rays of the sun, and say, "Hey! Yes! I own what I've been through. I see it in the clear daylight, and I'm not afraid to figure out how it affected me. Now, I will get on my yacht of self-care, throw on these chic sunglasses I saved up for because I look like a goddamn movie star in them, and relish the life I am living." Because if you don't, then you will let yourself be defined by crisis-to-crisis living, missing out on all of the joy that is around you. And I know you better than that. You are not just going to give up and let your life, the life you are ALLOWED to love, pass you by. You are a glittering, pulsating star that will shine on all of us. Please, illuminate the way.

Living the life you want to live is just about the *least* selfish thing you can do. You know in those airplane safety videos where there are a mom and daughter sitting (unrealistically) calmly as oxygen masks deploy from the plane's ceiling? And the mom puts the oxygen mask on herself first, *before* her fucking *child*? Did that ever strike you as strange? That she would take care of herself before her *child*? It's just like that. You can't help anybody, not even *your child,* unless you are healthy yourself, unless you can breathe. So if you want to be the least selfish version of yourself, if you want to contribute to this world, if you want to be a remarkable person, I recommend you grab that oxygen mask, strap it around your head, and breathe in, baby. Breathe in. We need you.

II

THE
BODY RITUALS

I Stopped Treating My Body and Physical Space like a Garbage Can, and So Can You!

A Fresh Start

Create Physical Habits That Work for You

OVER THE COURSE OF TWO and a half years, my rituals for calming my mind had paid off. No longer was I weeping in my cubicle at work, no longer was I walking around with an anxiety knot in my heart. Obviously, I still slipped up sometimes. There were still stretches when I let negative self-talk kick me down a few pegs, but now I was aware of what was happening, *and* I had the tools to get back on the path of self-care when I faltered. I was re-parenting the shit out of my mind, and, ladies and gentlemen, it was working. YAAAY! CUE THE MOTHERFUCKING BALLOON DROP!

As my self-confidence began to grow, unexpectedly so did my desire to move back to Los Angeles, the very place I had worked so hard to escape. I had pined for the East Coast as a kid, but I was tired of how difficult the reality of living in New York was. The subways that never ran when you needed them. The waitresses who would look at you with suspicion if you asked, "How is your day going?" I would find myself writing things in my journal like "Wouldn't it be nice to live in LA where there is SUN and NOT a polar vortex?" I suffer from seasonal depression (TBH, who doesn't?!), and since my New

York apartment had windows that let in only the shining light of the brick wall across the alleyway, I struggled with the darkness. I found myself scribbling, "In Los Angeles, there are more opportunities to be involved in entertainment, and since that's your passion, a move makes sense."

I was expressing my desire to get back to California in writing, but I couldn't figure out how to make the move without giving up the job I was coming to love and feel at home in. Then, dearest reader, the most off-chance-weird-NO-WAY-is-this-real? thing happened. I was in Los Angeles visiting the offices of the new show I worked on remotely, *Key & Peele,* when my boss called with some big news. "I'm moving to Los Angeles. I don't want that to freak you out—you'll still have your job. You'll just report to me from New York." My Brooklyn-hipster boss was moving to *LA*? Totally unexpectedly? DID HE KNOW *I* WANTED TO MOVE BACK? Was this a "tiny, little break" that Jon Stewart had described all those years ago?

Without thinking, as if moved by some invisible hand, I hung up the phone, walked straight into the office of the stars of the show, and explained that I could do a better job for them if I worked from their offices in Los Angeles. Didn't they think it was essential that I move? "Sure, whatever," they not-so-enthusiastically replied before returning to a heated debate over what to order for lunch. I called my boss back in New York and explained, "Keegan and Jordan said I *have* to work from their offices in LA. Why don't I move with you, and we can start up a West Coast division?" Luckily, no one checked in with the other, and the move was approved. It was a win for everyone involved: Keegan and Jordan got a dedicated digital producer for their show, which was *just* starting to create a little buzz; Comedy Central got better access to their talent; and I couldn't find an excuse NOT to move if everything was going to be so smooth. Though it felt like a magic piece of luck that this was so effortless, writing my intention so many times and being aware of what I really wanted cleared the path for me to jump when the opportunity presented itself. The invisible hand that moved me was my own.

Before I left New York for good, I took a trip to LA for a promo shoot. A promo shoot is when a shocking amount of time and money is spent filming the stars of a show for ads. You remember "ads," the things you fast-forward through? These shoots are usually way more extravagant than producing *the actual show,* with lots of downtime and a catering staff offering "ice-blended-kale-raw-honey-banana-smoothies" and tiny grilled cheese sandwiches sitting in cups of tomato soup. I spent my downtime with Ian Roberts, one of the showrunners for *Key & Peele* and a personal hero of mine. He was one of the founders of the Upright Citizens Brigade, which in addition to having been a groundbreaking television show is also a school and philosophy for how to make comedy. I had taken classes at the UCB and read the book, and whenever I spoke to Ian, I hung on to his words like I was in a master class. "So you're moving back to LA, huh?" he asked as a fog machine filled "the club" set we were shooting on with vapor. "Yeah, I'm thinking about it, but I'm a little worried. It's home for me and . . . well . . . home was a not-so-happy place." "The thing about moving," he said, "is it's a good way to shake loose whatever old baggage you have, or the old things that were true about yourself, and decide what you *want* to be true about yourself. It's the best way to make new habits that serve you." I felt shivers. Both from the mass amount of manufactured haze and from recognizing something true in his words that I had never considered before: In Los Angeles, I would have a clean slate to create whatever new rituals I needed most.

I decided I wanted to move to LA with the intention of

creating good physical routines for myself. I had spent so much time working on my mind, but recently, I had been noticing that in New York, it was entirely possible to avoid the fact that I had a physical body that also needed care and attention. In a city where it is normal to have drinks before you have drinks, where most of the year you are bundled and fully covered so that your shape most closely resembles an amoeba, where dim lighting is not only sexy but mandatory so no one has to see how pale we all are, I hadn't really confronted my physical self, beyond my morning jogs that were, for the most part, to clear my headspace. I had never really pushed myself to grow stronger. In Los Angeles, where it is sunny most of the year, you are forced to *see* yourself. Bolstered by Ian's words, the new me decided I'd move to LA *excited* to create new routines that took care of my body. It was going to be great and fun and I wasn't worried *at all* that this would be very difficult and demoralizing.

Under the bright California sun, I would learn to cherish my body.

~~EW, GROSS, BLECH, THAT'S NEVER GOING TO HAPPEN.~~

~~OH MY GOD, WHAT A FUCKING CRAZY THING TO EVEN THINK.~~

I Get Ready Like Cleopatra

Greet the Day like the Sovereign Ruler You Are

AFTER CRASHING AT MY DAD'S condo in Los Angeles for a ~~few months~~ year to save money (thanks, Dad!), one of my best friends also happened to make the pilgrimage from NYC to LA. I met Lauren my first day of high school when we both auditioned for the school play. (I was cast as Madam Zachanassian, an elderly self-made billionaire who returns to her destitute hometown to strike a disturbing deal: She will make the ailing town rich if they will kill the man who impregnated and then jilted her when she was young. Lauren played Grandchild Number Two. It was a very appropriate, not-at-all weird play for fifteen-year-olds.) I never had a roommate in New York and didn't think I wanted one now, but Lauren brought something important to my attention: If we pooled our *New York* rent, we could get a baller apartment in *Los Angeles* that would surely make all of our friends back in NYC living with four roommates separated by "walls" that did not go all the way up to the ceiling very jealous. I was sold. As we toured apartments, we noted what would make East Coasters the most envious: "I think these beamed ceilings with painted flowers are going to drive our friends *nuts*," I gleefully exclaimed. "I think the fact that this place has a dining room *and* a kitchen nook is going to make them just a *little* bitter," she added. "This washer and dryer IN the unit is going to make people set themselves on fire." (Okay, I went a *smidge* too far with that one.) We settled on a 1920s Spanish duplex in a so-so part of town because it offered us opulent space—no more tiny studio apartments for us!

I hadn't lived with another woman since college, and I was surprised to find that Lauren had many rituals for how she "got ready." "I'm going with my mom to Rosie's Nails to get a mani-pedi. I'll see you in a few hours, roomie." A few hours? What exactly was going to happen at Rosie's? Did her manicure come with Botox and a staged reading? "My mom and I are going to our makeup guy, Patrick, to get some new stuff for spring; see you around dinnertime." They had a *makeup guy*? Was *I* supposed to have a makeup guy? And, wait, was I supposed to get new makeup for *spring*?! One day, I came home to find Lauren and her mom sitting on her bed sipping chardonnay. "We're going to get our hair blown out before we see *Phantom of the Opera,*" Lauren explained. They were having pre-drinks and getting their hair blown out *for a play? Why?* Who was going to see them in the dark theater? If I was "going out," my routine consisted of slapping the tinted moisturizer I had been using since high school on my face and *maybe* flat-ironing my hair.*

At first, I thought the effort Lauren put into her physical appearance was . . . well . . . pretty vain. When she got ready at home, it always took at least an hour before she emerged from a cloud of perfume and powders. Wasn't it frivolous to spend so

---

* This has never been, and will never be, a good look on me. Yet for some reason, I keep flat-ironing my hair when I want to look "nice." Are other people suffering from this delusion?

much time, money, and energy on your appearance? But post–
"getting ready" Lauren always radiated. Not only did she look
great, but she seemed happy and confident. "Lauren, I don't get
it!" I confessed. "Isn't it annoying to spend so much time on
your appearance? Like, when you're getting your nails painted,
don't you just want to die at how long you have to sit there?
I've never left a manicure without smudging it because I didn't
have the patience to let it fully dry!" "Well, you can always get
a neck and shoulder massage while you wait," she offered.
"That's a pretty brilliant move," I had to admit. "But what
about how much the whole thing costs?!" She laughed. "How
much do you think a mani-pedi costs? It's not insane, and, honestly, it's fun." But, *again,* didn't she think it was wasteful and
superficial to spend so much time on her looks? "Well, I just
don't see it that way. These are things I learned from my mom."
Ah. Right. Enter the self-pity parade: Cue the cymbals, the
trumpets, the baton girl, and someone waving a big red ornamental flag with "mom issues" in gigantic bright yellow block
letters. Lauren had learned these rituals from her mom, and
since, as an adult, I no longer had a relationship with mine, I
had missed out.

Throughout my parents' divorce, which lasted through middle school, high school, and half of college—a fun eight years
total—I was deciding what to do about my relationship with
my mom. As you know, it had never been great, and I always
felt on my guard around her, ready to run away if her insults
got too intense or yell back if I felt like I needed to defend
myself. It often occurred to me that I could cut her out of my
life altogether, but I always returned to a central truth: I wanted
a mom. I thought, maybe, one day, by some miracle, she would
stop leaving me harassing voicemails, she would stop screaming
at me, telling me that I was "a terrible person with no values"
and that I needed "extreme psychotherapy to stop being a

pathological liar." One day, I still hoped, she would become a mom like the ones I saw in Nancy Meyers films: fun, loving, supportive, making chocolate croissants in the middle of the damn night. One day, my mom would be Meryl Streep, I hoped. (Do you ever wish for that? Tell me it's not just me waiting for Meryl? Or, guys, what about Diane Keaton *for your mom*?!)

I remember one morning during my junior year of high school, I was taking my sister to school because my mom wasn't feeling well. I was happy to drive from my dad's house to my mom's to pick her up; I would have done anything for some extra time with Diana, whom I rarely saw. It was our tradition at the time to listen to the soundtrack to the musical *Chicago* whenever we were together. We were in the middle of singing "Cell Block Tango" ("He had it coming! He had it coming! He only had himself to blaaame!") when my sister picked up a phone call from my mom. As she listened, I could see her face change from "fun-times-musical-sing-along" to worry, her forehead wrinkling and her eyes narrowing. By the time she got off the phone she was in a panic. "Something isn't right with Mom. Her words aren't making sense." We quickly turned around. When we got to my mom's house, I jumped out of the car, leaving the door wide open, and raced in to find my mom in the shower, semi-coherent. "Tara, is that you?" my mom called out. "I'm extremely ill. This is death. . . . I am dying. . . . I've gone septic." I wasn't sure what "septic" meant, but since I could remember, my mom had made histrionic claims that she was on the verge of death or incredibly ill, so it was difficult to know if I should take this seriously or not. Why, for example, if she was so sick, did she call Diana and not the hospital? I didn't want to question her or get into an argument, so I did the only thing I could think of: I dialed 911. "Operator speaking, what's your emergency?" "Well, my mom says she's dying."

When the ambulance arrived, the paramedics hurried through the house toward my mom standing naked in the shower, the water streaming down on her as she steadied herself against a wall. In my memory, the paramedics were kind but taken aback by the condition of my mom's house. Just like the home I grew up in, this one was so cluttered with cardboard boxes, clothes, and random equipment that it resembled what you might have seen on the reality TV show *Hoarders*. They affixed my mother to a gurney while she wailed, "Girls, I loved you. Remember that I loved you."

To this day, I am not sure *exactly* what my mom had. She said at the time it was typhus, which I thought sounded like something from *The Jungle Book,* but looking it up now, I see that typhus isn't all that exotic; it's an infection you can get from a simple flea bite. Sitting in that hospital, I felt pangs of guilt for questioning whether my mom was sick, but she had cried "wolf" so many times before that she had become an unreliable narrator for her health. I sat with my sister in the hallway outside my mom's room, eating chipped ice (the only perk to being at a hospital), shuddering lightly with fear that she may actually be dying this time. I emphatically decided that it didn't matter whether she was sick or not, it was time for my mother and me to put aside our tensions before it was too late.

I walked into her room, pulled up one of the visitor chairs, put her weak, IV-injected hand in mine, and explained, "Mom, I want us to love each other. I don't care who is right or how we got to this bad place, but can we move on and start over?" My mom, frail from her infection, looked at me and faintly smiled. "Sweetheart, I love you. Nothing else matters. I want to be a good mother to you." *Whoa. Is this the moment I have been waiting for my entire life? A reset? FINALLY.* I sobbed with relief.

This traumatic moment would be our turning point, I knew it; we would remember this hospital stay as the scary push we needed to finally fix our fucked-up relationship. My mom looked at me tenderly and raised her hand to my face. *She's about to tell me something I've been waiting my whole life to hear.* I leaned in. "Sweetie . . . I need you and your sister to write down everything that happened. Those paramedics thought I was just some crazy lady and not a *doctor.* They left the back door open in the ambulance and no one sat with me and exhaust seeped in and I could have suffocated to death. AND they took me to the *one* hospital where all my enemies work even though I told them not to. . . . We're going to sue them."

I walked out of my mom's room and sat down next to my sister. I pulled my knees up to my chest and wrapped my arms around my legs in a tight hug as I began to cry. My sister held on to me. "Tara, it's okay; Mom's going to be fine. She didn't die." I didn't have the heart to tell her that I wasn't crying about Mom's health. They were tears of a different kind of grief. If, on her supposed deathbed, if, at a time when her life had been supposedly saved, my mother was wrapped up in creating a conspiracy theory against the very paramedics who rescued her instead of focusing on the blessing that she was *alive* and that her two daughters were by her side, then it might be time to let go of the idea that she would ever be a nurturing mom. She was never going to be anyone other than who she was, and that person was not someone healthy in my life. There would be no reconciliation; there would be no Nancy Meyers moments. Meryl-slash-Diane was never coming to the rescue.

It took seeing that my roommate Lauren actually liked spending time with her mom to realize how much of a void had been left in my life. Look, I get that plenty of people don't have moms at all. I know that mother-daughter relationships are often complicated. I 100 percent understand that I am not technically alone, yet in my adult home, with my grown-ass roommate, I felt a sudden, petulant sadness for all of the experiences I never had. I never had a spa day with my mom. She never shared her makeup tips with me. We never went shopping together for a special dress for a dance. She never told me what kind of clothing might be the most flattering for my body. (*BTW, I still don't know. Do you understand these things? Please send help.*) I felt a heartache that I hadn't been granted access to those rituals, the ones that, while seemingly superficial, can feel so important in this culture of being a woman. I just wanted a mom who would show me how to *get ready*.

I wrote about this sadness until I was struck with a new, sensational thought: If I didn't have a mom I could emulate, then I'd just have to create my own rituals for getting ready. I would teach myself how to *perform* the role of being a woman. Maybe, in the end, I would determine that the "getting ready rituals" were just as stupid and wasteful as I suspected, but it would be *my choice* and not the result of having never been taught. I would not neglect myself.

I thought about all the women I admired for their look and how they carried themselves: Audrey Hepburn in *Breakfast at Tiffany's,* Ruth Bader Ginsburg at *all times,* Kerry Washington in *Scandal* (have you seen those power suits?! Those coats?! DAMN). Ultimately, I turned to my long-loved, aspirational icon: Cleopatra. Sovereign Goddess, OG Lady Boss. She was a shrewd, clear-eyed empress who at one point ruled over virtually the entire eastern Mediterranean in a palace made of onyx, garnet, and gold. Incomparably smart, she out-negotiated, out-strategized, and out-bad-assed her foes. She slept with only two men in her life, *but* those two men were Caesar and Mark Antony. The woman knew what she was doing. Ever since I first read about Cleopatra in a children's book about the mysteries of ancient Egypt, I have loved her. As a kid, I had a stamp set of hieroglyphics that I wore down to the nubs. As an adult, I have a signature summer bracelet, which is a golden asp that wraps around my forearm. It's a replica of one in the Metropolitan Museum of Art. It was given to me by an ex whom I would rather not remember, but I have a rule about jewelry: Its beauty alone can transcend any bad memories of the giver. That is a sentiment with which I am sure Cleopatra would have agreed.

Clearly, I couldn't ask Cleo how she got ready in the morning, so I imagined what it would look like. First, I put a postcard of Elizabeth Taylor as Cleopatra in a Tiffany-blue enamel frame and set it on the vanity table in my bedroom for inspiration. Then, because I figured the empress would keep her makeup brushes in good order, I took some pretty mason jars from the kitchen and arranged my measly instruments in them. I might not have had "a makeup guy," but it was easy enough to go to Sephora and buy a few essential items. I don't like the look of a face full of makeup, so I found an organic tinted moisturizer with rose oil. I splurged on a mascara called "Black Ecstasy" because it gave me those heavy faux eyelashes I think Cleopatra would have preferred. I experimented with the whole mani-pedi industrial complex. While I was right about manicures (I can't stand waiting for my nails to dry *even with* a massage), I discovered that a pedicure is one of the most luxurious activities in which one can indulge. I revel in the feeling of getting my feet super clean, having the gunk removed from under my nails, getting my cuticles cut, and looking at my nails after—like shiny, bright candies, ready to be eaten. Added bonus: You don't have to wait for them to dry. Simply put on your queenly sandals and move on with your day.

Now, in the morning, when I am getting ready for a new day, I take the time to act as if I am a powerful empress: confident, expansive, and enthusiastic about the work of the upcoming day. I blast Frank Ocean's "Pyramids" from my iPhone speakers. I smudge the air with sage. I might burn a black incense pyre called "Blood Countess." I let my bedroom get filled with music and vapor. I dot my wrists with a spicy French perfume, stand in front of the mirror, and breathe in the smoke (I am a *little* afraid this is not healthy).

What I have learned is that you are stronger when you give yourself incredible kindness. There is no better time to do this than in the morning. This day is yours. Sure, you might have to strategize around a boss who is undermining you. You might have to finally break up with someone you are dating, or be broken up with. You might get the worst news of your life today. You never know. But! While you are alone in your kingdom, while you have a moment of quiet, you can honor and respect yourself. It's a potent base level to start your day. And when you begin your morning recognizing that you are a goddess, you'll notice that the whole world will start to treat you that way. I'm not talking about vanity. I'm not talking about narcissism. I'm talking about acknowledging, first thing in the morning, that you are powerful and worth taking care of. I'm telling you, if it worked to just rush around and be mean to yourself in the morning, *I would do that*. It takes less time and comes quite naturally to me. But I tried that for so long and it just never worked.

If you can't believe me, believe our modern Cleopatra— Beyoncé. She sings, "You wake up, flawless. Post up, flawless. Ride round in it, flawless." Beyoncé's not saying that you need to be held to some unattainable standard, she's saying you are already *flawless*, the whole of you, just as you are. Look at yourself in the mirror, chant those words like an ancient prayer, and now go show the world your ferocious majesty.

A List of Ways to Treat Yourself like Royalty in the Morning

1. **Make yourself a witchy brew.** Yeah, coffee is great, but what about a *potion*? I mix espresso with Ashwagandha, an herbal antioxidant my doctor recommended that's supposed to help with stress. I have ZERO idea about the science, but the name alone sounds exotic and like something you would find on a trek to distant lands, so I'm super down with it. Sometimes I whisk in cinnamon or dried ginger or just plain old milk. But! The most important thing is, as I stir my concoction, I imagine it as an elixir that will bring me power.

2. **Light a fire. You heard me,** *light a fucking fire.* Be it incense, a votive candle, or a sage smudge stick, do something to sanctify the air. If you're running late, light a match and just take a moment to set the trajectory of your day. "Today, I will conquer many lands." "Today, I won't get swept into anyone else's bullshit drama." "Today, I will finally turn in my overdue expense reports." Breathe in. Imagine you are inhaling something smoky but wonderfully healing that will not damage your lungs.

3. **Pump those jams.** Play something that speaks to you in the morning. I've listened to Frank Ocean's "Pyramids" *a lot.* Sometimes Fleetwood Mac's "Gypsy" is in order. I play Beyoncé's "Flawless" *a lot.* Other times, I need to hear Kendrick Lamar's reminder to "Be humble." Paul Simon's "I Know What I Know" is another affirmative jam. Choose music that makes you feel giddy and powerful and gets your royal blood coursing through your body. Dance a little. I do.

4. **Make your face.** Every gender can take a moment to look themselves in the mirror and make sure they are polished to face the day. For me, this means painting on a light layer of my tinted moisturizer. For you, it might just be a spritz of a toner. Or maybe you use nothing at all. No matter. Just take a moment and *face* yourself in the mirror and make sure *this* is the face you want to bring into the day to show both your admirers and foes.

5. **Anoint thyself.** With gems, with rhinestones, with any amulets you may need that day. I wear a locket my dad gave me when I was eighteen because it reminds me that, though flawed and complicated, I am loved and can love. I can touch my locket and remember that. Dab your scent of choice on your body. I put perfume on the base of my neck, both front and back. That way, I am inviting the world to kiss the sides of my neck without getting a mouthful of perfume. How you adorn yourself in the morning is how you invite the world to interact with you. Clearly, I would like to be made out with.

6. **Say a prayer.** You are lucky that you were born a goddess. Thank the universe for your good fortune and let it know how you will carry your power. "Today I am confident, expansive, enthusiastic. I am enough, just me, standing here, in front of the mirror, being present. Today I will act with generosity." If you've been using any positive affirmations, this would be a great time to employ one like a blessing. "I am brilliant and talented" sounds pretty good right about now.

BUT, TARA, I'm at the gym! How the fuck do I do any of this at the gym/my lover's house/the dorm's shared bathroom??? Let me remind you that you are a queen/king/ruler, A MOTHERFUCKING GODDESS. Would a *goddess* skip her rituals just because it was a *little* inconvenient? Oh, hell no. Come up with a version that works on the go. If I'm at the gym, I have a sample size of oil I put on my wrists. I can't light a fire without freaking everyone out, but I can spray rosewater mist around me.

If You Can Play Nice with Others, Play Nice with Yourself

Do One Kind Thing for Yourself on the Daily

I HAVE A QUESTION FOR you: How nice are you to yourself? Not to your mom, not to your dad, not to your friends, not to the random stranger in line at the coffee shop who looked like they were having a rough day so you asked, "How's it going?" and genuinely wanted to know the answer. How nice are you to *yourself*? Don't know? Let's try a test. **Right now, write down ten things you like about yourself.** Go ahead and use the margins of the book.

Did that freak you out? Was your gut reaction *How about, instead, I throw this book against the wall?* Did you think, *TEN things? I have maybe* two? Did you think, *Presently, I feel doomed by my personality and trapped in a cycle of imagining all the ways I could have avoided becoming a terrible person but didn't?* Or was it easy? Did you think, *Just ten?!* Did you think, *I could go on about how much I love my hair, my laugh, the way I am thoughtful about my friends, la-la-la, this is a cinch?* Or did you find yourself a little confused, thinking, *I know it's important to be able to answer this* *question and there are things I like about myself, but I'm worried this is a stupid, self-centered exercise?**

If my question made you angry and think, *Only crazy narcissists* like *themselves,* then you really need this chapter. It's going to be painful, but I was once in your position, so *trust me,* we can get beyond this, together. If my question felt easy-peasy-lemon-breezy, then I bow down to you, Goddess. You have done a lot of work already, and I admire that you can recognize the good in you. This chapter will just be fun for you and help sharpen your self-love routine.

I smile at strangers. I hold the door for the person behind me (though it should be noted I feel a spiteful rage when others don't do the same for me; HOLD THE GODDAMN DOOR OPEN FOR OTHER PEOPLE). I buy thoughtful gifts for friends. I am "nice." And yet. I take when other people are not "nice" to me a little too much to heart. When a colleague once called me "aggressive," I had a total meltdown. DID EVERYONE SECRETLY HATE ME? WAS I RUINING MY CAREER?! I cried in my boss's office as she assured me that not only was I not "aggressive"† but that maybe one piece of "negative" feedback wasn't the worst thing in the world. It was an extreme reaction, but I want people to like me *so much.* There. I said it. Isn't that kinda what we all want, tho? To feel accepted and liked? When a magazine rejects an essay of mine, I often think, *See? Who were you to think you could write? They know better, and you suck.* When a boy I'm into, who I have been seeing four times a week, who claims he's "so into me," suddenly ends things because he is "not falling in love" with me and isn't sure he "ever will"—*OUCH!*—my first thought

---

*   BTW, these are all real things my own friends said to me when I asked them this question.

†   Can we please never, ever call women at work "aggressive"? The word is just too loaded. Let's just do away with it altogether, k?

isn't *How weird that he would tell me that in explicit detail when we've been dating only a month. I didn't even know I was supposed to be judging him on the love scale this early. This is clearly about his own issues.* My first thought is *Another heartbreak? What did I do wrong?* Taking someone else's criticism of me and doubling down on it is not a "nice" thing to do. If a friend told me, "I just got broken up with out of the fucking blue," I wouldn't yell at her, "Well, you must have done *something* for him to treat you so poorly!" I'd say, "That guy is a DICK! This has nothing to do with you. CLEARLY he has issues if that's how he handled it. You dodged a bullet. Can I take you out to fancy sushi?"

The *moment* I feel an emotional arrow pierce my heart, I do something kind for myself. When my boss says something I perceive to be even vaguely critical, I buy a Honeycrisp apple, even tho it's a dollar more than the Fuji apple, BECAUSE, DAMN IT, I deserve to eat apples I love. With every bite, I think, *I do good work.* When an essay of mine gets rejected, I draw a sudsy bath and tell myself, *It was nice they took the time to send me a pass instead of ignore me. What a sign that I am actually putting myself out there and am moving toward my dreams!* When I get spurned by a boy, I buy myself some seriously decadent sushi. THE SECOND I feel a hurt, I take a loving action and I think, *This apple is for you; this bath is to warm you; you are eating this delicious sushi because you deserve it.* It's intentional AF.

Finding a physical balm to soothe an emotional sting is one of the healthiest, most resilience-building practices you can bring into your life. Every single time you meet hurt with loving action, you train your body and your mind to think more highly of yourself. You stop the negative pattern of *Hey, what someone else did hurt me, so let me just really sink into it and believe whatever the fuck they think to be true.* That pattern is USELESS. Has it ever made you feel better or helped you accomplish more? No? Then it's time to let it go.

I challenge myself to do one nice thing for me every day, just because. Can you believe that? *Sometimes I'm nice to myself for no reason at all.* It's kind of astounding how hard of an assignment it can be. It's so easy to dismiss it as silly or self-centered or indulgent, but when you actually go through with being intentionally kind to yourself, you will be stunned by the results. You will feel more secure. You will notice how the insults and slights of the day, whether from internal or external sources, roll off you more easily.

I challenge you to keep a list of nice things you can do for yourself. I know it's natural to be mean to or hard on yourself, but you are going to have to trust me on this one. If you can let go of internalized cruelty, if you can instead say, "Fuck this noise, I'm going to spend twenty minutes making a Pinterest board about Paris because it will be fun for me," then you'll notice how negative feedback from your boss, fights with a lover, or just your own angry self-talk smoothly melts away. It's the delighting in our lives, luxuriating in the small details of our days, and not reprimanding ourselves that help us grow stronger.

In the morning, write down something nice that you will do for yourself and then think about it all day. Make time at the end of your day to do it. It's lovely to spend the whole day looking forward to the nice thing you are going to give yourself. You can't control how the outside world treats you, but you can and *must* decide how you treat yourself. When you do one nice thing for yourself, every single day, then you are guaranteed to treasure at least *one* part of your day.

I keep a list of things that I relish on my desk at home so I am never at a loss for what to do when I'm feeling a little hurt. I'm sharing that list with the hope that it spurs some ideas for you. Try doing one nice thing for yourself every day, and prepare to be taken aback when, one month from now, you try again to write down ten things you like about yourself and find that it's a breeze.

TOLDJA SO.

My List of Physical Ways to Shank the Emotional Haters

1. Taking a bath during the day. Wasting the sunshine just to soak.

2. Writing a letter, a postcard, or a thank-you note.

3. Using a fountain pen.

4. Replacing the ink cartridge of said fountain pen and feeling like a baller who knows how to take care of such things.

5. Traveling, even if it's just a day trip.

6. Traveling abroad alone: leaving the country, getting out of Dodge, buh-bye.

7. Taking Pilates.

8. Scrubbing my body down with a weird mitt I got at a Korean spa.

9. Post-scrub, taking *way too long* to slather myself in a creamy and soothing lotion.

10. Lighting incense. Watching it disappear.

11. Sage. In all forms. Burning it, boiling it in a pot of hot water to make a tea, using it as a garnish for lamb. Sage.

12. Opening a small gift. Even if I wrapped it for myself.

13. Sweating in a steam room.

14. Putting on makeup slowly in a cloud of incense.

15. Baking a treat, cooking with herbs, making soup from scratch, spending time in the kitchen making an elaborate dinner for one.

16. Baking a less elaborate from-a-box treat, but getting really pumped about it. I'm looking at you, Funfetti.

17. Putting fresh lilies in the bedroom. FRESH LILIES, YOU GUYS!

18. Adding Maldon sea salt to anything, including chocolate ice cream.

19. Listening to the sound of rain falling (an iTunes version will do in a pinch).

20. Standing in the rain, getting wet, going inside to get warm.

21. Reading *The New Yorker.* READING *THE NEW YORKER* IN THE BATH! THE PAGES SLIGHTLY DAMP. WHAT COULD BE BETTER?

22. Florals, florals, florals everything, bursts of flowers. Just googling "floral prints" online.

23. Going to a fancy bar, sitting alone, ordering an old-fashioned, and reading.

24. Dancing (alone).

25. Hiking and getting sweaty, going farther than I want to.

26. Driving down the Pacific Coast Highway, cold air rushing in through the open windows, Jay-Z blasting from my stereo, irresponsibly turning the heat way the fuck up to feel cold and warm air mixing at the same damn time.

27. Spending time with my sister. Or talking to her on the phone (if she'll pick up).

28. Cutting and pasting anything, using rubber cement.

29. Music. Listening to music, doodling to music, being in a cloud of music.

30. Paris. Just looking at pictures will do; just thinking about Paris will do.

31. Rereading, for the millionth time, *Eloise* or *Oh, the Places You'll Go!*

32. Buying a gift for a friend.

33. Going to a museum, any museum, and napping in said museum. Go on, try it. It's fun and scary.

34. Writing, even if it's just a list of things that make me feel good.

I Am a Bather. It's a Thing.

Find a Ritual to Honor Your Body

My BFF Fisch and I stood on the edge of a natural hot spring in Hakone, Japan. In the cold mountain air, we clutched our arms around our thin cotton kimonos to stay warm. I had come halfway across the world to treat myself to an adventure. Surveying the scene, I scanned women—some ancient, some young, some with big bellies, some stick-skinny—wading naked into the water. I was terrified. I just couldn't imagine taking the plunge and joining them. Hakone was a spa town, and we had traveled by train from Tokyo on the "Romance Express," passing Mount Fuji, all the way to this small town for the very specific purpose of getting in this water. There was one little detail, however, that Fisch hadn't communicated to me. "I *really* wish you had told me we had to get totally naked," I whispered, afraid the other bathers might hear the fear and judgment in my voice. "Tara, it's a cultural faux pas to get in the hot spring in a bathing suit, and if I had told you that you had to be naked, you never would have come." She was right; if she had explained that I would have to expose myself to strangers, and even worse, to her, I probably would have skipped the whole expedition.

My dearest reader, I had a problem: I had never, ever, not for a single day in my adult life been comfortable with my bare body. The idea of being naked in front of a mirror—much less other people—was so loathsome, so gross, so NO THANK YOU that I had successfully avoided seeing myself undressed for a good, oh-gee-I-don't-know, *twenty* years? (Is it just me, or do you also avoid looking at yourself in the mirror from the neck down?)

In middle school, I was the girl who went into the other room when it was time to change into pj's for a sleepover. In high school, I was the girl who changed into gym clothes by a series of contorted and perfectly choreographed acrobatics. From under my school clothes, I would unhook my bra, slide the shoulder straps down my arms, and thread the bra out through one armhole of my shirt before facing the lockers, strapping my sports bra around my belly, and shimming it up my torso until it was in position to slide over my boobs—all while still fully clothed. Even at home, in the privacy of my bathroom, I would put on a towel while I was still in the shower so I never had to look at my naked body in the mirror.

As an adult, I had never worn a bikini, I had never examined the reflection of my full body, I had never been naked in front of another person. Well, that's kind of a lie. Technically, I had been naked in front of boyfriends, but you can bet that I had a strict "ZERO lights on for sex" policy. If I was intimate with a partner, it was in utter darkness, under the covers, in a place where no one could make out my shape. Candlelight was acceptable, but only ONE candle, in the corner of the room. You can imagine how sexy I made my partners feel with all of these rules and regulations.

Some of my contempt for my physique came from the humiliation I felt when my mom intrusively investigated me as a kid, but that didn't fully account for why I thought of myself as decidedly gross and not beautiful, as someone who should never be fully *seen*. From around the ages of four to eight, like most kids, I had been totally unashamed of myself. I have troves of family vacation photos of me as a four-year-old in rhinestone bikinis doing karate kicks in Hawaii. I remember parading around the pool in Palm Springs in a leopard-print, off-the-shoulder, one-piece bathing suit, very much feeling like *the shit*. I loved pool time on vacations. My dad would play my favorite game, "The Little Mermaid," with me, during which I would swim to the deep end of the pool and he would rescue me from an imagined Ursula lurking beneath the water. Pool time with my dad was one of the few fun memories I had from childhood. After swimming, I'd make him take pictures with his fancy Nikon camera of me making funny faces and hitting karate chops. His love of "gear" combined with my love of performing for the camera made for some entertaining and epic photo shoots. We would go to the prettiest backdrop we could find (the ocean! the never-ending green lawn of a golf course in a desert!), and I would vogue.

I didn't think about the dozens of pictures of me modeling and frolicking until my parents' divorce a few years later. At the age of thirteen, in what I refer to as the "Archduke Franz Ferdinand assassination" part of the divorce—you know, the moment where something already bad turns into WWI—my mom claimed the bathing-suit photos of me were evidence that my dad was taking pornographic images of his children. The accusation she leveled was that he was a predator and thus shouldn't have custody of me and my sister. Every part of me was very publicly illuminated with humiliation. In my core, I knew my dad hadn't done anything wrong, but had *I*? Maybe there was something different about *my* body that made these photos of me illicit, while similar pictures in my friends' homes were A-okay? While I was confused and upset by the allegation, it sent my dad into a tailspin depression. He knew he hadn't done anything wrong, but my mom's allegation showed him *just how bad* the rest of this divorce would become. "Your mother has gone over the line. Even for her, this is disgusting," he lamented. Then, as a defense mechanism for himself, I think, and to thwart new accusations from my mother, my dad stopped hugging me, he stopped taking photos of me, he stopped commenting on my physical appearance except to tell me when he thought my clothes were too tight. (Let the record show that every single item of clothing I have ever tried on in front of him has been subject to the "it's too tight" refrain, including oversize winter coats.) Before prom, I would watch with envy as friends got hugs from their dads who told them they "look beautiful." My dad wouldn't even come to these gatherings. There was no "You're growing into a beautiful young woman." I went through high school yearning to be told I was beautiful. Can you relate at all? Maybe your mom didn't claim that your silly childhood photos were evidence of a *crime,* but do you know what it feels like to think your body is *wrong,* somehow? The lack of positive reinforcement, coupled with the steady diet of cruelty from my mother, calcified into a personal slogan of "I am not pretty and my body is something to be ashamed of."

Fifteen years later, after three-ish* years of re-parenting myself, I was aware that this "un-pretty" feeling was an old hurt that needed healing. On the edge of the hot spring in Hakone, I had a choice to make. Would I let my body-shame rob me of a once-in-a-lifetime experience in a far-flung corner of the world? Could I be totally naked in front of strangers and my best friend? GAAAH. I *really* did not want to. But as I looked around and saw how no one in the pool seemed to notice one

---

* THANK YOU, INSTAGRAM. I have mixed feelings about you (you take up too much of my time), but there is *no fucking way* I would have remembered all of the dates of my self-care journey had I not taken photos the whole way. You know the old saying "If it didn't happen on Instagram, did it even happen at all?"

another, and how no one was crying or upset or seemed to be having an existential crisis, I thought, *Maybe it won't be that bad.* I flung off my kimono and jumped into the water. When I emerged a moment later, I felt warm, soothing little bubbles all over my body and an exhilarating weightless feeling. I swam circles around the pool and laughed out loud. What had I been so afraid of?! I stopped thinking altogether and just enjoyed how my body *felt.*

My trip to Japan started what is now a full-blown love affair with bathing. On Sundays, after a long week, at four P.M. when the sun is still shining, I fill my tub with steaming hot water, pour in geranium oil bubble bath, and scrub my body down with a special kind of salt that turns hot when you rub it on your skin. I step into the bath and feel the salt fall away from my skin and dissolve in the healing water. I lie down in my tub covered in sunlight and suds. I pull a copy of *The New Yorker* from the floor and read. The pages become damp and my face gets sweaty and there is just about no better feeling in the world than a bath in broad daylight. As Sylvia Plath so knowingly wrote in *The Bell Jar,* "There must be quite a few things a hot bath won't cure, but I don't know many of them." Thank you, Sylvia. I feel the exact same way.

I've continued to push myself to be naked in front of people as a way to get over my discomfort with myself (but, ya know, not in a weird way—you won't find any public indecency records on me, sorry to disappoint). I like to get my skin sanded down in Korean spas. In a room full of other women, little old ladies hose me down and get all up in there with a mitt. They scrub under my armpits, down the sides of my body, under my boobs. They don't give a fuck that I am totally exposed and neither do I. While as a teenager changing clothes in the locker room was a feared but necessary part of the day, now I make a point to be unrepentant as I change in the gym locker room. I don't need to do a series of twists and turns to hide my boobs from other semi-naked and fully naked women. There is something liberating in being an anonymous body. There is something incredibly delightful in realizing that your nakedness just doesn't matter.

We get this one human body, and whether you hate it or love it, it's yours. Any time spent feeling uncomfortable or ashamed of it, past adolescence, is absolutely wasted. I urge you to find a way to feel at home in your skin. Maybe it's by forcing yourself to be naked in the gym locker room until that doesn't feel "weird" anymore. Maybe it's by going to a spa where you spend time with *other* women who are not ashamed of themselves. It may be as simple as wearing a bikini to the beach. In Nora Ephron's *I Feel Bad About My Neck,* which, BTW, is one of my bibles, she writes, "Oh, how I regret not having worn a bikini for the entire year I was twenty-six. If anyone young is reading this, go, right this minute, put on a bikini, and don't take it off until you're thirty-four." The first time I read those words, they leaped off the page at me as something incredibly important that I needed to tackle. I might one day regret *not* wearing a bikini? I might one day feel *remorse* for how I hid my body? I didn't want that. Whether or not a bikini is the right choice for you (maybe you like how you look in a super-stylish one-piece), I think Nora is talking about the fundamental need to be comfortable with our bodies. To stop worrying, stop complaining, stop feeling gloomy about the thing you inhabit every single day. Find a way to be grateful for and excited about what you *do* have. Buy a high-waisted bikini; buy a classic black one-piece; buy a super-cool neoprene wet-suit shirt with board shorts and go dance in the surf, your spirits lifted because you are aware enough to know that you are LUCKY to have this body and this moment on Earth. *That's what you meant, right, Nora?*

Taking a luxurious bath, cleansing yourself, sitting in a pool of water and thinking, *I feel good about my body,* is one of the most basic, accessible comforts available to you. All you need is a tub and some time. And if you can't make time to take a bath? I ask, quite politely, *Why are you even alive?*

A List of Places You Must Try to Dip Your Body into Before You Die

1. Your bathroom at four P.M. after a hike. Light a candle and let the daylight surround you.

2. A public pool, your friend's Jacuzzi in her apartment building, a hot spring just a little outside of town. Find a place that is close to you where you can swim and play and thrash about and lose track of time. There *is* a place like this near you. You may have to put in the effort to find it.

3. Olympic Spa, my favorite Korean spa in Los Angeles. It has a thing called the "Mugwort" bath that looks as if Harry Potter cast an ancient spell on a Jacuzzi—black water bubbles all around you. Find your local Korean spa and never let go.

4. Kyoto, Japan, in a communal whirlpool that shocks you electrically. It's not actually that fun, but don't you want to be able to say YOU'VE BEEN IN ELECTRIC WATER?!

5. A bathtub in Paris. Any tub in Paris will do.

6. Hakone, Japan, in a hot spring overlooking the Haya-
   kawa River, with your best friend at your side.

Go to the closest body of water you can find. The beach. A
lake. A small footbath you make in the sink. Get on the counter
and put some rose petals in there. Let your feet soak until they
are wrinkly.

I Have the Best Bras

How To Love That Thing About Your Body You Think You Hate

I BET YOU HAVE NICE bras too. But mine? Mine are the best. I buy bras that are see-through and embroidered with neon coral flowers. I buy bras that look like they have been painted on my skin with a blush-colored rose petal. I buy bras that are light pink with black polka dots and make my breasts look like two perfect softballs. I take pride in my bras because I spent too many years hating my boobs.

I've never met a woman who openly *loves* her breasts. Tolerates? Ignores? Feels compelled to have cosmetic surgery and, even then, continues to complain? Too flat, too big, too pointy, not pointy enough, droopy, too petite to droop at all, stretch-marked, I've heard it all and we haven't even broached the nipple complaints. Are they supposed to be quarter-size or is it okay if they are more like silver dollars? Does the color matter? My nipples are also kinda flat. Are they supposed to be more like thimbles? Who is happy with her nipples? Seriously, I'm asking. Also, dearest reader: How sad is it that I can't think of *one* gal I know who loves her boobs? If you are that woman, please contact me immediately.

I was cursed with my breasts early and by the ripe age of twelve could fill out a C, bordering on D, cup. I didn't really notice that my bust had grown so dramatically until other people brought that unfortunate fact to my attention. I remember opening night of the eighth-grade musical *Damn Yankees* like it happened last week. The show has a complicated plot about baseball and the devil and was somehow a modern retelling of Faust, but all I cared about was that I had been cast as Lola, the witty and tenacious lead. Lola worked as a homewrecker on the staff of the devil, who used her body to ensnare men (supz appropriate for eighth-graders), and if you've ever heard that song "Whatever Lola Wants," know that I sang it, very poorly.

Toward the end of the show, there was a big dance number where, in a moment of dramatic stunt casting, my character did the mambo with our school coach, Mr. Rodriguez. This is the same Mr. Rodriguez who had painfully watched me run/walk/crawl the mile every year. Not wanting to embarrass myself, yet again, in front of Coach Rodriguez, I practiced the dance every waking moment leading up to the show. On opening night, I put on my costume of a burnt-orange crop top and black matador pants. I shimmied my shoulders as hard as I could. My feet moved fast and with precision as I stamped out the beat of the song. Mr. Rodriguez and I straight-up *nailed* it. The audience gave us a standing ovation and I felt proud of my work. Backstage, a mom of one of the other cast members approached me with what I assumed would be praise. She got really close to my face and, with big eyes full of pity, softly said, "Honey, I'm so sorry you had to go *through* that." "Go through what?" I asked. "All of that shaking without a bra on, all of that jiggling; that must have been *so* embarrassing for you. You were all over the place."

WOW. Wow, wow, wow, wow, wow. It had not occurred to

me that my chest had been moving around, much less that it was a bad thing, something to "go through." I wondered if everyone in the audience had the same thought as this bitch mom and was snickering at me or, even worse, was mortified on my behalf.

This was not the sort of situation I could talk about with my single father, who, for previously discussed reasons, was ignoring my changing body. So I asked my babysitter to take me to the mall but refused to give her any details as to what I needed to do there. This was my humiliation alone to endure, and I needed to find the solution to my problem. I walked by Victoria's Secret but was put off by the strong odor of perfume and desperation that seemed to waft out of the overly bright store. I walked by a chichi lingerie store and was scared off by the window displays advertising "underwires," which sounded like cruel and unusual punishment. Finally, I settled on GapBody because it seemed safe. GapBody specializes in what I can only describe as "the boob shelf," a bra that smooshes both boobs into one formless mass. It's like a hammock where the boobs can take a nap. Unthreatening and on sale for "buy three, get one free," I had found my bras.

Still, my unhappiness with my bust only grew the older I got. In college, still wearing the exact same GapBody bras, I found myself legit depressed by the shapeless pile of boob attached to my front side. I would look in the full-length mirror of my dorm room and ask my friends if they thought I had a "matronly bosom." Add to this my ill-advised bob haircut and I thought I looked like a less attractive Velma from *Scooby-Doo*. I didn't want these boobs. I wanted to be a Kate Moss–style waif. I wanted tent dresses to look chic on me. I wanted to be so flat-chested that I could pass for a little boy.

I might have always lived this way if it hadn't been for my

semester studying* abroad in Paris. On a stroll, wandering the streets of the Marais, a neighborhood full of winding paths and the most *charmante* boutiques, I spotted a delicate pink silk slip dress in the window of a little store. It was love at first sight. I walked in and examined the frock only to see that the entire top of it was ruched, which is maybe the most unflattering look on a uniboob. That and the smock-style dress are the natural enemies of the large-chested. I decided to try on the pink confection anyway, and as I exited the dressing room, the saleslady, an impossibly elegant French woman, examined me. Skinny, with blunt bangs across her forehead, she was wearing black denim jeans and a blue-and-white-striped sweater; she might as well have been smoking a cigarette and introduced herself as Charlotte Gainsbourg, for how on point her look was. "I like this dress, yes. But . . . something . . . something . . . something . . . no, no, no . . ." she trailed off as she narrowed her eyes on the dress. "I know, I know, I can't wear things like this. I don't even know why I tried," I said, feeling defeated. "No, no. It's . . . not *you*. I think you need, maybe, a better bra? If you go to Le Bon Marché, they will have what you are looking for. . . . It will work." She nodded in affirmation. When Charlotte Gainsbourg tells you to do something, you don't question it. I bought the dress and made my way to Le Bon Marché.

From foie gras to leather jackets and rare perfumes, if it's expensive and the most high-end version of something, you will find it at Le Bon Marché. In the lingerie department, a no-nonsense woman threw me into a magenta-satin-lined fit-

---

* Getting v. v. v. drunk and high, never going to class, cavorting with a thirty-six-year-old French sculptor who *might* have only been using me for my apartment in the heart of the city.

ting room and began taking measurements before a single "bonjour" had been exchanged. She lifted and prodded my boobs with no ceremony, as if she were examining small canta-loupes for freshness in the grocery store. She asked how I wanted my *poitrine* to look. I didn't understand her. "What shape would you like?" I didn't realize you could *choose* a shape for your boobs! She left the small jewel box cabin and returned with arms full of intricate lace bras. They looked *nothing* like what I currently had on from GapBody.

In one bra, I had two pointy, perfectly compact boobs. They stared straight out at the world with ambition. In another, my breasts were rounder, soft, and playful. In another, a demi-cup, the top half of my bosom was *almost* spilling out of the top, like an overfull glass of milk that you have to take a sip of before you have a mess on your hands. There were all kinds of boobs to be had, apparently! Each bra was more expensive than *any* single item of clothing I owned, but for the first time in my life, I liked what I saw in the mirror. I bought two (after making a deal with myself to eat out less) and was *shocked* to see that with these bras, *all* of my clothes fit better. Dresses I hadn't worn in years because I thought I looked like an elderly, world-weary eastern European woman who needed to rest her boobs on her knees after living a *hard* life now magically flattered me. I no longer had boobs, I had *breasts*.

Today, I advise you to steer clear of Victoria's Secret. No GapBody. Save up for it and go to independent stores that spe-cialize in the highest quality of brassieres. It's worth the money; they last longer and make you look dope as hell!* Go to stores

---

* But *NEVER* put them in the washer or dryer. If you put these intricate, well-made bras in an electric machine, *that's a crime*. Hand-wash and hang dry your beautiful bras, and they can last ten years. Also, you need at least three good bras. Also, wear the same bra for two days and then switch to another to let the first one rest. Also, I have A LOT of opinions on bras.

where the idea is to work with what you have, not to project some look onto you. If a store is spending marketing money for Heidi Klum to run around in wings and a bra on a catwalk, chances are they aren't spending much on the quality of the actual goods. Also, I have nothing in common with Heidi Klum. Why would bras that fit her fit me? My beef is not really with Victoria's Secret or with my good personal friend Heidi Klum. I'm incensed by a store selling an image of a supermodel vamping around on a catwalk as something to aspire to. Aspire to be the most comfortable, best version of YOURSELF. And if a store like Victoria's Secret is the only one in your hood? Just make sure to take your time and look at how a bra shapes you and how it makes you feel. Don't get frustrated! It can take a while to find the right bra, but have faith that you will find it. You will have an "aha" moment where you see that one bra really does make a difference. And buy your bras for *you,* not so some other person can see them. I just bought a neon-pink and mesh bra that basically is one giant bow. My breasts spill out of it like a present. To be clear, I'm not dating anyone right now. The delight is purely for me.

Maybe you're self-conscious about your butt. Maybe it's "too big" or maybe it's a "pancake." Maybe you've always thought your calves are too muscular. I've heard women complain about their laugh lines, their foreheads, their noses, their thighs, their backs (which I hadn't thought to be self-conscious about until that moment, so *thanks* for that), their feet, their *earlobes,* the little fold of skin around their armpits; basically, I've heard every single body part ripped to shreds. Sure, you could get surgery to change yourself, but I have a solution that's cheaper and not nearly as invasive: Find a ritual that *celebrates* that thing you think needs work. Find a practice, a special piece of clothing, a favorite piece of jewelry, *something* that tricks you into liking your body. Sometimes you just have to take something you abhor about yourself and honor the fuck out of it.

My perfect, intricate bras pay homage to my breasts and are a wonderful solution to the self-hate I used to feel. My thongs are really bad though. They should all be thrown away.

Don't Let People Live in Your Garage

Fill Your Home with Treasures, Not Stuff

I CAME OF AGE IN a junkyard of sorts. My family may have had a "nice" house in the "right" part of Los Angeles, but we were the eyesore of the neighborhood. After my mom's medical practice collapsed, all of her office equipment was dumped in our front yard. The gynecological exam chairs rusted alongside rows of metal filing cabinets and swivel chairs. There was no care given to any of the objects, no tarp laid across them to protect them from the sun or occasional rain, no plan for getting rid of them. For more than a year, all of the items from my mom's former life sat on our lawn, decomposing.

Inside the house, rooms were so stuffed with goods that it was hard to move freely. Our living room was not only the place to watch *90210* on a big-screen TV, it also featured a home office, gym equipment, multiple zebra-print rugs lying on top of one another, a giant tanning bed from the 1980s, samples of slate rock for an ill-considered construction project, and racks upon racks of my mom's clothing, most items with the price tags still affixed. Each room in our house was like this.

The kitchen was swollen with appliances in their boxes and doubles and triples of ingredients that went bad before they would ever be used, and in the corner was a small desk with a phone and lots of paperwork, just in case you needed to do some business while making eggs. The dining room was rarely used because the ceiling had been ripped open after a hasty and now-abandoned renovation project, so when you looked up, you saw an eyeful of bare wooden beams and cotton-candy insulation. Inside the garage, there was an apartment where our live-in handyman, Barry, resided. And inside that apartment was a fully functioning but never used sauna, in which a lost youth named Dan lived. Yes. This is real.

Barry was a jolly, roly-poly man from Alaska. He had a white beard and a bald, shiny head, and he wore rainbow suspenders over his white Hanes T-shirt. He had a potbelly that stuck out over the top of his jeans and he was always laughing. He had a full set of false teeth that he would pop out of his mouth both to entertain and terrify me. With his teeth out, his lips clung to his gums like one of those lost souls in *The Little Mermaid*. He had a white van with no windows that signified both manual labor and kidnapping. He parked it proudly next to the heap of medical equipment in the front yard. It's *the* van your parents tell you to never get inside of. Actually, Barry is *the* stranger you should never talk to.

I have no idea why my parents thought we needed a live-in handyman, but here Barry was, living in our garage apartment. His little home inside our home always creeped me out, but what was even creepier was Dan, the troubled youth who lived in the sauna. AGAIN, THIS IS ALL TRUE. Dan must have been about seventeen, but as a ten-year-old, I thought he was *much* older. He had bleach-blond, '90s hair drapes. These were bangs, popular for men of that time, that framed the face like curtains. Dressed in board shorts and a novelty T-shirt (e.g., the

FedEx logo but instead it read "FedUp"), he would take me outside to catch rattlesnakes so he could kill them and collect their tails. He would expertly affix the tails to No. 2 pencils. When he finally left our house after a year or so, we found a stack of books on satanic worship in his sauna-slash-home.

This is all to say that my family couldn't be trusted to have nice things. There was too much chaos in our home to guarantee that anything would last. I took to hiding my most prized possessions in secret locations in my room. My collection of charms from cities I had visited sat in a secret lockbox under my bunk bed. My curated sticker collection lived in a Winnie the Pooh lunch box under my desk. My Beanie Babies were housed in clear plastic boxes that I proudly displayed on my bookshelf. *I HAD THE PRINCESS DIANA BEANIE BABY.* That was too cool to hide. I would try to protect my things, but often I would either forget where I had stashed my treasures or they would get destroyed. Where was the silver bracelet with hearts my godmother had given me? Or what happened to my favorite leather jacket covered in rhinestones and sequins? My mom always had the same response: "The housekeeper stole it." Why would the housekeeper want my collection of Bazooka Joe bubblegum wrappers featuring cartoons and jokes? I learned to stop asking questions.

As a kid, I loathed this kind of littered living. I always had the impulse to protect what was mine, but I didn't have the chance to successfully do so until I set off for college, where I took care to curate my side of the dorm room with precision. A Matisse poster hung on a wall illuminated by a red Chinese lantern. I bought a mini faux Persian rug at Bed Bath & Beyond and put it next to my bed so that when I woke up, I had something soft to step on.

Today I surround myself with objects that bring me pleasure. They aren't necessarily expensive; what makes them precious is the care I give to them. I have a ceramics collection that consists mostly of items I bought in the restaurant-supply district of Tokyo. These are not "fine" pieces. In fact, they ranged in price from inexpensive to dirt cheap. They're special because I bubble-wrapped them in Tokyo, lugged them to the airport, and then kept them safe on the twelve-hour journey to Los Angeles. They're valuable because I proudly and orderly display them on shelves. I whip them out for dinner parties and am always sure to hand-wash and dry them. In my home office, I keep my stationery in a lacquered box. The cards are divided by occasion (thank-you notes, holidays, flirtations). I collect pens from intriguing restaurants and hotels and put them in a special drawer in my desk right next to my collection of washi tape.

Given enough care, the objects you surround yourself with can become amulets, energetically charged with your love and attention. Your wooden kitchen table, which you wipe down with oil once a month and always use coasters on, is no longer just *any* table, it's a talisman. It's a symbol of how much you value meals with family and friends. Your sweat equity seals in the power of the table. Confession: I don't love Marie Kondo's *The Life-Changing Magic of Tidying Up*. I find the idea that there is only *one* way to organize your life off-putting. *I will maintain my sock drawer in the way I best see fit, please and thank you.* But I think she's onto something when she advises to "take each item in one's hand and ask: 'Does this spark joy?' If it does, keep it. If not, dispose of it." That's *fantastic*. We have the power, now, today, to keep only things that bring us *joy* in our lives. Make sure you are doing this with your physical space. While *stuff* can't make you happy, if you surround yourself with objects you are crazy about and then invest care into those objects, you *can* increase the overall enchantment you feel in your life. These treasures will shine all of the love and time you've invested into them right back onto you, casting a sparkling aura of self-love around you, giving you inspiration when you need it. That's why you can't just have *stuff.* Stuff can't hold magic.

Keeping a home full of treasures is a physical way you can protect and care for yourself. And it's fun! It's simply a more delightful life when you think, *Oh, perfect! I get to use that antique silver teapot I bought at the flea market as a vase for these roses.* We all know, however, that they are, at the end of the day, just objects. Try not to freak out when your roommate puts a gold-leaf cup in the dishwasher. She's not *trying* to ruin your life.

My Home Office Is a Sacred Sanctuary. Please Do Not Come In.

Take Up Space

I HAVE A SMALL OFFICE in my apartment. I colored the walls Middleton Pink, which the paint can described as being both "youthful" and "fun." Said walls are covered in notes to myself, photos of soups I've made, embarrassingly cheesy quotes, postcards from my favorite destinations, positive affirmations, multiple images of Saint Nora Ephron and Saint Coco Chanel, letters I have written both in praise of myself and attacking my Frenemy Within, loving emails from people I respect, and lots of glitter tape. Right above my desk I keep my Hype Men, Road Warriors, and ABSOLUTELY NOT/ARE YOU CRAZY/ DO NOT ASK FOR ADVICE lists along with my Idea Board. There's a small closet in my office, and on the wall next to it, I tape paper with the monthly goals I have set for myself written down. When I achieve one of these, I put a sticky note next to the goal that reads "YAAAY! I FUCKING DID IT!" It's deeply satisfying to be able to look at a wall and, at a glance, see all of the things I have achieved and all of the things I want to accomplish.

My home office is like the Etsy version of Russell Crowe's

office in *A Beautiful Mind*. Yes, there are "notes to self" taped on every wall; yes, there is an actual outline of my principles on the back side of the door; yes, there are photo collages of my hopes and dreams next to positive affirmations; and, yes, all of this looks *a little* overwhelming and like someone is trying to unravel a complicated conspiracy theory or figure out the lineage of a major crime family, FBI-style—but I use the *cutest* stationery and the *absolute best* tape.

This room is my HQ, my own temple of self-love. A place where I say, "I am worthy of a little pink room, damn it!" It's a place where I actively think about who I want to be, how I want to act, and what my dreams are. No person, thing, or idea can force me to be something I don't want to be when I'm in my little pink bubble.

The pièce de résistance is my desk.

. I have carried my writing desk and its chair with me for the past ten years. From college in Providence to New York City. From my ex-boyfriend's apartment in Greenwich Village to my little studio a few blocks away in the West Village. From New York City to Los Angeles. None of the furniture is perfect; in fact, the chair is pretty uncomfortable and I have to keep a blanket on it so it doesn't dig into my back, but I have a spiritual connection to my desk.

It's black and rectangular with round edges. It looks old-timey, with faux nicks and scratches that reveal red and brown wood beneath. I organize the inside of it with washi tape, gold glitter, and fountain pens. Everything has its spot. My desk is the first place I took myself seriously as a writer. In college, I very much did not have my shit together as a person, but I could always come back to my desk and spend late nights writing plays and papers, imagining what my life might look like if I were a respected playwright or a dope TV writer. Or maybe a journalist-turned-essayist-turned-filmmaker like Saint Nora

Ephron. At my desk, I could see flashes of dreams and then do the actual work to achieve them. Just sitting there meant I was showing up for myself; it only occasionally meant I was using the flat surface as a place to do drugs.

Despite all of the adoration I feel for my desk, I've abandoned it twice. Once, right out of college. In the haze of being depressed and anxious that my ~~life~~ education was ending, I decided nothing mattered, not my desk, not my dreams, not sleep, not friends, certainly not writing, not showering, and not *not* getting high. Why not sell my desk and make a little money? I sold it to the girl who was taking over my room. As I closed the door, I said, "Goodbye, desk," and felt like I was making a huge mistake, but one I was incapable of stopping. It was like I was watching the main character in a horror movie run at full speed into the basement, where *you know* she will be murdered. I wanted to scream through the screen, directly at her, "Stop right there!" but I could no sooner help her than I could help myself.

Once settled in New York and marginally calmer, I called the owner of my desk and pleaded to get it back. "I'm so, so sorry to do this, and I know I sold it to you, but do you think that *maybe* you could sell it back to me? Again, I'm so sorry for the inconvenience." I waited in silence, worried that she might have developed an attachment to the desk the same way I had and refuse to relinquish it. "Yeah, no big deal," she replied.

And on that day, I made a solemn vow I would never abandon my desk again.

That lasted a good year until I fled the apartment I shared with my ex, Keats. You remember Keats, right? Dude who swept up all of the broken pieces of me and delivered me to his apartment in New York after graduating college? I was grateful that Keats was taking charge of my life, but when I arrived at his place, it turned out it wasn't so much that his parents were *giving* him an apartment as it was they were *letting* him move back home. So, the actual plan, the one I had *not* been presented with, was that Keats and I were to live with his parents in their two-bedroom apartment. "Move in with me" is ten thousand times different from "Move in with me *and my parents*," but I had no backup plan. It took a good year for our tumultuous relationship to implode, and when it did, my friends came over with suitcases and boxes as Russian discount movers looked on in bewilderment. "Ladies, did you pack *anything?*" *Oh damn. You have to be packed BEFORE the movers come?!* "We'll be done in just a minute," we lied as we drank mimosas, did lines of coke, and tried to make this move something "fun" and not the necessary but still tough, tear-drenched "divorce" I considered it to be. "Miss, what about the desk?" Boris asked. *What about the desk.* "You can leave it. I don't need it," I decided. I didn't think I would have space for it in the itsy-bitsy studio apartment I was moving into, and I wasn't doing that much writing anyway.

Once settled into my new place, I would find myself in my kitchen (the space between my bed and the bathroom) wishing I had a place to write. I again felt that in leaving my desk, I had left a little healthy part of myself behind. Then, one night, I had a dream that my desk collapsed in Keats's apartment. In the dream, the desk was a pink cartoon version of itself. The legs toppled inward and the whole thing crumpled. The desk cried, "Tara, why have you abandoned me?" in a little woeful song. My desk wept. It wanted to come home. *I* wanted it to come home.

That very next morning, THAT VERY NEXT MORN-ING, Keats's mom called me. "Hi, Tara. It's Nancy. How is everything?" *Everything is really perfect and great and please tell*

Keats I don't miss him, don't care about him, and am definitely not having weird dreams about the furniture I left with him. "Things are good, really good," I lied. "Glad to hear it. So, this is strange, but your desk kind of broke and collapsed last night, and if you want, I'd be happy to rebuild it and bring it to your apartment." I was stunned. Had my desk *actually* spoken to me the previous night through a dream? And were Keats's parents really willing to rebuild and then carry the desk up five flights to my walk-up? *Was my luck turning?* "Please! Yes! Oh my God. That would be amazing. THANK YOU, NANCY!" "Okay then," she replied, a little weirded out by my gusto.

The times I have parted with my desk mark the times in my life when I thought I wasn't worth taking seriously. They are the times when I felt like my life was in shambles and I piled on with self-loathing. My senior year of college, I was lucky to meet and occasionally be taught by the brilliant, kind, encouraging playwright Paula Vogel. I asked if I could attend one of her office hours and she generously agreed to give me some of her time. Sitting next to her in a folding chair in the school theater, I told her I wanted to be a writer, or a creator—someone who put something of value into the world. I also told her I was afraid that it would lead to a life of chaos and financial instability, the two things I had been fleeing since I was a little girl. "I love making things, but should I be a lawyer? That seems like the best career for someone who likes words, right? It's so much safer than being a playwright, don't you think?" I appealed to her. "Let me stop you right there. The world doesn't need any more lawyers. I mean, unless of course you are *dying* to be a lawyer. But that doesn't sound like you. You sound like a storyteller. The world needs your thumbprint, your voice, the record of your time on Earth. What you need to do is take yourself seriously." *Take myself seriously?* I knew those words were important, but at the time I didn't have the power to fully understand them or incorporate them into my life. Instead, I wrote them down, committed them to memory, and promised I would keep coming back to them until they made sense to me.

I have spent the past decade ruminating on Paula's words, and I am very happy to announce that they make sense to me now. Taking yourself seriously means allowing yourself to have a dream, a vision, a hope for your life. It means putting in the work, little by little, to be who you *know*, deep down, you *are* and *want* to become. It means living your life in pursuit of your most authentic self, the self that wants to come out and dance and flirt and conquer the world. Taking yourself seriously means you don't fret and worry at the bottom of the staircase of your life. You don't dig your nails into the banister wondering if it's safe to start the climb. You take the first step with confidence. Then the next. Baby steps all the way. There's no reason to run up the next four steps super quickly. Simply be present with the one you are on. There, you can live it up. Stomp your feet, wake the neighbors, feel it in your knees, break the fucking wooden slats beneath you—this is your flight of stairs and you get only one.

Here is what I want to tell you: If you have dreams, even *big fucking* dreams that scare the shit out of you because they feel so impossible and difficult and you'd rather ignore them but they keep calling to you like a telemarketer who just won't give up, if you have fantasies about what your life *could be* but you are not pursuing them *in any way at all,* then it's time to take yourself seriously, my dear. Put your worry to the side and commit to one simple thing you *want* to do, today. Don't spend a second worrying about HOW IS IT ALL GOING TO WORK OUT IN THE END? Just get going. If it's starting

your own candle company, buy the supplies you need and *start.*
If it's finding your dreamboat husband, download an app and
get going. You don't need to do everything at once, but you do
need to do one thing, *today,* that moves you closer to where
you want to be.

Do you see now why my desk is so important to me? I take
my dreams so seriously that I carved out ACTUAL SPACE in
my life so I had *room* for my aspirations. I didn't quit my job,
take off to the countryside where I could "concentrate," and
upend my life so I could write; I created a small spot where it
felt safe, gleeful, and totally okay to create in. Then I set a timer
every morning before work and did the damn thing I wanted
to do. You can do one little thing *today* that moves you toward
your dreams. Not in three years when you're more financially
stable. Not in five years when you "have your shit together
more."

I think, on the whole, we get way too wrapped up in the
idea that to pursue our dreams we have to throw caution to the
wind—you have to be a lone entrepreneur, you have to
CHANGE EVERYTHING ABOUT YOUR LIFE *NOW,*
you have to run up the staircase of your life at lightning speed
even if it means breaking your ankle and tumbling back down.
Adam Grant, one of the most insightful and generous and just
so fucking smart people on Earth, describes in his book *Originals* how some of the most creative and successful people kept
their day jobs *as* they followed their dreams. The creators of
Warby Parker, the founders of Google, director Ava DuVernay,
Stephen King, T. S. Eliot—they all kept their day jobs *even as
they were pursuing their passions.* "Having a sense of security in
one realm gives us the freedom to be original in another,"
Adam so wisely wrote. For me, that sense of security, that safety
so I can write, starts with having a little room I can call my
own.

I will never part with my desk again because I'm never giving up again. I take small, thoughtful actions *every day* in pursuit of the exact life I want to lead. And it's always evolving. Virginia Woolf wrote about the importance of making space for yourself in *A Room of One's Own*. Though written in 1929, her words are just as urgent today. Her most quoted passage is probably that in order to create, in order to pursue her own passions, "a woman must have money and a room of her own," free from distraction and judgment. A lesser-known quote— but one I have memorized so it is now a part of the neural pathways in my brain—is her conclusion: "I find myself saying briefly and prosaically that it is much more important to be oneself than anything else." Yes, V. V. V. YESSS, VIRGINIA! She understood that taking yourself seriously, having a room of your own, is KEY to creating the most authentic version of you.

I actually don't show people my office when I give tours of my apartment. I find it hard to take dates into. It just feels too vulnerable. It's a room I have poured myself into: the hurts I've had, the goals I'm reaching for, the little nourishing phrases that help me along the way. It's the physical manifestation of all the things I love and my most authentic self. A little messy but mostly organized, optimistic but pragmatic, covered in glitter tape and soothing words. My office is a safe haven of love and creation where I get to be as cheesy and vulnerable and silly as I want to be. Nobody is watching me here. Nobody cares.

Do you have a space you can pour yourself into? Do you have a nook where you feel safe to be you? To be impractical and dreamy and not give a fuck about anyone else's opinions? Do you have a place to take yourself seriously and act on that thing inside you waiting to be born? A closet? A sewing nook? Part of the garage? If you don't, might I suggest you dedicate a pantry, a drawer, a shelf, or a little box that a cupcake came in to taking up space? You deserve a little space.

For you, I'm hanging on to a little purple box that previously held some delicious macarons. It has gold stars printed on the sides, and I think it would make the perfect home for some of your wishes.

Keep Your Home
Dinner-Party Ready

Treat Yourself as You Would Treat Your Guests

I DISCOVERED THE PLEASURE OF entertaining my sophomore year of college. My dorm room was a three-bedroom suite I shared with my three closest friends. We cleverly dubbed it "The Sweet Suite." We were thrilled to have a common space big enough to host parties, and we meticulously decorated our "living room" in the style of Louis XIV after watching the movie *Amadeus,* stoned. We filled it with a spray-painted gold clock, candelabras from Goodwill, and a yellow brocade sofa that didn't look so much "Sun King" as it screamed "a grandmother definitely died here." We opened the door to the utility closet that we had been instructed, very specifically, never to use; threw a mattress in it; draped hippie-inspired cloth on the walls; and christened it "The Opium Den." We hung a red lightbulb from a pipe just to seal in the look of "seedy, gross, bad things happen here." Looking back, it would have been more apt to call it "The Fire Hazard" for the amount of weed we smoked in such a confined space covered in cheap, highly flammable cloth. Since not many students had access to this much space, we hosted epic dance parties with jungle juice (generic vodka and Kool-Aid, yum!), pretzels (that's enough food, right?), and lots of vomiting on my part. The truth was, our dorm room was not nice. But this was our little home, and we treasured the shit out of it.

The morning after a night of too much jungle juice, a night in which I had apparently accused some partygoers of being "fascists," a word I had just learned and was *very* excited to use, I stumbled out of my bedroom to see my roommates in yoga outfits cleaning. I was surprised. We had *just* had the party, why clean up so soon? What was the rush? Having grown up in a house that was *always* in disarray, I didn't understand that in order for a place to be clean, *you had to clean it.* Back at home, if our dog peed on the rug, then the rug was just permanently stained. Sometimes there would be an effort, days later, to erase the splotch, but it was always done in a resigned fashion. We would meekly scrub the now-set-and-impossible-to-remove mark as if it was just another example of the futility of life.

I tiptoed around my friends vacuuming Cheetos off the floor and spraying down every surface with Formula 409. When my friend Jess caught me slumping around, she arched her eyebrows and asked, "Tara, are you going to watch or are you going to help?" "Of course, I'll help. But isn't it dumb to clean up if we're going to have another party soon? *AND,* why do we have to clean up so quickly? Can't I sleep off my hang-over a little more?" I thought she would see the reason in my pragmatic argument, but, alas, she stood up from the floor and explained, "I love you, Tara, but that's pretty disgusting." She walked over to the coffee table and picked up a "sculpture" of at least fifty pieces of chewed gum we had drunkenly created the night before and asked, "Do you really want to be in a dorm room with this?" There is something viscerally sordid about a stack of chewed gum, something about seeing the teeth marks and the spit of lord-knows-who that make it particularly foul. She was right. I didn't want to be within five feet of that eyesore. As she dumped our gum art into the trash, she explained, "It's just way easier to clean up now than to let all this filth sit and soak in." It never occurred to my roomies that it was acceptable to live in a mess. That morning, hungover but impressed by the cleaning hustle of my friends, I learned that you can't wish for your home to be nice; if you want a clean household, you have to make it so. No hemming, no hawing, no waiting.

I have a rule chez moi: I keep my home Dinner-Party Ready. I should not be embarrassed if someone comes over unexpectedly. That's the test. Would I be self-conscious or feel like I needed to apologize if someone dropped by today? If I would, then I absolutely need to clean up. It's okay to have a few things disorganized in a kitchen drawer, but it's not okay for the sink to be overflowing with the remnants of this morning's elaborate chia seed, avocado, blueberry, protein-powder smoothie. It's okay for my bathroom mirror to have a little schmutz on it, but it's not okay to have the bathroom trash spilling over with dental floss, cotton balls, Amazon packaging, and, for some reason, an apple core. It's okay for the sofa in the living room to have the pillows and a throw blanket balled up to one side, but it's not okay to have the glasses from last week's cocktail party, sticky and frozen in place, on the coffee table. I'm not trying to build a dirty-glass memorial to fun times gone by.

I'm not Marie Kondo–style obsessed with keeping things organized. Again, I'm not the biggest fan of that book. *Okay,* I get it, you're an expert at "tidying up" and have been doing it since you were a child, Marie Kondo, but *are you saying you're better than me?* What I *have* noticed is that when my home is in order, I am in order. This is true of all the spaces I spend time with: gym lockers, hotel rooms, offices. I turn them all into safe, tidy, enjoyable dwellings where I can look around and feel calm.

By keeping my home Dinner-Party Ready, I guarantee that I am living in a way that brings me zero shame. When I look around, I feel proud of where I live and the world I have created for myself. It might not be *perfect,* but there's nothing to hide. I would not mind if you were to drop over with a friend right now. I would seat us in the living room and make you and your charming guest fresh ginger tea. I would not have to scramble around, hiding old mail in closets, picking up laundry from the floor, and apologizing for myself. And that's kind of the point. I treat myself, on a daily basis, with the same consideration I would treat a guest. If you are anything like me, you will treat a visitor a million times nicer than you will treat yourself. How backward is that? How odd to extend so much graciousness and consideration to someone else but deny yourself the basic hospitality of a clean space?

I am sure there are plenty of people who have nice, clean homes and are mean to both themselves and others in different ways. But what I'm talking about here isn't the discipline of keeping a flawless home. I'm not trying to get into *Architectural Digest;* I'm not talking about being a maniac and making sure everything is controlled within an inch of my sanity. I'm talking about the sheer delight in looking around and thinking, *Oh yeah, I live here. Awesome.* Even if you are not living in your dream home, even if you are living in *a far cry* from your dream home, by treating your space with care, attention, and a little organization, you will feel better about your life overall, because you will have made active choices about how you want to live. You can bring order to your physical world no matter your circumstance. Still living at home with your parents where chaos reigns supreme? Treat your room like it's a palace. Don't have your own room? Take the greatest care with your bed. Living in a fucking mansion but everything's a mess of clutter? You are in control.

If your home is always ready for guests, it will lead to more festivities and quality time with your friends. It's so much easier to have people over when cleaning is not an impediment or even a consideration. The kitchen is ready if you just put the Bed Bath & Beyond coupon that's sitting on the counter into its special drawer; the clean dining room table can be set in a flash; and no one has to know that what you are serving them at this impromptu dinner is really frozen food from Trader Joe's. Why tell them that the Mushroom & Black Truffle Flatbread they are raving about actually costs four dollars and the only thing you did was put a fried egg on top to make it look fancy? Your secret is safe with me.

A List of EASY, Not-Horrible Ways to Keep Your Home DPR (Dinner-Party Ready)

1. **Always make the bed before you leave the house.** Going on a trip and dragging yourself out of bed to make your early flight? Make the bed. Hungover and just not in the mood? Make the bed. Running late to work? Make the fucking bed! Just throw the duvet up toward the pillows and be done with it. You have time! Coming home to an unmade bed is unsettling and easily avoidable. Make the bed for a week straight, and I dare you not to feel better about life in general.

2. **Clean the bathroom sink every day.** EVERY DAY? Yes. Just keep a delicious Mrs. Meyer's surface cleaner (rn I'm using "Rosemary") in the cabinet, and spritz,

baby, spritz. It takes like ten seconds. I like to do this at night before I go to bed so that in the morning I wake up to a nice smell and a clean sink. It's a small thing, but what a way to start your day!

3. **Clean up the party *at* the party, BUT not in an insane way.** This is controversial, but as a party is winding down, start to put dirty glasses in the dishwasher, make sure trash is being put in the actual trash can, and when your friends offer to help clean, *never* decline. I'm sorry, but you're not Emily Post. You have nothing to prove. This is not 1920, and good housekeeping is not the only way to prove your worth. Put your friends to work.

4. **Don't treat your dining room table like a landing zone.** Same goes for the kitchen table, the coffee table, the TV dinner tray, or any other flat surface on which you might be tempted to "temporarily" store things. This is not a purgatory for your groceries. I always set up ceramics on the dining room table in a pretty display so I'm not tempted to clutter it up. You won't be throwing a phone book (yes, someone is still sending me a phone book!), lightbulbs, and that package you *must* return to Amazon onto your dining room table if on it there is a delightful display of colorful ceramic plates you bought in Mexico City.

5. **Upgrade the basics.** Do you know why families (not mine) pass down silverware and crystal and fine china? One, because of weird customs having to do with dowries and "hope chests" and other unpleasant things, but, *two,* because it's nice to sit down to a pretty display

when you eat. If you were not lucky enough to inherit a special set of plates for holiday meals, might I suggest you go and buy your own? Maybe Goodwill has some pretty floral ones you can mix and match. They don't have to be expensive; they just have to make you feel special. I upgraded my paper napkins to Japanese textile pieces. They weren't costly, but they are very *me* and I love them. I made my place mats by hand-dyeing squares of linen in indigo. The whole project cost maybe fifteen dollars, but every time I set the table I think, *How lovely.*

6. **Set the table for one.** I often eat dinner alone, and I go *all* out. I'm talking lit candles, a place mat, napkins, silverware, flowers on the table, Ella Fitzgerald playing in the background. If it's so nice to set the table for guests, why wouldn't *I* enjoy the same experience?

7. **Put things away after you use them.** I *know*. Duh. I'm sure your parents told you that a million times. Actually, I'm not sure, because I wasn't told that. *But!* If you put your stuff away *right after* you use it, you can avoid a mess and, even more important, losing things. When I'm done with my rose-gold pen, it goes in its place of honor in my desk drawer. When I'm done with my journal in the morning, it goes straight back into my bedside table. My purse always goes on the little shelf next to my bedroom door. It's so much easier to know where your things are when you intentionally put them away.

8. **The moment you are back from a trip, unpack.** I KNOW. IT'S HORRIBLE. But it works. Within an hour of being at home, even if my flight got in late, even

if I had to drive all day to get back, I unpack my bag. Because otherwise, I might never unpack. To help, I keep my dirty laundry from the trip in a pretty travel bag that reads "Please Wash Me" and closes with a big black bow. I keep my underwear in another bag with the words "On Vacation" embroidered in pink. I can easily chuck these cute, presorted little bags into where they belong: the laundry hamper.

9. **Give yourself one corner of disorganization. But I'm talking *one* corner. A *small* one.** Sometimes, you just don't know what to do with a broken record player that you *know* you could get fixed one day. And what about the plastic container full of pictures from high school and letters from your grandmother? Someday I will make a scrapbook, but for now, I have a corner in my home office, hidden by a sofa, where my disorganization lives. It's about two feet by two feet of stuff I'm just not sure how to handle. While Marie Kondo might say I am living in chaos and the absence of joy, I'm telling you, I feel no less blissful about my life because of it. Of all the things to feel bad about in my life, I am not letting a *tiny* bit of disorganization be one of them. Sorry, Marie. You can't make me feel guilty. Not today.

10. **Forgive yourself if your home is not DPR.** I was not born into a DPR home, nor did I take pride in maintaining one until I was almost thirty. It took me *that long* to value how awesome-pinch-me-YES-amazing it feels to live in a place you fucking love. Start small. Don't get overwhelmed thinking that EVERYTHING HAS TO BE PERFECT. It doesn't; who said that? Put the plate in the dishwasher, return your running shoes to the

bedroom closet (how did they make it into my home office?!), throw away that *crazy*-long CVS receipt-slash-coupon you're never actually going to use, and move on with your day.

Don't worry, I'm still learning too.

It's Not the Open Bar's Fault You're a Mess

Think Before You Drink

LAST YEAR, I WENT TO see my general practitioner, feeling pretty good about my health. I was no longer smoking weed (whaaat, take *that*, weed!), I was working out (whaaat, take *that*, PE!), and for the first time in my life, I thought my doctor might be impressed by me. Sitting on the exam table, I felt a combination of confidence and cold because doctors' offices are always so chilly. Why is this? We patients are wearing gowns made of paper that don't fully close in the back. Why keep the thermostat at sixty-six?

My doc entered the igloo and asked me if I smoked. "NOPE!" I proudly proclaimed. Do you take any drugs? "No way! I'm afraid of drugs now." YAAAY ME! And then he asked about drinking. "Do you drink?" "Well, yeah, of course I drink." "How many drinks would you say you have in a week?" Well . . . let's do the mental math on last week's drinking:

On Sunday, I accidentally had at least four glasses of wine. As a rule, I don't drink on Sundays, but this was a *fun* Sunday on the beach, so of course I had rosé all day. Monday through Thursday, I had one-ish or *if we're being real* two-ish drinks each night. So that's four accidental Sunday drinks plus an optimistic

four, but really more like eight, weeknight drinks, which equals
something like eight *to twelve* drinks before the weekend. On
Friday, I should get lots of credit because I drank NOTHING
in preparation for a wedding Saturday (Mature! Saintly! Adult!).
Saturday tho . . . Saturday night I proceeded to drink all of the
drinks *in the world*. I drank so many drinks that there was no
way to guess the number. So, my grand total for the week was
somewhere between twelve and infinity drinks. I looked my
doctor square in the eyes and told him the truth: "I had seven
drinks this week."

"Watch it!" he scolded. "For a woman your size, seven is the
absolute *max* you should drink in a week and *never* more than
three in a day." *Totally,* Doc. Totally.

Reader, I am not so good at saying no to an open bar situation. Usually an open bar is at a fun event, be it a wedding or
birthday party or house party dancing with friends on the met-
aphorical grave of your ex-lover. At art gallery receptions,
where most people have one of those little plastic cups full of
Trader Joe's–brand wine, I have five. I feel like it's my duty to
keep drinking as long as the open bar is still serving. My rea-
soning is that I'm usually with friends and I enjoy the ritual of
drinking with them. How fun are shots, toasts, the clinking of
glasses, the corralling of your girls to "get another"? The very
act of ordering another drink is a vote to stay out with your
friends! Plus, an open bar is FREE. Fun times with friends that
I don't have to pay for? Of course, I try to maximize the shit
out of those blessed occasions! But here I was, semi-naked on
the exam table, baldly lying to my doctor. It didn't feel right.

On the Saturday night in question, I had attended a wedding
deep in the winding hills of Malibu. It took an hour to get
there, and by the time I arrived, I was famished. The wedding
was at six P.M., so I didn't eat beforehand. I assumed we would
be knee-deep in heavy apps by seven and then on to wedding

food by eight. But by eight-thirty, the only food that had been served was tiny bites of puff pastry filled with a mystery substance. Spinach? Cheese? Meat? I couldn't tell you. The open bar, on the other hand, was flowing and full of fun people, including a hipster boy in a three-piece suit wearing Converses. *Oh boy.* That whole hipster/nerd look is a real weakness of mine. Ignoring all my previous experiences on planet Earth, I thought, *Maybe it wouldn't be so bad if I had just a couple of glasses of wine on an empty stomach?*

At the bar and guzzling rosé with a boy who looked as if he could have been a member of The Strokes circa 2004, I could feel the booze catching up with me. My cheeks were getting hot and my face started to feel a little bloated. I knew I should stop drinking, but we were in the middle of a fascinating conversation about all the people we both knew and hated. There's really no better way to bond. We were soon summoned to the dance floor by friends, all with full glasses. I was in so deep, could another glass of wine really be that much worse? I continued to drink even though I knew I was too drunk already, because, I reasoned, we were at a wedding and weren't weddings supposed to be fun? When the hipster boy asked if I wanted to split an Uber back to LA, all I could answer was a slurred "Yeaaah, I *do*," feeling confident that a make-out sesh was on the horizon.

I knew the road would be twisting, but now that I was completely full of booze, it was tortuous. I felt every turn in my stomach, and a cold-sweat trembling took over my body like it does when I'm sick. Oh no. I *was* sick. Now I was scared I would throw up on this pretty hipster boy, and so, in something I have come to acutely regret, I asked him to hold my hand.

"I'm just feeling so carsick and scared," I explained to him. *WHY, TARA, WHY???* He dutifully took my hand in his as I demanded that we stop at a gas station to buy Smartwater.

"Not just any water; get Smartwater," I instructed him. In my head, I could see images of the Jennifer Aniston ads. You know, the ones where she has perfect skin and looks like the picture of glowing health with a Smartwater in hand? Yeah, that brand of water was *definitely* going to change the course of the night.

Needless to say, I made out with the pretty hipster that night and we started dating shortly thereafter. KIDDING. There was no make-out sesh.* I barely remembered the moments before I went to sleep. The second I woke up the next morning, I knew I *never again* wanted to ask someone to hold my hand because I was drunk and scared. I took out my journal and began to write about my war with the open bar. Why didn't I stop myself? And after almost three decades in this human body, after all the self-care, how could I continue to get *that* drunk? "If the caterer served more food, you would have been fine," I scrawled. I began working myself up. "The hipster boy shouldn't have insisted on drinking," I wrote in a fury. "It's the *open bar's* fault you're a mess!" I finally charged in big scribbled letters. I looked at the pages. I laughed. First of all, I was so hungover that my handwriting looked like that of an angry, drunken preschooler. Second, it was definitely *not* the caterer's fault, not the hipster's fault, not the bar's fault I got so drunk. I continued to write and realized something that had never occurred to me before: There was no fated amount I was supposed to drink or not drink. This was no one else's decision but my own. I had to make more conscious decisions about drinking.

I decided to take the next month off from imbibing. Not because I thought I had a problem but because I hadn't expe-

---

* In fact, it's totally awkward when I see him now. I only made things worse by asking him to have "friend tacos" with me one Sunday morning a month later. What's a "friend taco" you ask? I think it's when you are so ashamed of how you behaved that you try to normalize the situation by defining the relationship when there is no need to do so. I already defined the relationship as *never, ever happening*.

rienced a whole sober month since college, when I first started drinking. I thought the month would be difficult and I would find it hard to go out with friends as they did shots and made toasts (two of my favorite rituals), but it was surprisingly easy. I could hold a soda water and lime all night, and no one even knew the difference. I spent that month asking friends how much they drank, googling what liquor is least likely to give you a hangover (quality tequila), and rereading Nora Ephron's *I Feel Bad About My Neck,* because I remembered that somewhere in the book she talked about how much liquor she could handle. Nora Ephron is someone I look to for advice on everything from men to writing to how to host a dinner party. She inspires me so much that sometimes I write letters to her in my journal and then answer the letter back in a very shoddy impression of her voice. *These letters are not embarrassing at all.* I found the passage I had been looking for: "The reason you're waking up in the middle of the night is the second glass of wine." That had me shook. The second glass of wine? The *second* glass of wine, *Nora*?! I simply could not live by that. What I could take away from her advice, though, was that I needed to find a way to *mindfully* drink. That was the missing key for me. Often, when I would drink, I would have no idea how much I had consumed. And that blind drinking, that "as-long-as-the-open-bar-is-still-going" mentality, had clearly not served me.

As the month went on, I wrote my own rules for attentively sipping, which I have continued to tweak to this day. You might ask, "If you need rules for drinking, then don't you have a drinking problem?" And I would say to you, "This book is a label-free zone, thank you very much." What I have found is that so many of us live our lives on autopilot. We wake up, go to work, go to bed without really ever being present for the experience. Nowhere is this truer than in eating and drinking.

We learn to do these things instinctually but don't necessarily talk or think about it. I started drinking Smirnoff Ice in high school but didn't have a real, thoughtful conversation about how liquor affected me until my late twenties, because it never drastically affected my life in a negative way. It seemed that for people like me, people who drank socially and whose lives weren't disrupted by booze, there was nothing *to think* about. I need the rules not because I have a "problem" but to remind myself to be present and pay attention to the fact that I am, indeed, drinking.

Do I always stick to these rules? Nope. Not even close. Last weekend, I went to a bachelorette party in Austin, Texas, where I mainlined sweet-tea vodka at a respectable one P.M. We were on a boat, ladies! I had to. Sometimes you have to break your own rules because it's just plain fun. But did I feel wretched after? Did I cry on the floor of the party bus that picked us up about the "unrealistic beauty standards imposed by society"? Yes, I did that too.

That night, still in a bathing suit and flannel shirt, I swore I would stick to my rule of never day drinking again. At least until the next bachelorette party.

T$'s Rules to Drinking

1. **Always eat.** This is so basic that I find it surprising some of my friends—grown-ass adults—have not figured it out yet. Do not rely on the wedding food, do not expect there will be snacks at the party; have a nice little meal *before* you do *any* drinking. What about an apple with almond butter? Some homemade avocado toast? Both are easy and delicious solutions. Is that the sound of you thanking me?! *No problem.* This way, you will *never* find yourself drinking on an empty stomach.

2. **Count each drink and have a limit.** I mentally say to myself, *This is drink number one,* after I order my first. I usually stop at two, but three is my absolute limit before a super-fun night turns into a humiliating night and an excruciating morning. Another great thing about keeping an exact number in mind is that it holds you accountable. Alcohol *always* invites more alcohol. You know how after you've had three glasses, the fourth just seems like it wants to be invited to the party? "I mean . . . why not?!" that fourth glass screams. If you hold yourself to a limit, you won't let booze make choices for you.

3. **Know your drink combinations.** What works best for you? I have found what works for me: two cocktails and one beer; one cocktail and two glasses of wine; two glasses of wine on their own but *never* a third; or three beers and absolutely-no-liquor-you-cheater, and I'm in the clear.

4. **Don't drink on Sundays.** Ever. If you drink on Sundays, your sleep will be messed up Sunday night, and isn't Monday morning rough enough without adding the insult of a hangover? Don't throw off the entire week's sleep cycle because of Sunday. There is no drink worth that.

5. **Choose how many nights a week you want to drink.** I limit myself to three nights total, every week. You might do well with one glass of wine with dinner five nights a week. I can't do that *at all,* but maybe you can! The point is to figure out what works for your body. And it's okay if you don't totally stick to that rule; again, simply having a plan helps you be more aware.

6. **Don't get drunk alone.** Ever, really. A solo old-fashioned at a stylish bar just because you want to? *Love it.* A glass of white wine on your patio at home because it's summer, damn it? *I'm very jealous of your patio.* Getting so fucked-up alone at home that you wake up wondering why there is spilled red wine resembling a murder scene on your white sofa? *Not so much. ALSO: WHY WOULD YOU EVER BUY A WHITE SOFA?!* I understand that drinking a bottle of Pinot Grigio while watching reality TV alone *seems* like a good idea at the time, but isn't it odd how that bottle of wine usually invites something else that isn't a super-great idea either? A text to an ex, a pint of ice cream, online shopping, *another* bottle of wine. Avoid all of this by taking precautions not to get drunk alone.

7. **Don't drink in a crisis.** This is not the time to take the "edge" off of shit. The edge might very well be saving you from the abyss. When something horrible happens—when your dad gets sick, when you get robbed, when you get laid off from work—that's exactly the *wrong* time to take a sip. You do not need to add booze to the storm clouds that are already raining down on you.

8. **Don't day drink.** Did I just lose you? I get how a drink at brunch might be fun for some. I get how people are now saying "Sunday Funday" without being totally embarrassed by the excruciating lameness of that turn of phrase. I get how delightful day drinking is in concept. But booze when the sun is shining just makes me sleepy and cranky. I usually have to take a nap to

recover, and then my whole day is shot because of a stupid Bloody Mary. But remember! You can break the rules. I *just* told you about my own day drinking at a bachelorette party. But having this "rule" means I am less likely to day drink in general.

9. **When in doubt, have soda water with lime.** Every open bar has soda water and lime. If I don't want to have a "real drink," I have a soda water with lime because it tastes good and looks like a tequila/vodka soda. If I know I can have only three drinks, then in between "real" drinks, I have soda and lime to stretch out my three-drink max. This will keep you hydrated while looking sophisticated. Huge win.

10. **And if you remember nothing else from this list: When you start to ask yourself,** *Should I have another?* **the answer is almost always a hard** *no*. You wouldn't be asking if it was a good idea. *Tara, I'm talking to you.* Do not drink tonight. You are already hungover because you drank three glasses of wine last night like an amateur.

What Are Vegetables?

Nourish Yourself

IN MIDDLE SCHOOL, MY TYPICAL lunch was takeout from Panda Express. Or maybe a Subway turkey sandwich with extra mayonnaise, please. I would eat Lunchables, Gushers, Shark Bites, Cheetos, all processed, portioned, unnaturally shiny foods. High school was not much better. Most days I would subsist on a bread roll, ranch dressing, carrots, and a chocolate chip cookie from our surprisingly health-*un*conscious cafeteria. My single dad didn't have much time to cook dinner during the week, so I would often get a giant burrito from Baja Fresh made "enchilada-style" (doused in cheese and sauce). There was no adult overseeing my diet. There was no parent teaching me the difference between nutritious and "Jesus-that-cheeseburger-with-chili-has-four-days'-worth-of-calories-in-it."

It wasn't that I didn't know anything about gourmet food. As a kid, I had been lucky to eat in fancy restaurants. The issue was that I would order the steak or the cream-drenched pasta with bacon before I would ever order a salad. Why would I waste part of my meal on vegetables? In my family, food was something decadent, a luxury, something to show off with, not something nutritious. When I went away to college, I actually *lost* weight because my eating habits had been so dismal at home. When I came back after Thanksgiving that freshman year, my friends worried I had an eating disorder. Having grown up a chubby kid, I had never been more flattered.*

I don't think I'm alone in not knowing how to feed myself in a healthy way. Though it seems so basic, I have plenty of friends who came from stable, wonderful households who complain about this: How are we supposed to eat? One day Greek yogurt and quinoa are touted as miracle cures for all of society's ills, the next we find out that the process of making Greek yogurt actually creates a toxic, acidic byproduct that's blamed for killing thousands of fish and that quinoa production is ethically questionable for the farmers in the Andes who grow the ancient grain. What about coconut oil? One day it's in *every* supposed healthy food, the next it's panned as nothing more than snake oil. WHO CAN WIN? What are we supposed to eat?!

In the absence of some gracious adult instructing me on good eating habits, I have had to learn how to feed myself. While there's a lot I have left to learn, I have cobbled together what I know from friends' parents, the interwebs, and cookbooks.

From Isabelle's parents, I've learned that vegetables seem to be important. Every time I have dinner with them, I notice that leafy greens are one of the main events, not just a sideshow to be ignored. Swiss chard is not a new European band but a hearty, even yummy, leafy vegetable with surprisingly bright red roots. From my own experiments, I've found that red meat will make me lethargic. I try to stick to fish and chicken— proteins that don't make me want to take a nap. But it's also not

---

* I was a naive college freshman at this time who did not understand how mentally and physically destructive eating disorders are. I would be very off-put, bordering on horrified, if someone said this to me now.

the end of the world if I have a cheeseburger at a barbecue; I just know I might not be doing much else the rest of the day. From my gym's blog, I've learned that drinking seventy-two ounces of water every day will keep me "hydrated" and feeling more alert. I thought this was total bullshit until I tried it for myself. After a few weeks, I found I was less fatigued at the end of the day. I also learned that oftentimes when I felt hungry, I was actually *thirsty,* and that water satisfied me far more than a bag of pita chips. Now I count out four rose-gold S'well bottles of water a day, make sure I finish them, and feel a million times more refreshed and awake. My water bottle is so pretty that it encourages me to drink more. My friend Fisch's mom gave me a recipe for Chicken Marbella from the classic *The Silver Palate Cookbook,** and now I can make the most delicious, life-giving chicken. It's made with prunes and capers, two things I would have never put together, but is such a surefire party-pleaser that it's now my go-to recipe when I have friends over. And having friends over, sharing a meal you made with people you love, is one of the best ways you can nourish *yourself.*

While my dad didn't teach me a whole lot about nutrition, he did instill in me the value of having family traditions around food. On Sundays, he would make me, and sometimes my sister, roast beef. He would buy a slab of prime beef and slather it in Heinz Chili Sauce. The beef would marinate overnight, absorbing the sweet-and-sour bright red paste. The next day, we would eagerly await the moment he would put it in the oven, where the fat and chili would combine into delicious crispy chunks. Homemade roast beef with a side of mashed potatoes may not win any diet awards, but it was the most loving, soulful, caring food my dad could offer us, because he put his full

---

* P.S. This is a LOVELY cookbook full of stories on entertaining told by two wise and fun female chefs. It's so soothing that sometimes I read it before bed.

attention into the meal. It's one of the few traditions I kept from my childhood, and today, I've taken it on. Every year around Christmas, I have my dad, sister, aunt, and cousins over to my apartment, and I make my dad's roast beef. We drink too much wine, we willingly submit to the sleep-inducing qualities of the red meat, we laugh, we tell stories. It's incredible how healing a meal can be when you make a little bit of a to-do about it.

Dad's Roast Beef Recipe

Made first at the Schuster home in Milwaukee, Wisconsin, 1942.

1. Pick some nice "prime beef." About one pound a person is perfect. Freak out that it's possible one pound a person won't be enough *and* it will be way too much.

2. Marinate the beef overnight in Heinz Chili Sauce. Two bottles should be good!

3. Take the beef out of the fridge *well* before you want to cook it so it gets to room temp. This will make you uncomfortable. "Should meat be left out this long???" you'll ask your dad. When he responds, "It'll be fine," trust him.

4. Set the oven for 450 degrees. If you have an oven like mine, which is *never* at the right temperature, buy an internal oven thermometer *and* a meat thermometer. The internal oven thermometer will hang from a rack and tell you what the fuck the actual temperature is inside the stove. To get to a real 450 in my oven, I have to set it to 500. Once I did this, I realized it wasn't *my*

fault it had taken an extra half hour to cook everything! The fucking oven was lying to me the whole time!

5. Cook the entire roast at 450 for fifteen minutes.

6. After fifteen minutes, lower the temperature to 325. It takes about twelve minutes for one pound to cook. So if you have eight pounds, that's ninety-six minutes of cook time. *If* I'm doing my math right. You should def check me. I already told you I hate/am very bad at math.

7. Have a glass of wine. Or one stiff drink. Or one stiff seltzer water with lime. Check on the beef frequently *but not so frequently* that you let the hot air out. Now use the meat thermometer so you can tell the exact temperature. I like my meat rare. That's 120 degrees in the center.

8. Once you've hit 120 degrees, take the meat out, let it rest for a half hour, and pray to the meat gods.

9. Slice your feast using a gorgeous ornamental carving knife you "borrowed" from your cousin. *She's not getting a knife this nice back. Well, at least not until Thanksgiving.*

T$'s Food Rules for Eating Actual *Food* That Nourishes Me and Makes Me Feel Good, Not Gross

The following is a set of rules I developed after reading the excellent *book* Food Rules: An Eater's Manual *by Michael Pollan (which I highly, highly recommend), flipping through a million cookbooks, heavily googling, watching other families eat in a (mostly) noncreepy way, and just paying attention to my own eating experiences.* Note: This has NOTHING to do with losing weight or being "skinny." *I'm really tired of people talking about being* skinny *like it's some achievement. You didn't climb Machu Picchu, you didn't complete your master's degree, you just subsisted off of celery and hummus for a week while being* the most *stressed-out version of yourself the rest of us had to suffer through.*

1. **No diets.** COME ON! You know this! *There is no miracle cure for weight loss.* No special pill or juice or cleanse that is going to give you the body you want. I'm so sorry! I wish there was! I would do it. Don't drive yourself crazy with something that's never going to work. Also: Food is a *good* thing. We are lucky to have food. Please, let's not stress about every bite.

2. **Eat food.** Not low-fat, low-sugar, "lite," protein powder, it-came-in-a-package-that-said-"natural"-so-that-means-something-right? Food made in a lab is not food at all. It's science. You are not a lab rat. No need to run an experiment on your stomach. I have an exception to this: I keep a (simple) protein bar in my kitchen and at my office for emergency situations. Nothing is worth a hangry version of me.

3. **Eat food that makes you feel good, not sick.** Again, simple, but it took me YEARS to learn this one. I stopped eating almost all fried foods simply because I always felt sick after eating them. There is no discipline to this other than realizing that I *always, always* had an upset stomach after eating fried chicken and deciding I didn't want to feel that way anymore. Listen to what your body hates. Let your body's hate be your guide. Namaste.

4. **If you are having trouble figuring out what your body likes, keep a (low-key) food journal.** *What is it with me and journals?* It took me a while to figure out what foods *felt* good and what put me into a food coma, so I kept a little journal in my purse of what I ate and how it made me feel. Salad with tofu for lunch: HANGRY THE ENTIRE FUCKING DAY. Salmon and lentils for dinner: pleasantly full and energized. Special doughnut for a colleague's birthday at four P.M.: crazed with sugar, like a baby who just had her first bite of cake and wants MORE NOW, unable to pay attention in a meeting when I *really* needed to pay attention. Write down for just one week what you eat and how you feel; you'll be floored by what you learn.

5. **Don't make food choices when hungry.** Have you ever noticed that if you go grocery shopping on an empty stomach, you'll leave with a basket of ice cream, carrots, and a block of cheese? How are you supposed to make dinner with that? Seriously, can you tell me? Because I've been there so many times and have never been able to find the answer. I am incapable of making any choices about food when I am already ravenous. I also tend to get into arguments around this time. "No, what restaurant do *you* want to go to??? If you have a preference, just say it!" Try to make your food choices when not on the verge of eating another person.

6. **Make your freezer a precious miracle solution from the heavens.** Keeping a freezer full of healthful meals, or meal components, is one of the best ways you can make sure you are nourishing yourself. When I roast

chicken, I always make a little extra so I can dice some and put it in the freezer. Same with soups. If I make a chickpea stew, I make a couple of extra servings, pour them into ziplock bags I decorate with Sharpie-drawn hearts, and freeze them. My freezer is stocked with fruits, spiralized zucchini, muffin-tin frittatas, turkey meatballs, and other real food. This way, I'm not tempted to buy a box of microwaveable mac and cheese and call that dinner. Tho, occasionally, there is nothing better than a box of Annie's mac and cheese.

7. **It's okay to go on a cleanse, but it's not okay for that to become your personality.** I've done a bunch of the juice cleanses. I've had the charcoal water that costs twelve dollars and "detoxifies" your blood. I've done the whole fasting thing. These drastic changes to your eating habits can be good for shaking things up every so often, sort of like the food equivalent to cleaning out your closet, *but* they are not a long-term solution. DO NOT BECOME SOPHIE. Sophie is the girl standing in front of us in line at the wedding buffet talking endlessly about her juice cleanse and how it "totally and utterly" changed her life and how she "never really liked full meals any-way." *You "never really liked" meals, Sophie?* YOU'VE NEVER FELT THE ECSTASY OF STRAIGHT-UP *DESTROYING* A FULL PIZZA, *SOPHIE*?! YOU HAVEN'T *LIVED, SOPHIE!* Never be the one who is endlessly talking about some cleanse, some cure-all, your new diet, the new BEST food trend, etc. You have more interesting things to talk about than what you eat.

8. **Keep a yummy, healthful treat around.** At the end of the night, if I want something sweet, I have a few

dried mango slices. They are delicious but not something I want to demolish in one sitting. What about a whole-grain toaster-oven waffle with a little honey? Three dates with a cup of mint tea is an elegant and tasty treat. The point is, always have something you ENJOY around you. You're less likely to binge on things you *don't like* when you have something that does satisfy you around. I'm looking at you, can of Pringles I don't even like but I can take down in three minutes flat. How did you even get in my house?

Clonazepam Communion
Use the Tools You Need

MAJOR DISCLAIMER: I AM NO doctor.

Can you believe that? I bet you were reading this book thinking the whole time, *Man, she is so scientific and logical in her approach to life, she must be a medical professional!* Alas, I don't know anything about science. As I am not a doctor, I'm not going to talk to you about more serious mental health conditions. I don't have any insight into those. Instead, I am going to talk about my own experience healing and coping with my anxiety and depression and what worked for me. Take all of this with a grain of salt.

Let's go back in time. Way, way, way back before the beginning of this book. Before I turned twenty-five and decided to get my life in order. Let's go back to the ancient year of 2008, the historic year in which *Sex and the City* went from being a TV show to lighting up the silver screen,* fifteen-year-old Miley Cyrus took a wrecking ball to American standards by— *gasp*—exposing *some of her back* on the cover of *Vanity Fair,*† and the country elected President Barack Obama. I was twenty-

---

*   Young millennials and the *even younger,* this means "movie screen." I don't know how or why, but doesn't it sound nice?

†   Doesn't this seem quaint now? What would you give to go back to the pop culture of 2008? Everything? Yup, *everything.*

two at the time, and in the spring of '08, I felt like college was unfairly casting me away like a discarded lover (a.k.a. I was graduating). I was suffering through extreme anxiety, far worse than anything I had experienced up to that point in my life. This was the kind of anxiety where I couldn't sleep—at all. I would roll around in between my sheets, get up, pace across my room, get back in bed, profusely sweat even though I was cold, cry, rub my feet together for what seemed like hours BECAUSE THEY REFUSED TO STOP MOVING, get out of bed again, cry at my computer while reading celebrity gossip, and wait at my desk for the sun to rise. In the morning, when it was acceptable to leave my room and start the day, I was a ghost of a person. I lived in a permanent panic attack, during which I would clench my jaw so tightly I had come to fully understand the phrase "weeping and gnashing of teeth." You know, the cheery description of hell from the New Testament.

I dreaded the future. I had spent my entire life trying to get to college, and now I would have to find *something else to do*? I hadn't spent a single moment thinking about life *after* college. I had bet my life on the magical healing power of Brown University to save me, yet it hadn't. Sure, I was smarter, sure, I had amazing friends, but here I was, unable to *function* let alone enjoy the fact I was graduating. It seemed to me that there was nothing left to hope for. My friends, who were watching me disintegrate, forced me to go to the mental health services office to find a psychiatrist.

I was cynical to say the least. Pills always seemed like too much of an easy way out. I thought that maybe I was just being a baby about graduating. I felt guilty that I couldn't handle my emotions like my friends could. I thought medical solutions for mental health problems were reserved only for "crazy" people, and I wasn't crazy, was I? I worried that drugs might permanently alter my identity and turn me into a different person. As

I morphed into this weeping, sleep-deprived ghost girl I realized I had *already* become a different person and I desperately needed a way back to myself.

At my very first appointment, Dr. Klein—a kind woman with warm brown eyes who was *covered* in chunky turquoise jewelry reminiscent of what an art gallery owner living in Albuquerque, New Mexico, might rock—explained, "I think you are clinically depressed and anxious. I suspect you've been this way for years, maybe since high school, but graduation has triggered you to enter into episodes of severe anxiety and depression." I was *clinically* depressed and anxious? Somehow, having a diagnosis made me feel immediately a little better. I had a label instead of a wash of emotions I couldn't get out from under. She asked me about my family history and bluntly explained that I "could go crazy" if I declined treatment. Cool, cool, cool. Was a psychiatrist supposed to use the C-word? I pressed her on what that meant. "Listen, given the shape you're in, and your family's mental health history, I would say that if you aren't careful, you could tip into manic-depressive. I'm not saying that you are right now. I'm just saying, untreated, this could get much worse." Her sage parting words to me were "And no cocaine. That could really push you over the edge." She prescribed an SSRI to help with my depression and a drug called clonazepam to (hopefully) break up the permanent anxiety attack I now called home.

I had never heard of clonazepam, but its effects were immediate and powerful. Even at a low dosage, the pill made me feel like I could step away from the anxiety and live in my body again. I imagined my anxious layer of skin lifting off me and floating away. My real body was now free from the shackles of angst, if only for a few hours. Sure, the underlying causes were in no way solved, but I had some time back in which I could try to understand why I felt this terrible. Sometimes, I even had an entire day back in which I did not feel like I might die. I had a day back in which I could get some motherfucking sleep. And the sleep! YOU GUYS, THE SLEEP. The sleep was the key. In an anxious, unrested state, *everything* was upsetting. But with the eight solid hours of sleep that the clonazepam gave me, I could better deal with and actually *show up for* my life. It gave me the ability to simply see that it was *possible* to do other things with my day besides weep and pace. The medicine helped me return to *myself.*

I was talking with an especially insightful friend recently about the unfair stigmas placed on medication and the idea that it can actually help us return to ourselves. "What about when you have a pounding migraine that makes you miserable and curl up into your sofa, totally incapacitated?" she asked. "If you take maximum-strength Advil and suddenly feel like yourself again, did that *change* your personality? Or did it get rid of the horrible migraine that was keeping you from who you really *are?*" I realized she was onto something. For me, it's the same thing with mental health. If I need to take medication because I have been swallowed whole by the whale of anxiety and depression, if I feel like I am deep at the bottom of the sea and will never make it to the light again, there should be no shame in allowing science to help lift me back up to the surface.

To be clear, the clonazepam did not fix everything (obvi, since you know what went down in the years after college). It solved *none* of my problems. I had my twenty-fifth birthday fiasco *while being treated by a therapist* and *with* the aid of drugs. I got to that rock-bottom place even with the help of pills and treatment. But. In the days and weeks after that birthday, I do think the clonazepam gave me *some* space to breathe—to see that I had a life worth taking care of and that I could do it if I really worked hard.

I have been taking clonazepam on and off since 2008 as needed to deal with my anxiety attacks. It's a yellow, chalky, flat pill that looks like a mini Communion wafer. I put it on my tongue and swallow it down using my own spit. It's tasteless, and if I take it when I feel a true anxiety attack coming on, I can prevent said attack. In the past few years, however, I've experimented with not taking it altogether.* Often, I can now deal with my anxiety through my rituals, but I don't think I would have had the space or ease of mind to build my stability without the leg up clonazepam gave me: enough time away from anxiety that I could find other solutions that work for me. You can't fix a car that's on fire as it careens down the highway. You have to pull to the shoulder of the road, smother the flames, wait for the smoke to settle, and *then* you can assess the problem and fix the car. Clonazepam was a very important fire extinguisher for me.

So why tell you any of this? Why go into the details of taking pills to help with anxiety and depression when this is a book about the rituals I have built to nurture myself? Are the pills a cheat? I WISH! I *wish* there was something you could swallow right now to make your life whole and happy and fun. Medication was just one important weapon in my self-care arsenal. I tell you all of this because if you need extra help, if you need a little room to breathe, if you are suffering from something that is debilitating, there should be no stigma in taking something that can help you. There are many treatment options if you are deep in the shit. With the help of your doc-

---

* BTW, when I go on or off medication, I do so with the help of my doctor and at a steady pace. I once STUPIDLY went off an SSRI cold-turkey and immediately felt like there was an electrical storm raging in my brain. I googled it and learned I was suffering from "brain zaps," a withdrawal symptom that makes you feel like the inside of your skull is being shocked. Doesn't that sound like fun? Don't be dumb like I was. Talk to your doctor when going on or off any medication.

tor, and a little trial and error, you might be able to find some relief. Pills are never *the only solution,* but they can help set you on a more stable path where you can find some reprieve and deal with the bigger issues affecting you. In my case, the medicine simply helped build a floor beneath me so I could stand on my own. The pills didn't build a beautiful, stable, joyous life for me. I did that.

I'm excited to see what you will build for yourself.

Anjelica Huston Blessed Me

Climb Up Things You Don't Think You Can Climb Up

HIKING IN LA IS THE most #Basic of behaviors. Every model-turned-DJ-turned-B-list-celebrity "hikes." It wasn't like this when I was growing up. When I was a kid, you were supposed to shop indoors at the mall on the weekend. This is, after all, the city that paved over its river, turning a bountiful, vibrant water bed into a bulging, concrete vein that now runs through Los Angeles with a polluted trickle. This is the city where a boob job is often given as a high school graduation present. It's not a city that embraces nature. Or so I thought. When I returned to Los Angeles after almost a decade on the East Coast, I was stunned to find that the city was making an effort to keep natural preserves pristine and to—*gasp*—enjoy them. All of a sudden, friends who didn't even own sneakers wanted to take their dogs for hikes down the meandering Westridge Trail. Formerly, I had known it only as the place where the druggie kids did shrooms. I never knew it was actually a twenty-thousand-acre urban park where you could hike for miles without seeing anyone else. Los Angeles had changed, apparently—and, luckily, so had I.

Remember how I had promised myself I would not be skeptical after I moved to the West Coast? How I had told myself I would embrace the triteness and the health-obsessed culture and I would give this whole "look at your body" thing a try? Well, in theory, I was very much on board. In practice, I was very, very, *very* out of shape. Yes, I had been running in New York, and that had done SO MUCH for my mental health, but it hadn't really helped me grow physically stronger.

One of my best friends from high school, Evan, offered to help me on my path toward a more active lifestyle. Evan has always been somewhat of a caretaker to me. Maybe "caretaker" is not the right word—he's not feeding me applesauce after taking me out for my daily constitutional. It's more like, in high school, when my parents weren't paying attention to my education, he was the one who suggested I study for the SATs. When my college counselor recommended I go to school in California, Evan was the one who looked at my black horn-rimmed glasses and the scarf I had wrapped around my neck in the eighty-degree heat and told me I didn't need anyone's permission to move to the East Coast. In addition to being one of my oldest friends, Evan is . . . hot. Like, Instagram model hot. With a six-pack and, under that, a V-shaped "love line." Ya know what a love line is, right? Those grooves right below the abs that lead to a man's nether regions? The kind you see on David Beckham in an H&M underwear ad? Not that I have extensively googled this or anything. . . . My point is that Evan is in distractingly good shape. "I'll help you get out there!" Evan offered via text. "Meet me at Runyon."

Runyon Canyon is both a hike and a *scene*. Here, women in full faces of contoured makeup sporting platform sneakers attempt to climb up the eastern side of the Santa Monica Mountains. Men in Greek-statue physical condition easily bound up the hills while taking perfect selfies. Fifteen minutes into our expedition, I was already winded. "Evan [*breathes heavily*], can we take a rest?" I pleaded. "Um. Well . . . the hike hasn't really *begun* yet. This is the walk from the parking lot to the trail, so . . ." I was not yet entitled to rest.

As we climbed farther up the hill, I began to feel self-conscious. This hike was *hard,* far more difficult than I'd envisioned. I was barely keeping up with Evan, who was jumping off rocks and darting up hills while insisting I do the same. He was *smiling* and *enjoying* himself as I gritted my teeth and just tried not to fall too far behind. When we came face-to-face with a hill so steep I thought it wasn't even an option to explore, Evan motioned toward it and called out from up ahead, "Come on, Tara! Let's get this!" I glared at him; he was barely sweating. I looked at the peak, which appeared so steep I didn't think *anyone* could get up it, and I can tell you that I genuinely hated my old friend Evan in that moment. I was already doing something hard! I couldn't get up that hill! That hill was for hikers with "gear" who said things like "On belay!" Why did Evan want to humiliate me? And while we're in my rage spiral, why was Evan *jumping off shit*? What was *that* about? Show-off. I was annoyed. I was sweating so profusely that my light pink tank top was now a shade deeper. I was done. "Evan, I can't."

"Oh, come on, it's just a little hill! You can!"

"Evan . . . I *can't.*"

Evan looked at me like he didn't understand. It took him a moment for it to register that I was giving up. We walked away from the steep hill and back toward the trailhead in silence, stopping once to take a picture with a horse so our lives would look perfect on Instagram. #Smile #SquadGoals #Blessed

That statement "I can't" pricked my ego like the spine of a cactus. One of those tiny, translucent spines that are hard to get out with tweezers because they are so small and sharp that they lodge themselves deep into your flesh. "I can't" stuck with me for weeks. I knew it wasn't *that* big a deal. After all, it was just a hike, but what bothered me so enormously was the very idea that I would ever say "I can't," then proceed to give up. I wanted to be the kind of person who *could*! "West Coast Me" was supposed to be the kind of person who at least says, "Eh, okay, let's try."

I needed to learn how to hike. It didn't need to be Cheryl Strayed, Pacific Crest Trail–style hiking. I wouldn't be confronting trails where you could possibly freeze to death or plummet off the side of a cliff. I just wanted to be able to explore the semi-wild hills of California with confidence. I wanted to force myself to hike up things that looked impossible to mount. Alone, with no one to judge me, I started my hikes with small, gentle goals, just like I had done with running:

1. Time yourself for ten minutes going up this hill and then come back. Repeat it if you can.

2. Make it to the tree in the middle of the trail; then you can come back, go home, and take a bath.

3. Time yourself for twenty minutes, ~~walk the entire time,~~ take many breaks, then walk back to your car. Get yourself a latte for your efforts.

Little by little, I tried things that I didn't think were possible:

1. Walk slowly up that hill that's basically a ninety-degree angle.

2. Take the harder path that is reserved for the mountain bikers.

3. *Oh my God, get down from this godforsaken biker path; how do people do this ON FUCKING BIKES???*

4. Okay. Now try to go up the biker path again. But super slow. You have all the time in the world. You don't have to be anywhere.

Alone on these hikes, sweating and dirty, my fingers swollen because I am allergic to all grass and most trees, I impressed myself with what I could actually do. I could actually go up a thing that looked impossible. I could actually *run* a trail. There was a lot I was capable of, and I could see it in a very physical way. I would listen to the sounds of Californian woodlands in the wind as I moved. I would listen for my inner guide, and, very often, I would hear something I needed in that moment. (Does that sound kinda earth-child-supernatural to you? It should; it's both divine and spooky as hell.)

Temescal Canyon is a particularly special hike for me. It's right off Sunset Boulevard in the Pacific Palisades, and the entire first leg of it is uphill. It's brutal but *good* brutal. You get breathless, and the physical act is so hard you kind of have to stop thinking, and then, BAM! You are smacked in the face with sweeping views of the mighty Pacific Ocean. I go on this hike with my dear friend Hilly almost every Sunday. Hilly is annoyingly good at life: She looks like a brunette Daenerys Targaryen, owns her own home, and fully embodies the word "fierce." On one morning hike, I was complaining to Hilly about a work problem I had. I knew it wasn't a big deal; I had sent in my expense report late, my boss called me out on it, and I felt like a fool. I took his criticism of my work as criticism of my character and was having a very tough time diffusing my anxiety about the situation. My mind was obsessively chewing on the idea that this was actually a grave mistake: *You're a chump. What an easy thing to avoid getting dinged for. What's wrong with you?* I was in such a trance of questioning myself that it was making it difficult to enjoy our usually relaxing hike.

"Can you separate the anxiety from being with me right now?" Hilly finally asked. "Like, can you think of the anxiety as something that doesn't exist with us? Can you leave it at the office?"

I honestly didn't know. I imagined the anxiety sitting in my swivel chair at work, right behind my computer. I saw myself closing the door and walking away from the office. I saw myself transporting to this hike. Here I was, moving forward. One foot goes in front of the other. I feel sweat on my lips, and I love that salty taste. I am under the sky, under the sun, next to someone I love. I am here. Oh yeah, I am *here*. I AM FUCK-ING HERE. It was a lightning-bolt moment. An "oh-shit-maybe-spirituality-is-real" jolt of electricity that charged my skin with a buzzing, cold vibration. Before I could explain anything to Hilly, I was suddenly struck by the apparition of a woman in a white visor, white shirt, and white tennis skirt zooming by us. There was something radiant and ethereal—yet familiar—about her. I thought I knew her. Maybe she was some friend's super-hot, yoga-practicing mom? We kept walking, and then it hit me. I stopped and grabbed Hilly's arm as I realized: That vision in white was Anjelica Huston.

Anjelica Huston, whose memoirs I had just devoured. Anjelica Huston, whom I had been writing about in my journal. Something about her books made me feel like she would have sage advice for me. She was just such a gangster. A woman who did what she wanted and reached for colossal desires, a woman who played *Morticia Addams*. What a boss. I turned around to see if I could get a better glimpse of her, expecting to see her walking away, continuing down the path. But instead, there she was, facing me, standing still. She smiled. She nodded. She stayed there for less than a second, but it was a moment that felt so long I could have taken a nap in it. Then she turned around and went on her way.

It was so fucking weird.

I feel certain that Anjelica Huston blessed me that day. She consecrated me in the exact moment I finally felt present. There I was, able-bodied, awake, and aware enough to see something sacred. Anjelica Huston showed me that when you expand what you think you are capable of, *that's* when you become truly capable. The key is, you have to get out on the trail, say, "Yes, I can," and, suddenly, as if by magic, you will find you can climb farther than you thought possible. It's not magic, really. It's the practice of having faith in yourself. It's the habit of deciding you are capable of great things, putting on your hiking boots, and getting on the dirt path. And maybe I am stretching by looking for meaning in glimpsing Saint Huston. But so what? I would rather stretch and see blessings all around me than not.

Anjelica Huston blessed me, and today I bless you.

I don't have an Oscar to my name, but I've scaled some difficult, shitty trails. I've fallen down. I've bruised and skinned every part of me. I've watched blood and soil mix. I've also cleaned myself off, I've healed, and I've gotten back on the motherfucking climb. I'm at the trailhead to tell you that you are capable. You are worthy. You can do things you don't think you are able to, so you must go out and try them. There is good news for you and bad news: The good news is that the things you want, the hills you want to climb, you can have them. You absolutely can because it just takes work, and you are capable of work. The bad news is, you have to *do* that work. There's no staring at the hill and saying, "I can't." There's no second-guessing allowed. Have faith in yourself, in your abilities, in your capacity to blast through the limits that either you or others have laid down on you.

Having trouble finding faith? Don't worry. Faith is a practice. It's a habit we can *all* build. All of the loving body rituals you are learning about are aimed at training your body to *feel the faith*. Getting ready like Cleopatra, doing one nice thing a day for yourself, taking baths, learning/tricking yourself to be comfortable in your body, collecting amulets, having a physical space to take yourself seriously, keeping your home as nice as you would for guests, nourishing yourself with food, avoiding substances that make you feel bad, seeking medical help if you need it—these are all ways we build the faith that we can lead the lives we want to lead, lives we are proud of, lives full of delight.

Take that hike you're curious about that seems a little out of the way, wrap up your hands and get in the ring for your first boxing lesson, take a ballet class at your gym that sounds fun even though you worry you won't be any good. Be prepared to be *fucking jubilant* when you do something you didn't think was possible. See the power that was *always* there in your body. You may not do it perfectly. Your pirouette may be severely lacking and you may look more like a toddler who is just learning how to use her legs than a trained ballerina, but that doesn't matter. It does not matter *how* you perform, just that you show up and try. And there is no other time than right now. Do you get that? That this is actually *it*? To have faith in yourself, you must *build* faith in yourself, and the best way I know to do that is through physical activities. Get that faith in your joints, in your muscles, in your sweat. Little by little, you will feel it course through your blood until it becomes NBD to take on your next challenge.

Please, do not put a limit on who you think you can be and what you are capable of achieving. Shrug off that cloak of doubts that weighs you down, and climb, baby, climb.

On fucking belay.

I'll be right there with you.

III

THE RELATIONSHIP RITUALS

You Can't Control How Others Treat You, but You Can Control What You'll Accept

A Sad Meditation
Where Do You Find Love?

I'M NOT SO GOOD AT meditating. My Headspace app tells me that I'm supposed to let the clouds of thought pass by in order to see the endless blue skies of a truly open mind. It sounds heavenly, but I find meditation impossibly difficult. Every time I try to do it, my mind immediately wanders to such high-level thoughts as *What am I going to eat next?* and *Ugh, when will I do the laundry?* And then I feel like a failure for not "nailing" the meditation. It's no fun at all. Yet the idea of quieting my mind, of being present and aware while sporting an on-point yoga ensemble, is still highly appealing to me. So many people I admire meditate: Oprah, Elizabeth Gilbert, the Dalai Lama, *Oprah*. As you know, I am a thief of good habits, and an Oprah habit is as good as gold in my book.

After years of haphazardly attempting to meditate on my own and beating myself up for my shortcomings, I decided to visit a real-deal meditation studio. A friend told me about a new place in LA called Unplug. It was supposed to be fancy, like SoulCycle, and in the same way that SoulCycle hides the horror of cardio under the veneer of a luxury experience, Unplug was supposed to make meditation feel more like something pleasurable and less like the torture I had come to expect. I drove to the studio on a lunch break from work, walked in (through the merch store, of course), signed up for two weeks of unlimited classes (I was *totally* going to come every day), and took my seat in the way, *way* back, where I figured I'd be the least likely to be judged for my fidgeting.

I sat down and felt the cool, clean wood floor support me. A calming purple light, much like that of a Virgin America flight, bathed the room. The teacher, who looked suspiciously like Vin Diesel (bald and ripped, with a could-save-the-world vibe), entered, and with him came a sense of calm. He moved deliberately, and it's hard to describe, but his steps were somehow . . . *kind*. As if with each motion he was summoning compassion into the room. As he took his seat at the front of the class, I had a feeling this was going to be my first fruitful meditation.

"Close your eyes," Vin instructed us. "Breathe in and breathe out. On a count of four, breathe in through the mouth and fill your lungs and belly with the sweet air. Now on a count of four breathe out through the nose. Feel the awakening of your body through the sensations of the breath. Feel yourself come into presence." I was breathing in and breathing out for sure. Was the air sweet? Not particularly. Did I feel myself coming "into presence"? Well, I was *here,* wasn't I? After this meditation was over, though, I should get some lunch. Maybe a smoothie? An acai bowl? What even is "acai"? *DAMN IT, TARA.*

As our teacher continued to guide us through our meditation, I tried as hard as I could to stay with his words. When I caught myself drifting to some other thought, I imagined that I was sitting on the top of a mountain gazing out, and that each idea that popped into my head was really a train car passing by, far below in the valley beneath me. I was starting to relax when Vin began explaining the theme of today's meditation: love. "Love is available to all of us, in every moment. I want you to think of a time when you felt *unconditionally* loved. When you felt safe and shrouded in love. Maybe it's a time your mom held you close to her. Or a time your father read you a story before bed. Let the first thing you think of sit with you, and feel its warmth radiate through your entire body."

I began searching my mind for a memory of unconditional love. *Um . . . okay . . . this shouldn't be so hard . . . think of a moment when I felt accepted and loved. . . .* I brought to mind pictures from family vacations in which I was smiling. I remembered one photo from when I was really young, maybe five years old. I was in my mom's arms, on the beach, my head pressed to her chest, the surf blurry behind us. It should have been a nice, normal moment, but as I looked at the picture in my mind, my body felt the revulsion of my little-girl self. I smelled my mom's sweat. I felt the heat of her body and how it made my heart race and want to flee. As a kid, these sensations drove me to spring from her arms and avoid all contact with her. Maybe my mom was *trying* to love me unconditionally, but, in her grip, I always felt constricted and somehow violated. As I flipped through more childhood memories, I mostly saw fights and heard the voices of others telling me I wasn't good enough or that there was something wrong with me. I couldn't find anything that made me feel the unqualified, unrestricted, full-on LOVE that Vin was asking us for.

Tears pooled behind my nose and flowed upward toward my eyes as I was struck by a pounding, hollow beating in my chest and stomach. The more I thought about it, the more I saw quite clearly that my most fundamental "ancient wound" was that I had never felt worthy of unconditional acceptance and affection. Instead, I was always, as Brené Brown, the research professor and radically wise storyteller, says, "hustling for worthiness," striving, *struggling* to get my parents' consideration or at least a little approval. When that failed, I learned to accept *any* kind of treatment, so long as someone was paying attention to me. It took Vin Diesel in Virgin America lighting to illuminate where the knife of neglect had cut me most deeply.

To calm myself, I brought to mind the love I knew I had: my own. I had been working on taking care of myself for so long that I now had an arsenal of tools to give myself love. I once heard the magnificent, enlightened Elizabeth Gilbert say that "true love liberates the beloved. You are your beloved. You liberate yourself." Those words called out to me like a benevolent siren song, impossible to ignore. (And as you can guess, they now live on my Idea Board—held up with gold glitter tape, obvi.) Instead of choosing a moment with my family, I looked for the times I had soothed and loved and liberated *myself*. I recalled a particularly warm and decadent bath I had recently drawn after a boy had broken up with me. I remembered playing with the warm suds around me and saying aloud, "I am good." I thought of a solo hike I had taken on a trail in Malibu. I had gone farther than I thought I was capable of. I felt the orange sun wash over me as I leaped between boulders, exhilarated and free and a little scared but totally at peace with myself. I could see the lilies I bought regularly simply because I believed I was worth lilies. Unconditional love started with me deciding that no matter whether I was successful, no matter what other people thought of me, I would always believe in myself. *I* was my beloved.

Sitting in the meditation with my legs crossed and my hands in my lap, I knew that my next step toward self-care would be thinking more about this whole "unconditional love" thing. While I was getting really good at treating myself well, I now needed to figure out how that worked in relationships. How could I fill my life with people who would nurture me? Were they even out there? How could I build bridges and establish guardrails with my own fractured family? I knew I couldn't control how other people treated me, but I *could* decide what I would accept.

A bell rang and the meditation was over. I picked myself up off the floor and walked back into the gift shop. I bought a glass water bottle with the word "love" on it to keep on my desk at work. That would be some kind of start.

Lady Harem
Find Your Friend Family

A MAN I WAS ON a dinner date with recently called me out for saying, multiple times, that multiple people were my "best friend." "How can they *all* be your best friend?" he wondered. He told me that by the way I talked about my friends, you would think that each one was the most interesting, thoughtful, exciting, unique, sparkling snowflake of a person. "Can all of your friends really be *the best*? I mean, you're using a lot of hyperbole." Ya know what, *guy*, I'm not sure who made you the language police, but all I can say to you is *yes*, an enthusiastic, I'll-never-take-it-back, I have the fucking best *best* friends, HELL YES. I keep a harem of kick-ass, smart, spiritually and emotionally generous, ride-or-die best friends. Each one is a life partner I have actively sought out, intentionally nurtured, and done my very best to deserve. Our friendships are now eternal and unconditional. Check, please!

I didn't always feel so sure of my friendships, nor did I always value them. I know this will sound weird, but growing up, I didn't know *how* to have friends. The adults around me were not setting good examples from which I could learn. Instead, I was told by my parents that nearly everyone we knew was a potential enemy of the state. One day I was being held by my

favorite babysitter, Anja, and the next my mother was screaming at me, "Anja is fired! You're never going to see her again.
She's only interested in money. She's a thief and a bad influence!" Even though I was only ten, I was pretty sure Anja was
just a lovely French ex-pat and part-time masseuse and not
some criminal mastermind who was gunning for the total de-
struction of my family. After all, Anja had once given me a glass
bottle full of purple oil and glitter that she told me would protect me from my mother. Maybe she knew too much and that's
why she was fired. . . .

My parents' friendships never lasted. Suzanne Somers (yes,
that Suzanne Somers, the *Three's Company* Suzanne Somers, the
Step by Step Suzanne Somers) was my mom's best friend and
my godmother. When I was seven years old, we would go to
her house in Palm Springs, and I would nuzzle in Suzanne's
platinum hair before she would "gift" us yet another Thigh-
Master to add to the growing pile we kept at home. I remember I *loved* spending time with her. She was warm and strikingly
beautiful and a little mystical. Her house was full of crystals and
dream catchers and I want to say feathers, tho I can't be one
hundred percent sure on the feathers front. In my little-girl
mind, it was supz witchy in the best possible way. In Suzanne's
arms, I felt affection and acceptance. Suddenly, however, and
under never-explained circumstances, my mother cast Suzanne
as a Traitor with a capital T, someone who had deeply betrayed
her, someone who was no longer to be spoken about. "Suzanne
doesn't love you, that's for sure," my mom plainly told me. Only
days before, Suzanne had been the next in line to take care of
me and my sister if something happened to my parents, but
now she was expunged from our family altogether. Adults came
in and out of my life like this with ferocious speed and barely
any explanation. Even my paternal grandparents were villain-

ous, according to my mother. "They ruined your father's life; it's better if you don't have a relationship with them," she would tell me repeatedly.

All of this drama, this continual threatening that people were "out to get us," left me with the distinct impression that "family" and "friends" were always just one step away from being enemies. They were to be viewed with suspicion, and I had to keep my wits about me. Sure, Lindsay Safran *seemed* like a nice first-grade playmate. She had the brunette pigtails and dimpled smile of someone who *looked* like she could be trusted. But I wouldn't be fooled that easily. I would keep her at arm's length. We could play all the Mario Kart she wanted, but I would never tell her my secrets.

It wasn't until college, when I started going to therapy on my own, that my doctor told me one of the most important things I have ever heard. I don't remember what tangent I was on exactly, but I remember Dr. Klein told me something that immediately struck a chord in my heart: "The *only* thing that matters in the long run is the bonds you create. You won't be on your deathbed wishing you'd worked more or achieved something greater professionally. You'll be looking back on your friendships, your kinships; you'll be thinking about the people you love and who loved you. Your bonds are what give your life meaning. Your relationships give you strength." *Damn.*

Of course, I was not able to develop deep and lasting friendships overnight. And I did not start auditioning potential BFFs the very next day. *But,* from that moment on, the way I approached all of my relationships *was* fundamentally different. While I wasn't born into the family I would have wished for, I began to understand that my friends could become my family.

Today, I have a Lady Harem. A group of friends whom I love unconditionally, who, in turn, give me *their* love without restriction. I'm not just talking about my acquaintances or people

I like to have dinner with. This is a group of people I consider sacred.

The Fisch, as I call her, treats my feelings so gently that when I'm with her, I feel like I actually come from a loving home. Over the years, she has shown me that she has my back, and whenever I'm down in a deep, dark hole and lonely and feeling like a fucking loser who can't *even fathom* returning to elevated ground, she will take my hand and lead me back into the sunlight. In return, if she's ever feeling anxious, I will show up, fully, for her. This might mean talking on the phone, this might mean driving down to Orange County to help take care of her daughter for the weekend, but it has also meant going to the desert with her to meditate on rocks or simply sitting in her car for hours, remembering and laughing about the time our college landlord told us there were to be "no alcohol parties on the premises." *DEAR LANDLORD: IT'S COLLEGE. GOOD FUCKING LUCK ENFORCING THAT ONE.* My Hilly is so fierce, so spectacularly, annoyingly "good at life," that when she praises me for something, I feel a rush of pride and a thrilling sense of accomplishment. I covet her approval because I admire the hell out of her. For my part, I try to make her feel cherished. With postcards from every city I visit, with visits to the new city she has just moved to, I do my best to show her that she is always in my thoughts. Julia, who introduced me to running, is both so beautiful and kind that it's frustratingly unfair. How one person can be that gorgeous inside and out is outrageous. She is THE most generous wingwoman in the history of the game. Though happily married, she will suffer through *horrible* bars, introducing me to men she thinks might be a good match. She also picked me up from the airport once. WHO DOES THAT?! Only fucking *saints* do that. I'm not sure how I can ever repay her. Maybe I should give her my firstborn child? I try to be someone she can talk to about anything without fear of judgment. I ask her questions because I know that sometimes it's hard for her to seek the support *she* needs.

When I lived in New York, Isabelle welcomed me into her parents' loving home every Sunday night for dinner. Through example, she has taught me some of my best self-care habits—journaling, gratitude, thank-you cards, vegetables. She is the most empathetic person I know, willing to put herself in someone else's shoes even when that line of thinking is inconvenient and difficult. I try to remind her that just as she takes care of her friends, she deserves to take care of herself. I send her self-care packages: oils, notebooks, and candles that I think will help her be nice to herself. And then, of course, there is my Lauren, my roomie and my BFF. I met her on the first day of high school when I was still in the habit of hiding myself—performing the role of "the artsy girl who's super smart but always super high." She immediately saw through my bullshit and tried to get to know the real me. She is the kind of friend who, when I asked for hot chocolate on my birthday, surprised me not only with cocoa and marshmallows but also with a spread of rose macarons and champagne. She goes above and beyond to make the people around her feel special, and I try to make her feel the love that she gives. I will curl up with her on the couch and listen to her rail against "fucking Dave," her incompetent boss, for hours, for as long as it takes for her to sufficiently vent. I will explain my elaborate plans to burn down Dave's house until she laughs. When she finally quit her job this year, you know I organized our friends to send her a big blast of orchids to commemorate her victory. *Take that, Dave. I might still burn down your house, BTW.*

I would tell you that these friendships are all about give and take, but really, they are all about give, give, give. My Lady

Harem doesn't treat one another with kindness in the hope of getting something back. It just feels *good* to be generous. It does something for your own soul when you pour out love to another. I write these women Valentine's Day cards every year. I bake them homemade bread when they come over for dinner. They don't all live close by, nor are they a cohesive group, so I'll travel to wherever each lady lives (San Francisco, New York, Tokyo, Orange County). And if I can't afford the ticket just now? A Google hang with a glass of wine is a great way to catch up. A twenty-minute phone call on my way to work just to ask how they are doing is enough. Underneath the actions, my intention is always to value them. I also send good wishes for my friends into the world, daily. I write about them in my journal; I think about them on my hikes; I include them in my daily gratitude lists. If that sounds bogus to you, then I am sorry, but it feels nice to live in a world where good intentions matter.

I'm able to treat my friendships with such care because I've made space for them in my life. I've weeded out the people who deplete me. If I leave lunch thinking, *Ellen didn't ask me a single question about myself, yet again,* then I don't tempt fate by continuing to make plans with Ellen. I no longer hang out with people I don't want to hang out with. Did you hear that? I NO LONGER HANG OUT WITH PEOPLE I DON'T WANT TO HANG OUT WITH. That seems so obvious, but how many times have you *dreaded* dinner with Steph but have grudgingly shown up because you "have to"? How many times have you thought, *Steph, enough already with the endless self-promotion and talk of your new, AMAZING diet that everyone really should follow.* SUBSISTING OFF OF WATER, LEMON JUICE, AND CAYENNE PEPPER ALONE IS NOT A DIET, IT'S STARVATION, STEPH! Listen to me very, very carefully: You don't *have* to make plans with people you don't want to make plans with. I stopped hanging out with people whom I only saw out of a sense of obligation, and NOTHING bad has happened to me.

I want to be clear that my relationship with my Lady Harem is not always perfect. We are not always hugging and making crafts together and singing 2000s-era Britney Spears (tho that does happen with some frequency). Sometimes one lady will cycle out of my harem for a time because our relationship has changed or we are in different phases of our lives. Sometimes we fight. Sometimes we need to take intentional distance if someone is feeling hurt. Sometimes we can even be a little petty and shitty and selfish. Or at least, sometimes *I* can be a little petty and shitty and selfish. These relationships bend and grow over the years like trees, branching out and stretching and shedding leaves so they can bloom again later. But. There is one thing that is always constant in a Lady Harem: At the end of the day, our friendships are so deeply rooted that even the ones that are damaged can always heal. If called into action, we can quickly get over our shit and show up for each other like damn warriors. Ready to defend, love, and keep vigil with one another.

The people you surround yourself with make up the quality of your life. These are the people who influence you, whether consciously or subconsciously. They serve as a reflection of your values, your hopes, what you think of yourself. These are the people you are sharing your precious, finite, never-guaranteed-but-always-tick-tock-slipping-away time on Earth with, so my advice to you is to be fucking greedy and ruthless. Choose ONLY the people who lift you up, who are reaching for higher things themselves, who MAKE YOU FEEL AWESOME. Grab on to them, hold them, scream "Mine, mine, mine," and do everything in your power to be good to them.

Never let go of the people who treat you like *the shit* and who are *the shit* themselves.

You will meet all kinds of people in your life. Some you can trust with your deepest vulnerabilities, some are just fun to share a glass of rosé with, others you will feel you need to keep at a distance to protect yourself. You'll be able to identify these people by the chips on their shoulders. By their negativity. By the fact that they never seem to be genuinely happy for you. These people are not bad, damned, or unworthy, rather they are just working out their own shit. But let me remind you that *their* shit is not *your* shit. You do not need to "save" them. That idea is, in fact, both impossible and kind of insulting. I love you very much, but you have only the answers for yourself. Instead of trying to save them, shed them. Shed them now. Don't waste another second on people who don't make your life better. Harsh? Maybe. BUT WE'RE TALKING ABOUT YOUR LIFE HERE.

And if you can't take my advice, then maybe you will listen to the eternal wisdom of Drake. You know *everyone* wants to be Drake's friend, so he has had to be discerning about whom he lets into his inner circle. In Lil Wayne's song "Right Above It," Drake sings, "Fake friends write the wrong answers on the mirror for me. That's why I pick and choose. I don't get shit confused." I think what Drake is saying is that you don't need a million friends on the surface. You don't need sycophants who just agree with you; you don't need people who mirror back behaviors you find draining or not in line with how you want to lead your life. What you do need is a small circle of friends who bring their real selves to the table. People you trust and admire and just think are the bee's knees. You need to banish the people you DON'T WANT TO BE AROUND and embrace the people who make you radiate with joy and ease and love and warmth and laughter and OH MY GOD, ARE

YOU GETTING THE PICTURE OF WHAT FRIEND-
SHIP CAN BE YET? What you need is a family of friends.
What you need is your own Lady Harem.

Did I get all that right, Drake? I know you're reading this
book.

A List of Things to Look for in a Ride-or-Die Friend

*I'm not saying that each member of your Lady Harem
(or militia or cartel or posse or whatever works for you)
needs to have every single one of these qualities.* But that
would be nice! *And I'm certainly not saying your acquaintances need to have all of the following. But here
are things to keep in mind when looking for the people
you want to call your family. Also: Don't worry if your
harem isn't in place just yet! Simply start by getting a
really clear picture of what you need. Once you have the
space and the intention for a Lady Harem, watch how
the right people seem to tango into your life.*

1. **Kindness. Over everything.** Do you feel that this
   person is fundamentally *kind*? Or are they given to shit-
   talking, drama, and constant criticism of others? If you
   have a friend who is super judgmental behind people's
   backs, rest assured that she is going to be JUST as judgy
   about you when you are not around. Sorry. There is no
   fucking time for people who want you to fail.

2. **Confidence.** It takes a confident person to love fully. It
   takes confidence to see the achievements of someone
   else as a wonderful thing. One thing all of the members
   of my Lady Harem have in common is that they are
   confident enough in themselves that they can shower
   love on others. The Lady Harem reminds you of your

own power. They are able to celebrate and support your latest adventures and achievements because they don't have chips on their shoulders. And when you fall flat on your face? They give you a hand up and show you the way back to your satin throne. Look for people who have the backbone to see your good-natured self as something awesome, not a threat. Remember, NO FRENEMIES ALLOWED. Not the kind who live in your brain OR the kind you meet in the real world. Please and thank you.

3. **Self-awareness.** How aware is your friend of their own behavior and how it affects others? Do they have perspective? Or did you fly all the way to Texas to be at her thirtieth birthday, but she is crying because you can stay for only two nights of the four-day weekend? When you come upon a friend issue, which you inevitably will, can you have a real conversation with this person? Can you say, "It hurts my feelings that you have re-scheduled so many of our dates lately" and know that they will take that in? Are they aware enough that they can investigate themselves, or do they get super defensive and shut down? Picking a self-aware friend at the onset pays off at every single turn in a friendship. You can talk through the rough patches with someone who is aware.

4. **Curiosity.** Look for people who ask you questions and are engaged in your life while also letting you in to their stories. It's too draining to have a friend who dumps emotional baggage on you without asking about what you're going through, but it's *boring* and unfulfilling to have a friend who won't share their emotional life with

you. How well can you actually know someone who is not open enough to share their feelings with you?

5. **Secret sauce.** There is some little piece of you that is, well, a little needy. And that's okay. It's healthy to "need" something from your friends. My secret sauce is that I look for people who come from a "good family." I KNOW THIS IS UNFAIR. I DO NOT COME FROM A "GOOD FAMILY." Yet I am aware enough to know that it's healthiest for me to be around people who don't have baggage identical to mine. Otherwise, we get our black suitcases of neglect mixed up, and suddenly I'm dealing with someone else's mom issues. What's the thing you need the most from friends? Maybe it's loyalty. Maybe it's humor. Think about what is important to you specifically and don't be afraid to go look for it.

6. **If all else fails: Do you feel *good* in this person's company?** Do you feel like a better version of yourself when you're with them? Do you look forward to seeing them? Do you feel like you can be your actual silly self around this person, or are you performing some idea of yourself? Get honest. If you have a friend who doesn't make you feel good, or who makes you doubt yourself, why are you calling this person a friend at all? People who make you doubt yourself are not your friends, they are your frenemies. And again, NO FRENEMIES ALLOWED.

And if they don't fit this criteria, then they might be wonderful, they might have the most enviable Instagram account, they might be the hottest, coolest, buzziest, most well-traveled interesting person of all time, they might be Zoë fucking Kravitz, but let's not go further than an acquaintance, shall we?

Nobody Cares, at All.
In Regard to Everything.

Choose Pronoia

ARE YOU PARANOID THAT YOUR boss thinks less of you because your banter at the office was subpar? When you asked how he was doing and he replied, "Tired," you said, "You look like it." *UGH!* It was funny in your head, but the moment you said it out loud, you wished you could grab those words from the air and stuff them back down your throat. Are you scolding yourself on the inside, wishing you had responded with more wit or at least a bit more tact?

Are you scared that the wonderful woman you almost went to work for secretly hates you because, at the last minute, you didn't take the job she offered? Yes, you made up with her over email, but are you still terrified to run into her at a party, even though that was TWO YEARS AGO, and the reason you turned down the job was that it *really* didn't feel right, and you were even proven correct when the company went bust a few months later? Are you STILL scared that you disappointed her?

Are you worried that you didn't get your best friend's brother's boyfriend an expensive *enough* birthday present? What you gave him was FOR SURE nice and thoughtful and you don't know the guy all that well, TBH . . . But was it nice *enough*?!

Or is that all just me?

I used to suffer from a deep-seated paranoia that people, in general, didn't like me. Or at least, I figured, they were judging me at all times. I assumed that, at a baseline, I was in a "meh-to-negative" zone with everyone I met. I would endlessly obsess over external feedback, playing back the most mundane conversations in my head, torturing myself over all the ways I felt I had screwed up.

As a kid, if a teacher chided me for turning in my homework late, I took this as a personal assault. The teacher must hate me. In college, if a new, cool-looking hipster from New York looked at me the wrong way, I assumed they thought my outfit was lame and that I was not worthy of their company. As an adult in the workforce, if I received any criticism of *any* kind, I took it in as a personal failing and assumed that my superior now despised me. My boss might have prefaced the conversation with "I'm only giving you this feedback because I care about you and your development," but all I heard was "You suck. I don't like you anymore."

To combat the "fact" that everyone was judging me, I worked my ass off to give them no reason to criticize me. I thought that with enough work, I could actually *control* how others perceived me. I was *always* teacher's pet. I would do the extra, extra credit; I would stay in at lunchtime; I would show up at the protest my AP bio teacher had encouraged me to attend even if I had *zero* idea what the protest was about. (Anti–dry cleaning maybe? Is that a thing?) As an adult at work, I would always go above and beyond in such a way that it could be oppressive to others. Did I really need to be the most proactive, communicative, overworked person in the office? Was it necessary for me to reply to every email the fastest, to come to every meeting with new, innovative ideas that I had elaborately researched (even when no one had asked for them)? Was it necessary for me to not only *crush* my presentation but also surprise the room with cookies from the best bakery in town? Was it worthwhile for me to treat every single project like it was a greater statement about my value as a human being? Just whom, exactly, was I trying to prove myself to?

It's exhausting—and, it turns out, impossible—to try to manage other people's judgments. A hustle I couldn't maintain. And, of course, my eagerness to please often backfired. At work, people took my enthusiasm as a sign I was gunning for their jobs or trying to show them up. Some people thought I was insincere, that there was no way on Earth I cared about my projects the way I claimed to. I aroused their suspicion when all I desperately wanted was their approval. It turns out you can't command the perceptions of others, and the more you try, the more you risk losing your own sense of self-worth and alienating people. It took decades of running myself ragged trying to gain acceptance from others for me to learn a fundamental truth I would now like to share with you:

No one cares. No one is watching you.

No one is tallying the total of your decisions, judging you from afar. They are not doing this because they are too worried about *themselves*. They are making all kinds of judgments about their own lives and worries, and I love you very much, but they are just *not* thinking about you right now.

Let me prove it.

Are you thinking about all of your friends right now, going through a list and picking apart their every move? Are you mad at your buddy who had to cancel dinner plans last week? Or are you thinking about what you need to order on Amazon? I am considering a new organic laundry detergent and a mega order of toilet paper so I never run out again, EVER. Are you thinking about your co-worker right now and how she was nervous during a major presentation? Are you laughing at the semi-awkward moment when she repeated herself? Or did you find that moment endearing and lovely because you know how much she cared about the project and then *immediately* forget about it?

We spend so much time concerned with what other people think of us when other people are generally *not thinking about us at all*. They are wrapped up in their own stories, and when they *do* think of us, it's probably about something good. At least that's what I've taught myself to always assume.

I have built for myself a good case of pronoia—the belief that people are secretly plotting for my well-being. It's a state of mind that's the opposite of paranoia. When I walk into a house party full of people I don't know, I now assume that everyone in the room instantly likes me. If I'm scared of meeting new people, I tell myself, *Everyone in this room adores me*. I assume that the tall boy in the camouflage jacket is part of a vast conspiracy for my own good. He is happy that I introduced myself and genuinely interested in our conversation. I give this same honor to the new people *I* meet: I suspect everyone is cool and worthy of my time and courtesy until proven otherwise.

Pronoia has been an INCREDIBLE tool for creating a more joyful life. It *works*. If you take for granted the fact that you are awesome and liked, you become a magnet, pulling people who are happy with themselves into your orbit. There is something SO attractive about a person who not only believes they are fundamentally worthy but also sends that energy back out into the world. There is something SO alluring about someone who isn't trying to prove anything. And! It takes so much less energy than being paranoid. I'm not talking about ego here. This has nothing to do with thinking you are *better* than anyone else. ICK. GROSS. NO. *You are no better than anyone else, and you are also no worse*. Train yourself to think that you are just as good as that very smart, elegant lady in the sparkly mermaid-cut dress across the room, with degrees from everywhere and friends in all the right places. *Oh my God, is that Amal Clooney? OH YES, it is! You, my friend, are just as good as she is. YOU ARE JUST AS GOOD AS AMAL CLOONEY AND SHE IS VERY GOOD.* You are just as worthy and bright and deserving of respect as she is. Why not go say hi?

Try it! Act as if everyone likes you this week. When you walk into a room, think to yourself, *Each person here values me.* When you talk to a stranger, think, *This person actively wishes me well.* Even try it on someone you believe *doesn't* like you. Have a conversation with a colleague you think isn't a fan of yours and tell yourself, *This person DOES like me; anything they show me that suggests otherwise is more reflective of THEM than of me. Maybe they are insecure? Maybe they have not learned to like themselves yet? I wish them well.* Watch as someone who used to get under your skin becomes just another fan. Try pronoia and come tell me that it doesn't work.

Actually, don't wait for that moment because it will never come, and I would like to meet you sooner than never.

Congrats! I'm Dating My Dad. Again.

Find Your Relationship Pattern

A FEW YEARS INTO MY self-care routine, I was feeling excellent. My mind was mostly at peace, I understood that I *had* a body I luxuriated in taking care of, and I was filling my life with friends who were loving and generous, friends whom I now considered my family. I felt a huge sigh of "YAY! MY LIFE IS NO LONGER A DISASTER BUT IS IN FACT *FUN!*" It was a major triumph that I had certainly not thought possible that morning after my twenty-fifth birthday. In fact, that twenty-fifth birthday and major swaths of my mess-wreck-disaster childhood now felt distant, as if they had happened to someone else. And, in a way, they had. The person who had experienced so much neglect as a kid was healing. In her place, a more confident, joyful, sparkly woman had emerged. But there was still one tiny-itsy-bitsy-little area where I couldn't seem to make any progress *at all*: romance.

Every relationship I had been in for the past fifteen years felt eerily similar. I would find a partner who was *great* on paper: He would have gone to the "right" school, he would have an impressive job, he would be someone I thought I *should* like. But he would always have so much emotional baggage that our dating would end in disaster. Of course, we all have our own baggage we carry into relationships. I, for sure, have steamer trunks full, but I went for guys whose luggage was currently *on fire*. As he rolled his carry-on of flaming issues down the aisle, he would set the entire plane ablaze before we ever got off the tarmac. These were guys who, on the first date as we waited for cocktails, would unload on me that "my dad murdered someone . . . but don't worry . . . he committed suicide . . . in jail . . . I'm just not sure I will escape the overwhelming despair I feel." *DON'T WORRY??? YOU'RE NOT SURE YOU'LL EVER ESCAPE THE DESPAIR?* Our bruschetta hadn't even arrived yet! That's a lot for Date One—ya know, the date where it's just supposed to be "What do you do?" and "How many siblings do you have?" It seemed like I was seeking out men who were so damaged, so wrapped up in their past traumas, that they did not have the capacity to be kind or emotionally giving toward me. Instead of looking for genuinely confident people who knew themselves, like I did for my Lady Harem, I would find men who were so insecure and in such constant crisis that they could give nothing to anyone, not even themselves. I would ignore all the warning signs that they weren't a good partner and instead doubt *myself,* endlessly wondering what I could do to fix them. Then I would predictably be upset when the relationship ended. And it always ended.

By the age of twenty-nine, when most of my friends had already found their "person," I had just started dating a very depressed, seemingly sweet man named Ben, who was exactly the kind of trouble I liked. He had been an accomplished advertising executive who moved in swanky circles. Check. He had gone not only to Harvard but Harvard Business School. Double check. He had flamed out of his career, was taking a "break from life," and lived with a labradoodle named Nikola Tesla, who was "the only person who gave life meaning." I let the "person" part slip. Nikola Tesla, however, FUCKING HATED Ben and would dash out of the room the moment he walked in. I had *never* seen an animal reject his owner in the way this dog rejected Ben. "See, even those who love me run away," Ben would lament. One night at his apartment, as we were watching TV, Nikola started biting at my hand and barking for me to get off of "his" (Ben's word) couch. I asked Ben why Nikola was in such a foul mood. "Nikola bites everyone, even me, and he definitely can't be around children. . . . It's just sorta his thing," he explained nonchalantly. When I asked if that was *maybe* something a trainer could work on, he looked incredulous as he replied, "I wouldn't want to change Nikola's personality. If he wants to bite me, if he wants to hate me, that's his way of expressing himself." "BUT WHAT ABOUT THE KIDS, BEN?" I didn't ask.

Being with Ben felt like a bad case of déjà vu. I knew it was weird that I was trying to "save" our relationship one month into dating, but I felt certain that *if only* I spent more time with him, my optimism and newfound stability would rub off on him and, voilà, just like in a children's fable, Ben would shed his narcissistic skin and my prince would emerge. I would break the evil enchantment that had turned the accomplished, box-checking, good-school-going Ben into his current dejected, hated-by-his-dog-but-unwilling-to-do-anything state. I explained this to Ben—how I would be patient with him as he went through his almost-midlife crisis. "You're wonderful," he replied. "But you should know, I depress even my therapist. I'm not sure you're going to have any more luck than she's had." *Oh, Ben,* I thought. *You just don't know how special I am yet.*

For a date night, Ben was supposed to join me at Fisch's house to watch a movie with her family. This is the same Fisch who persuaded me to go to Tokyo and is a card-carrying member of my Lady Harem. Whenever I enter her parents' house, I

feel total and utter peace, as if my soul has taken a heavy tran-
quilizer. The house itself is physically welcoming. Family photos line the warm wooden walls of the hallways, and practically
every room has a couch that calls out, "Take a seat with me and
share something about your day!" And her parents just make
you *feel* like you *belong*. Her mom always shouts "Taracita!"
when I walk in, before she hugs me and checks in on how my
life is going. Her dad is one of my most important Road Warriors; I can always go to him when I need a little career perspective. Fisch's childhood home, both the actual place and its
state of being, has always been the model of what I want my
own family to look like one day: stable, loving, inviting. I had
explained all of this to Ben and was excited for him to experience something I considered sacred.

Fisch, her husband, her parents, their dog, and I were sitting
around the TV waiting for Ben to arrive so we could watch a
movie when he texted me. "Sorry, I have to bail, I haven't
worked out yet." *HUH?* I felt a prick of anger and disappointment. This was an important night for me, the night my new
dude met my best friend and her family, and he was flaking at
the last possible moment? "What do you mean?" I quickly
typed. "If I don't do my squats for the day, then I won't have
accomplished anything and I'll feel like a loser," he shot back.
He didn't care that he was making *me* feel like a loser by ditching me. He didn't even apologize. I suddenly felt a surge of
embarrassment and exhaustion. Not only had Ben disappointed
me, every version of him I had dated before had let me down.
I explained to Fisch and her family that "Ben has a stomach
bug" and excused myself to the bathroom to have a good cry.

As I walked down the hall, I felt my eyes water and a sharp
stab of self-disgust pierce my heart. How did I keep making the
SAME FUCKING MISTAKE? How was I in the position *yet
again* of dating someone who didn't have his life together

enough to stick with a plan to *see a movie*? Then I turned the corner and saw the "family history" quilt that Fisch's mom had sewn. Fisch had once explained to me how, with intricate, laughably precise stitchwork, the quilt represented how tightly her family was sewn together. One square featured the Statue of Liberty with the New York City skyline in the background and a ship in the foreground to show how her grandparents had emigrated from Germany. Another showed her parents under a chuppah, exchanging their wedding vows, holding hands, looking out onto their future while two blue doves kissed above their heads. Each child had their own square, and, in each stitch, in each deliberate choice, the quilt was a representation of how committed and enmeshed their family was. Looking at it, I had an epiphany: You can't sew quilts, you can't build homes, you can't start the foundation of a life with men like Ben. If I kept dating the Bens of the world, the emotionally damaged navel-gazers who were incapable of giving me much of anything, then I would never have my own quilt to sew. Tho, to be real, I'm never going to sew an *actual* quilt. How the fuck did Fisch's mom sew that quilt? HAVE YOU SEEN A QUILT? I can *barely* sew a button onto a shirt!*

That night, I went home, grabbed my journal, and wrote about my past relationships. I had a hunch that if I could uncover the unconscious pattern I seemed to be following, then *maybe* I had a chance of escaping it. For the next week, I called friends, my sister, and exes with whom I was on good terms; looked back at old journals; and wrote out common themes and events. As I wrote and reflected, it was shockingly easy to see my pattern. It was so intricately and precisely stitched that I guess I did have my very own quilt. It looked like this:

---

*   In fact, I *can't*. Any shirt that loses a button remains buttonless, *forever*.

Step one: Find someone who is good on paper but bad at life. Look for someone who went to a "good" college, someone with a "good" job, someone you think is ambitious and will "succeed." If he comes from a "good family," bonus points! Completely ignore that this person is CLEARLY, FUNDAMENTALLY in an emotional crisis of some kind. Decide that you can fix him, or, even better, come to the conclusion that something is actually wrong with *you*.

Example: He is a fancy finance executive who owns his house and is established in his career (YAY!). BUT *up front* he explains that he "must be wasted to enjoy sex, and that's not going to change." Think to yourself, *That's not great, but he hasn't gotten to know me yet.*

Example: He is a successful producer with mutual friends, but within a month of dating, he tells you, "I'm not sure I can date a woman with a big career like yours. . . . I might need someone who has less going on." Instead of immediately ceasing contact with this CLEAR AND PRESENT DOUCHE, you think, *Maybe it's bad I love my big job? Maybe my priorities are out of whack? Should I be less ambitious? Should I shrink?* BEGIN TO SHRINK.

Example: He is a lauded writer with a history of gallivanting (red flag?), went to Harvard (check, but also red flag), and works in comedy (double red flag), and he tells you, "I know what you're thinking—that I'm this player who went to Harvard and thinks he's so smart and great and mega successful, but don't worry, I'm actually one of the good guys." UGH! GROSS! NOOO! Instinctually understand that *GOOD GUYS DON'T TELL YOU THEY*

ARE GOOD, THEY JUST ARE. Decide to give him a shot anyway. *Maybe you are being too judgy?*

Step two: Get emotionally invested too quickly. Based solely on how good he looks on paper, ignoring the fact that you feel lonely in his company, despite your body screaming, "Nooo, we've been here before!," give him a chance and convince yourself he is someone you want in your life despite all evidence to the contrary. Or, if he's not the person you want at this very moment, maybe you can repair him for future use? Project all of the good qualities you want in a partner onto him. You will make this very new relationship work, no matter the cost. *Why? Not sure, kiddo! Just follow the fucking pattern and stop asking questions.*

Example: He has a dog, and even though you have complicated feelings about dogs, this shows he is caring and responsible, which are qualities you *do* like. Completely ignore the fact that he is in a codependent relationship with said dog and watches surveillance video of his Yorkie-poo WHILE YOU ARE ON DATES. You'll be having a drink and he'll stop mid-sentence to check in with the dog. Look at the grainy closed-circuit live feed on his cellphone that shows the dog sitting still on the couch where you left her, watching the front door. Pretend you don't hear your date say, "Do you see how much she misses me?! She just sits there, staring at the door! I could watch her waiting for me all day." *Don't feel hurt that he clearly likes his DOG better than he likes YOU.* BURY THIS SADNESS RN.

Example: After an electric first date, he asks if you'd be interested in going to a Korean spa the next morning!

Could he pick you up at eleven A.M. so you could continue talking about your mutual love of Tokyo? You have
shared interests, yay! Take this all as a sign that he's open,
honest, and not interested in playing games. I mean, a
second date, *the very next day?!* Completely ignore the fact
that he asked MULTIPLE times to sleep with you, didn't
take no for an answer, and when you were at your wits' end
and finally said, "Listen, I don't have sex on the first date,"
he actually pouted and crossed his arms over his chest like
a child who didn't get the candy he wanted. Pretend that
the image of him sulking in his garish electric-blue BMW
didn't make you vomit in your soul. *You can fix this.*

Example: He went to MIT, which must mean he is exceptionally smart. *Smart* is something you are SO attracted
to and want in a partner. Forget the fact that someone
going to a "smart" school is not the same as them being
emotionally intelligent. Shake it off that your "date night"
to see a movie turned out to be just a "stop" on his run.
When the movie ended, the dude, dressed in a full workout ensemble, said, "That was fun; now I have to go back
on my run." WHEN THE MOVIE ENDED, HE SAID,
"THAT WAS FUN; NOW I HAVE TO GO BACK ON
MY RUN." *You picked a winner!*

Step three: Try to persuade the boy to like you. Obsess
over text messages, trying to decipher "what it all means." Be
whatever person you think he will like best, but DO NOT
BE YOURSELF! Never consider if *you* actually like *him*. You
are now a new person, the person you think he wants you to
be, which is tricky because it always seems to be changing.
*Isn't that fun and not soul-crushingly-oh-my-fucking-God-why-am-
I-even-dating exhausting?*

Example: Now you like dogs! Now you don't mind a dog sleeping in the same bed as you. You are still scared of dogs, but now you "like" them because *he* likes them.

Example: You are willing to completely rearrange your schedule on the off chance he *might* want to hang out. You will cancel any plan, change any beloved routine, just in case he wants to see you. Tell your sister you might need to move your annual excursion to Disneyland because he *might* text you. Get very upset that you are no longer doing the things you want to do.

Example: He is jealous of ANY dude in your life. So lie if your BFF Evan calls and pretend it was someone else. Cut all male friends out of your circle in order to appease the man you've been dating for a month. What if he's *the one*? YOU'LL FIGURE THIS OUT *LATER*. Maybe you can secretly call Evan once a month? From your work phone, tho, so there's no evidence? But even then, best to erase your call history! And eventually the new guy has to come around! Right?! *Right.*

Step four: Get progressively resentful of having to act like someone you're not and then go CRAZY when the relationship doesn't work out. Cry on the floor of your bedroom. Bang the steering wheel in your car while masochistically listening to Neil Young's "Harvest Moon." Blame yourself. Do every destructive thing until you become the kind of depressed where you don't shower for days and only want to sleep BUT CAN'T FUCKING SLEEP DUE TO ANXIETY, then rise from the ashes, phoenix-like. Swear to yourself, to your journal, to your friends, to your co-workers, that you'll *never* get hung up like this again. You see the pattern clearly and are going to change it, damn it! *YES, WE CAN!*

Step five: Repeat steps one through four.

My detective work in my journal showed me that at the center of my relationship maze was a truth I hadn't yet healed: From an early age, I had learned that love meant being neglected, mistreated, or told that I needed to change in order to be worthy of affection. *Paging Dr. Freud.* I say this with empathy toward my parents; they lived in such turmoil, they simply did not have the capacity to treat me tenderly. So, little problem-solver that I was, I learned to take *all* of their treatment as *love* because that was better than nothing. When my mom screamed at me that I was stupid and bad at math? Love. She just wanted me to do better. When my dad ignored me and never asked questions about my life? Also love. He must have trusted me enough to have it all figured out. I survived, thrived, and came to expect cruelty. My romantic relationships, it seemed, were simply repeats of my relationship with my parents: superficial, draining, and deeply unsatisfying.

I think that over time, we all develop patterns based on what we believe we deserve in relationships. Once in the habit, it's incredibly difficult to change course because it's *what we know.* This isn't just in romance. We repeat the same destructive behavior with friends, bosses, siblings, mothers, and fathers. In the wilderness of relationships, we walk on the same path, over and over, stepping on the wildflowers, crushing the leaves and mud beneath our feet until we've cleared a path we are comfortable walking. Once we have that path, it becomes easier and easier to find again, even if we don't want to be on it. That path might have poison ivy all over it. That path might have a fucking snake pit in the middle of it. But it's *our* path. It's the one with the worn-down ground that we know how to return to again and again. It feels like the safest route because we always know where we will end up.

If you can simply *see* your pattern, if you can describe it, then you have a chance to break it and create something new. There is no magic trick to this other than becoming aware. So I ask you: Do you have any relationship patterns you are tired of repeating? Is there a friendship pattern that's not serving you? A romantic pattern like mine? If there is one area where your relationships feel stuck, get out your journal and let's work through this shit together, shall we? We shall.

How to Find Your Relationship Pattern*

An inexpert guide that I developed out of pure necessity and an unwillingness to keep doing the same fucking thing over and over again. Who has time for that?! I DID, APPARENTLY. For fifteen years!

1. **Get out your journal.** If you have not bought a journal at this point in the book, I'm not sure what to tell you. Other than *Buy a fucking journal, my love.*

2. Okay, it's just you, me, and the journal right now. No one else is around. **Identify your pattern.** Sometimes it's just that simple. Sometimes, the thing that is true about us lives on the tip of our tongue, just waiting to be articulated. Take a moment to identify the truth. Do you pick people who are not ready to be in a relationship? Do you attract folks who are prickly and brash when you want a sweetheart? Write it down.

3. Didn't come up with anything for the above? **Write about your past three to five relationships.** Maybe

it's "They all had strained relationships with their families." Maybe it's "They were all people who I slept with so quickly it was hard to build past date five because we had gone too far too fast." I have been in both situations. Spend some time highlighting, circling, and reflecting. Prepare for an aha moment.

4. Don't have it yet? **Ask your friends.** Say, "I am trying to better understand how I relate to men/women/ whomever; do you see anything that I am doing repeatedly?" You could also ask them, "Is there anything you have continually thought 'OH NO' about me when I'm in a relationship?" I used this technique myself with Julia, who revealed, "You always try to fix things, even if it's super early in a relationship when things should be easy and fun." I knew that about myself, I KNEW IT, but I wasn't willing to recognize it until Julia verbalized it. *Fucking Julia. Again.*

5. **Ask an ex.** This is a tricky one and totally counterintuitive, but if you've ended a relationship with someone amicably and some time has passed, this person will very often have good intel for you. DON'T ask an ex with whom things ended poorly, though. Those dickheads are not reliable narrators.

6. **Keep on thinking and writing.** It can take a while to uncover your pattern. And sometimes, just when you think you've done the excavation and found the bedrock of how you repeat yourself, you'll discover some new shaft that leads to a whole other mine of issues. *Oh great, there is MORE shit to dig up?* you'll think, but be patient. You are doing the work and that is all that mat-

ters. This is a process and you are on the road. Or in the mine? Something like that.

7. **After all that hard work, be good to yourself.** Give yourself something nice. A favorite candy you never let yourself buy, a nice pen, a lavender hand lotion that's too expensive. Treat yourself affectionately. Commemorate that today you took the time to reflect and get to know yourself a little better. How amazing are you? It's hard to be honest with yourself. Also, how you treat yourself is often a clue to others about how they should treat you. If you are not sweet to yourself, why would anyone else be? Start showing the world the affection you deserve *today*. I'm going to get myself a sparkly silver blazer I've been coveting. What about you?

This Is Not the Oregon Trail. There Shall Be No Settling.

Find Yourself a FUCK YEAH Lover

SO, YOU KNOW ALL THAT stuff about how I found my pattern? Remember how I investigated my history, reflected on it, and was ready to escape the maze of relationships that lowered my sense of self-worth? Remember how I was so badass and self-aware and ready to change this thing once and for all? Well, it turns out, knowing your pattern is a whole hell of a lot different from breaking it. I'm *so* sorry.

After almost five years of dating in Los Angeles but with no relationship that lasted more than two months, I decided I didn't care if I had a pattern that I couldn't escape, I didn't care if most of my romantic relationships made me sad and cry and wonder why people dated at all. Instead, I decided I needed a proper "boyfriend." I needed to prove to myself and the world that I was desirable. Why? Well, I was worn out from colleagues asking why I wasn't in a serious relationship. I was told I was a "catch." One well-meaning adult in my life suggested that I should be "finding a guy while you're still young." A less well-meaning co-worker said, "Your problem is that you need to get laid!" As much as I wanted to smack that person in the face, the idea stuck with me: Because I didn't have a boyfriend, there was something wrong with me. It was yet another problem that needed solving. *WHY WERE THERE SO MANY PROBLEMS TO SOLVE?*

I was increasingly annoyed about having to explain my singleness to my married and coupled-up friends. At dinner parties, where I was always the only person going solo, couples would gather around my phone and ask, "So how does this whole Tinder thing *even work?*" They would "ooh" and "aah" as I demonstrated swiping left and right with the elegance of a World's Fair presenter. "Step right up, ladies and gents! It's incredible! With an easy swipe of the finger, you can say 'nope!' to an entire human being!" My married friends would chirp with self-satisfaction, "We didn't even *have* dating apps when we met!," comforted that they had done something "right" to avoid the horror and humiliation of Internet dating. They would tell me they "could *never* do online dating" in the same way someone will tell you they "don't drink coffee." You know that if they were being honest, the next words to come out of their mouths would be "because I am better than you."

I became fatigued from defending myself against constant questioning and unsolicited advice from mostly well-intentioned friends. More than that, though, all this talk of my dating woes, over time, grated at my self-worth and made me feel like I had something to prove. I wanted to show not only my friends but myself that I was worthy of being loved after all. Forget that my career was taking off. Forget that I had built a fantastic community of friends around me who DID LOVE ME. Forget that I had re-parented myself to the extent that I was actually feeling good in my daily life and proud of the work I had done. The only *real* way to prove that I was worthy of love was to get a boyfriend. I would post photos of our relationship to Instagram, and then everyone would see that I was redeemable and wanted, and then, *finally,* I would be happy. *Oh boy.*

I was on the warpath and told everyone I knew, and many people I didn't know, that I was "in the market" for a setup. "Who do you have for me to meet?" new woman who is waxing me. "If you don't set me up, who will?" complete stranger I have met at a work event and have talked to for under seven minutes. A co-worker I adored said he knew *just* the guy: Danny. Danny was a top-notch finance guy. He had an established job, he had recently bought his own house, and he had horn-rimmed glasses. Check, check, check. You know I love a guy who checks the boxes.

On our first date, Danny was getting into old-fashioned number two when I realized he had not asked me a single question about myself. As I nursed my first tequila soda, he gave a monologue about how great and interesting he was. Did I know he was one of *Forbes*'s "30 under 30"? Did I know he was featured in *Bloomberg News* as one of the best and youngest "iBankers" in the industry? *What's an iBanker? Does it have to do with iPhones?* Did I know that he hung out with "Lin" after the fourth time he saw *Hamilton? Who is "Lin"? What is he talking about? OHHH. He's name-dropping Lin-Manuel Miranda, the creator of Hamilton! Cool, cool, cool, cool, cool.*

I was turned off by Danny's endless torrent of self-endorsements, yet I was incredibly comfortable with the fact that he had yet to show any interest in me. I *knew* from my prior investigation that he was perfect for my pattern: He had all the outward signs of success that I had learned to value as a kid, he wasn't too concerned with my life, and I wanted to fix him. I *knew* all of this! I knew *all* of this, and on *the first date,* I actually said in my head, *I'll settle for Danny.*

I was confident that I could change him. I was sure that I

could make him into someone I was interested in. And if I couldn't do that, then at least, I don't know, at least I'd be dating *someone*.

On one of our early dates, we sat in Danny's house on his custom-made sofa. He showed me how he had rigged the lighting in his living room to put on a light show. Through the use of colored bulbs and an app, if he pressed one button on his iPhone, we were lit as if we were in "sub-Saharan Africa," bathed in a dry white-and-yellow glow. If he pressed another, we were in "Iceland," a jarring combination of pink and blue more reminiscent of a nightclub that's trying too hard than Reykjavik. "Isn't this the best? Can you believe I set this up?" he asked, anxious for my approval. "Yeah, it's great," I managed to mumble, even though I thought it was just about the most on-the-nose "bachelor pad" thing I had ever seen.

I had come prepared and determined that on this date, I would force us to be more intimate. I whipped out my iPhone and presented Danny with the *New York Times* test "The 36 Questions That Lead to Love." I explained that it's a series of questions that fosters closeness by bringing up vulnerable subjects. "I love tests; I always ace them," he replied. "You don't need to ace this," I said, laughing. "It's just supposed to help us become closer. I'm pretty sure it's not something you *can* ace." "Uh-huh. Well, we'll see," he challenged.

I asked Danny one of the questions, "Would you like to be famous? In what way?" "This is such an easy one," he said. "Of course I want to be famous. I want to be remembered." "But in *what way* do you want to be remembered? Like, how do you want people to think of you?" I pressed. "It doesn't matter what way. It could be good or bad. I don't care if people hate me. I just want to be remembered forever." Um, *what now, Danny?* It was at that exact moment that I should have run.

But I didn't run. I dated him for an additional NINE

MONTHS full of red flags. We had a fucking red-flag baby! There was the time he secretly got high before we went to a holiday party, even though he knew I was sensitive about weed. Red flag. And how, in conversation, he would condescendingly announce "Correct!" after I made any point at all, as if he could determine which opinions were valid and which were not. SUPER-ANNOYING RED FLAG. Then there was the time we were at a wine tasting and he told the sommelier to "get rid of cable. You don't need it. It's a dying industry." EVEN THOUGH I WORK IN CABLE TELEVISION. EVEN THOUGH THAT'S HOW I MAKE A LIVING. That might have been the douchiest red flag of all because it showed that he was completely inconsiderate of me.

I had known the relationship was doomed since Date One. But that didn't stop me from proving our love on Instagram. Here we were, mid-hike, next to a sign reading "Lover's Lane," playfully pointing at each other. Here was another of us posing with monkeys at the San Diego Zoo. MONKEYS, YOU GUYS. We were *so* happy. I wanted the image to be the thing. And the image is never the thing. The thing is the thing. And the thing was empty. With each passing month, I felt like I had sold myself short. I had.

After a lot of journaling and talking the situation out with friends, I invited Danny to my house for a final date. I roasted a chicken, gave him some Aesop bath products, and told him it was over. Maybe that is a weirdly elaborate way to break up with someone, but I wanted to honor what little of a relationship we had. I did feel some amount of affection for Danny, and I wanted to be kind to him. He was not a bad guy; he was just not *my* guy. Also, I wanted to remember in my heart and body that if I were to follow my pattern again, I would end up at the same table making breakup roast chicken. By making this a memorable separation, one I had planned and cooked for, I hoped that I would finally learn that if I start a relationship *not* excited about the guy, I will never get there. It's like trying on shoes at a store. If the glittery *perfect-looking* stilettos don't fit the first time, they are never going to fit, honey. It doesn't matter what the salesperson says; there is no amount of stretching and wearing in and putting in inserts that will make them work. It was the first breakup of my life where I knew what I was doing. There were no final hookups, no late-night texts. I felt relief. I was actually shattering the pattern.

If you find yourself actively settling on someone because you want to feel loved, or because you're afraid that if you don't take this person *right now,* you will never have another shot, or because you don't believe you deserve more, let me tell you right now: **YOU ARE NOT READY TO SETTLE. WHY WOULD YOU EVER BE READY TO SETTLE? YOU HAVE FUN EATING POPCORN IN YOUR AWESOME BRAS.** Maybe it's just me on the bra-and-popcorn part, but why-oh-why would you *ever* settle? If you are worried that this person is just "okay" and thinking, *Who am I to be picky?* then allow me to yell at you, **YOU ARE ALLOWED TO BE PICKY.** If you are allowed to be paleo or vegan and drink only Fiji-brand water, you are sure as shit allowed to be picky about whom you spend your time with. I'm not talking about finding yourself a guy or gal who will bankroll you; money has absolutely nothing to do with it. I'm talking about the fact that we all deserve to be loved in a genuine way that makes us feel pumped and excited and happy and OH-MY-GOD-YES! That's what we all deserve. You deserve to find the person who will raise you up like the queen or king you are. You also deserve the opportunity to treat someone else as a precious priority and feel your heart expand as you take them in.

If you are, right now, unable to believe that you are worth more, if you are currently settling or considering settling, then let me also tell you this: Settling doesn't work. All of those feelings of loneliness that you are trying to solve with the person who is "fine" will follow you into your relationship and you will feel alone together. And there is just about nothing worse than feeling lonely in the intimate company of someone else. It's a certain kind of despair to feel like paper dolls, rigidly moving about, playing house, acting as if you are in love, but in reality, you're just thin, fake replicas of the real deal.

The real deal is out there for you. I don't know when you will find it. I can't offer a prediction for the future, but I can tell you, unequivocally, that the more time you spend with people you know are *not* right, the more you put off finding love. You simply can't draw the right person into your orbit if you are busy with the wrong one. For my part, I am trying to attract the sun. Someone who is secure, optimistic, and loving. Someone I am not *afraid* to be intimate with. Someone who is my true partner and, in the long run, a supportive friend. I want a guy I feel "fuck yeah" about, or I don't want to be with anyone at all. I want to tap-dance and sing from the top of the Hollywood sign about how much I admire him and how I feel so fucking superb in his company—otherwise, I would rather hang out with my Lady Harem. ACTUALLY, I want someone I am thrilled to *introduce* to my Lady Harem so we can all hang out together. I want this person to bring something bright into my life, and I want to do the same for him. I want to get out of my own damn way. I'm ready.

If you know of such a person, would you mind an intro? After all, if you don't set me up, who will?

A List of Questions to Ask Yourself When You Start Dating Someone That I PRAY TO FUCKING GOD Will Help You Break Your Old Patterns and Find Something Better, EVEN IF You Are Really, Really Ready for This "Whole Dating Thing" to Be Over

1. **Is there a connection?** Is there a spark? Is there an attraction? An "OH YES! I FEEL THIS!"? Or. Did he put his hand on your shoulder and your skin crawled? When he kissed you did it feel like his tongue was jamming itself down your throat as if to suffocate you? Is there *something*—it does not need to be physical—in this person that draws you to them? It's not mean to answer "no" to this question. But it *is* a waste of time to go any further.

2. **Is this person kind and thoughtful?** It's easy to tell: Did your date ask questions about you? More than an obligatory "What do you do?"—did they show genuine interest in getting to know *you*? Again, don't feel bad if the answer is "no." But, again, know that it is a GIANT FUCKING WASTE OF TIME to go any further.

3. **Can this person take care of themselves?** Can they handle their own shit? Or do they constantly talk about what a "disaster" they are, how "hard" their life has been, and how they "have no clue how to fix any of it," before lighting up a second bowl of weed and explaining that they "wouldn't blame you if you left right now"? If this happens to you, LEAVE RIGHT NOW. I've been here enough times! You never have to stay! You need someone who takes responsibility for their own life. End of story.

4. **What does your GUT say?** Forget about the other person for a second and check in with yourself. They may be hot, they may have gone to the best school, they may make lots of money and offer to fly you somewhere cool, or maybe they just impress you with the offer to take you on a date to the movies because somehow *that* is impressive nowadays, but do you have a feeling that this person is *just not your person*? Did they check their reflection in the window behind you so often it made you feel a little "ick" about them? Were they dodgy about whether they were actually single and your stomach said "byeeee" even as you continued to have a glass of wine? Were they perfectly wonderful and cute but you just weren't *into* them? IT'S OKAY TO HAVE A GUT FEELING THAT SOMEONE IS NOT RIGHT FOR YOU. Trusting your gut is not being unfair to other people. If it's true that you don't like this person now, it will also be true when you break up with them in three years. How *not nice* is that? Trust your gut.

5. **But my gut is all fucked-up from years of following a destructive pattern! CAN I EVEN TRUST MYSELF ANYMORE?!** Yes. If you are doing the work of being aware, then chances are your gut is getting better at discerning what's good for you versus what you're merely used to. If you want to become a ninja of self-love and self-trust, you need to keep developing the faith that you know what's right for you. Trust your gut even if you are afraid to.

6. **Are there any red flags the person has shown you?** No? Let me ask again: *Are there any red flags the*

person has shown you? I just want to be sure you are answering honestly. This is not a time to say, "Yes, he mentioned he is completely hung up on how his last girlfriend broke his heart and referred to her as a 'psychotic bitch,' but, whatever, let me forget that detail." You don't have to end things immediately, but you do have to take careful notes. Please do not disregard red flags; they are used at the beach to warn of severe hazards in the water. Would you ignore a red flag firmly planted in the sand in front of ginormous, crashing, scary waves?

7. **Can they meet you where you are?** (I don't mean are they conveniently located. Tho that is always a plus!) Is this person in a stage of life that is similar to or complements your own? If you are established in your career and looking to settle down, it will be painful if they are a total mess who doesn't know how to take care of themselves. Likewise, if *you* are in a scattered state, maybe it's not the best time to try locking down someone you think will *give* you stability. Ask yourself this: Is this person in a place in their life where they can be fully present with me? Can *I* be present with *them*?

8. **Does this person break your pattern?** Instead of being vague, write down how this *new* person plays into your pattern. Do they? Or do they break it? For me, a pattern-breaker would be someone from whom I can accept kindness. For you, it might be a guy who is not super jealous of all the men in your life. Or maybe it's a guy who is not so busy with his career that the only plans he can make with you are in three weeks when his

life "calms down." Whatever pattern you are seeking to break, ask yourself if this new person is at least different from your old ways.

Whatever you do, be sure to take a minute to reflect. Do not let yourself get swept up: You are not dirt. Maybe it's the fault of dating-app culture where everyone is swipeable, forgettable, and ghostable, but I find that we tend to get back on the relationship horse too quickly, before we've had a chance to clean ourselves off from the pile of shit we were flung into after something ended. I find that sometimes I move too swiftly into a budding relationship because OH MY GOD THERE IS REASON TO HOPE AGAIN. "You *CALLED me to confirm a plan?* Let's get married!" Take a moment at the start of a relationship to think. Answer the above questions. Go on a long walk and let it all percolate. Talk to your Lady Harem. Take stock of how you feel about this new person. Do you feel confident in their company or uneasy? A little time now will save you days, months, years, marriages, and divorces later.

Thank-You Notes to the Boys I Believe Wronged Me
You Can ALWAYS Learn Something

WHILE IT'S TRUE THAT I'VE been in my share of bad relationships, not a single one of them was a waste of time. Okay, maybe *one* of them was a waste of time. I'm looking at *you,* engineer obsessed with *The West Wing* who told me you had "trouble considering other people's needs" and that you "would never be satisfied" with a relationship unless it was as "perfect as your parents'." It should not have surprised me that you were terrible in bed, *Joshua.* Mostly, though, I've found that each relationship has taught me something about myself—about how I relate to others and about what I absolutely MUST, *at all costs,* avoid in the future. Even some of the bleaker moments, baked with a little time and a dash of humility, have risen to become my favorite, funniest memories. SO MUCH GROWTH, YOU GUYS. I've learned tremendously from these affairs, and I would like to acknowledge the gentlemen who made this all possible.

This is such a good-for-the-soul-CATHARTIC-cleansing-learning-healing exercise that you, my dear reader, should most definitely try it.

Thank you, Keats, for teaching me that the guy who lurks outside your dorm room, the guy your friends all describe as "creepy" and "possessive," is not someone you want to date for two years and then live with in his parents' apartment. Thank you for showing me that my friends are wise and always looking out for me and that I should listen to them more. Thank you also for teaching me that if you start a relationship by cheating, it is DOOMED. At first, cheating feels sexy and important and intriguing because you can't have the person free and clear and easy but you crave them *so much* and—OH, THE DRAMA! But once you cut the bullshit and actually date them? *Oh boy.* Then you find the magic is gone, the passion is lacking, and you are dating a cheater. Much worse, *you have become a cheater.* UGH! Let's never do this again, please and thank you.

A debt of gratitude is owed to you, Danny, for telling me I could never get anything published in *The New Yorker* even though it was my life's fragile dream and I explicitly asked you to be gentle with that dream. You taught me that when someone tells you what's not possible for *you,* they are projecting their own limiting beliefs about *themselves.* Thank you also for the happiest moment I can remember, when I got something published in the "Daily Shouts" section six months later and felt like I was dancing on your grave in a field of fire. Honest to goodness, *thank you* for that exhilarating moment of pure victory.

Also, Danny! Let me not forget the AMAZING kernel of wisdom you gave me at the end. You told me that every time I talked about how thrilled I was to be writing, you thought it was my way of saying, "You, Danny, are a loser who can't create anything." You showed me very clearly that you are INCAPABLE of thinking about anyone but yourself. I WAS TALKING ABOUT SOMETHING THAT MADE ME HAPPY AND YOU MADE IT ABOUT YOUR OWN INSECURITY. I had read in books about people who literally think everything is about them, but it was nice to meet an example of this kind of person IRL! Thank you for bestowing upon me a cum laude PhD in recognizing self-absorption. Maybe I can give a college commencement address on the topic?

Thank you, Ben Fast, for having a GREAT first date full of laughter. Thank you for kissing me—and then disappearing forever. Are you dead, Ben Fast? Also: great name.

Where would I be without Adam? You taught me that if your new boyfriend gets so drunk at his work party that you have to keep him upright as he stumbles into his house and then he takes his clothes off in the kitchen and his flaccid dick sticks out of his boxers like a mushroom seeking the sun and you are appalled and grossed out and just want to throw up, YOU CAN BREAK UP WITH HIM. Getting that wasted early on is enough of a reason to break up with someone. Actually, you don't need a reason to break up with someone other than you *want* to break up! If you are reading this right now and want to break up with someone but feel like you aren't "allowed," I give you permission. Rip off the Band-Aid.

Big thanks to Robbie for sweeping me off my feet with a series of grand dates. An Ethiopian feast where we ate with our hands! A day exploring Venice Beach! A BRUCE SPRINGSTEEN CONCERT! I knew nothing about Bruce

Springsteen but that felt impressive! Thank you for a romantic month of adventures. Thank you also for calling me to say that I was a "serious person" and that you weren't sure you could be with "an actual, legitimate adult." Whom do you want to date, Robbie? A child? Thank you for ghosting forever after I, somewhat confused and a little exasperated, responded, "Yeah, dude, I have my life together." It was nice to find out that some men really are looking for a hot mess.

Thank you, Joshua, for breaking up with me mid-hike and *then* going on to recommend a podcast about Donald Trump's effect on constitutional law. Ain't nobody got time for your podcast recommendations, *Joshua*. Also, maybe next time you want to break up *post*-hike? So we aren't, ya know, forced to be on our own trail of tears?

Thank you, Thomas, Chris, and Matt, for screaming at me. It took three of you, but I learned something key for all future relationships: I never deserve to be screamed at. Never ever ever. It doesn't matter if I'm flagrantly in the wrong; it doesn't matter how passionate or upset anyone is. Screaming is not an option, and I will no longer accept that behavior. Each one of you had your own special ways of screaming at me (in your car, outside a bar, when I talked to any male at all),* and when I shut down because I am conflict-averse, it was nice to find out that your reaction would be to scream *some more*. Seriously, this is a huge thank-you for helping me build my standards and boundaries.

Owen, I want to take a moment to call you out in particular. Many thanks for asking me what my bra size was

---

* Maybe this could be my own Dr. Seuss book?

over text before we ever went on a date. What I thought might be a joke very much was *not* a joke, and you showed me that some men are truly gross. It's on me that I went on the date with you and not surprising at all that on said date, you told me that the fact I wouldn't sleep with you made me "old-fashioned" and I "had too many rules." Thank you, also, for ghosting on me *right after* you spent a night trying to sleep with me. You taught me that if you actually listen to a guy and take his words at face value, you will quickly learn who he is.

Dudes Tell You Who
They Are. Listen.

Stop Hearing What You Want To Hear

"You remind me a lot of my mom. I have a *very* weird relationship with her."

"I hate myself and can't be trusted to be nice to anyone. Can you help me?"

"I'm like a rigid old man. I'm selfish and can't change."

"I don't know if I would be a good match for someone with super-ambitious hopes and dreams."

ALL OF THE ABOVE ARE real-life things that grown-ass men have said to me. Maya Angelou once wisely pointed out that "when someone shows you who they are, believe them the first time." It took me thirty years to understand these sage words. I'm pretty sure Dr. Angelou meant that people—the folks you date, the friends you have, your parents, your siblings, basically *all* of the people you encounter on a daily basis—are constantly telling you who they are through their words and actions. They *can't* hide it! There's no magic to understanding them other than making sure you are watching, listening, and paying attention to what is genuinely happening. Nowhere is this truer than in dating.

My problem is that I am SO good at hearing what I want to hear. If someone tells me they aren't looking for a serious relationship, I interpret that as "I didn't know someone as special as you could exist, which is making me rethink everything I thought I knew." When, on a first date, a dude says, "I'm currently living my life from a place of vengeance where anger is my fuel,"* I hear, "I'm an open and honest guy who will turn into someone optimistic under your guidance." Has anyone said anything remotely resembling my interpretations? HELL to the no. But that doesn't stop me from living in an alternate-FANTASTIC-yet-doomed universe of what I want to be true.

I once dated a dude who wore blingy, chunky, ostentatious, why-does-your-ring-have-a-dragon-on-it-do-you-love-dragons David Yurman† jewelry for men and had retired early from his career (at the age of forty) because he had, in his own words, "already achieved everything." *Everything?* Everything. On our first date, over a delicious glass of Montepulciano red wine, he explained, "The entire human race is doomed. We are just ants running up and down a hill. Any notion of free will is a farce. I'm thinking of becoming a vegetarian so I can stop doing harm to others. . . . All I seem to do is harm others." "ALL I SEEM TO DO IS HARM OTHERS." Did YOU hear that?! Did you hear *any of that*? I DID NOT! It should have made me run for the Hollywood Hills, but instead I dug in my plat-

---

*   Real thing, really said.

†   After we broke up, *every single one* of my girlfriends told me that the David Yurman jewelry had been a detail they had picked up immediately and it was a dead giveaway that this was not my dude. What's wrong with David Yurman jewelry for men, you ask? *Everything.*

form heels. As I eyed his giant octagonal-cut gold ring and the shiny leather rope bracelet with a silver clasp wrapped around his wrist, I heard, "I've had a rough time, but I'm sweet and a winner under all of this mess. Save me from my negativity spiral."

When he told me he was chronically tardy and said, "Don't take it personally when I will, for sure, be late for our dates," I heard, "I have an acknowledged problem with being punctual, and since I like you, I will change." OF COURSE he showed up an hour and a half late for our New Year's Eve date. I was pissed, but I brushed off my anger because I knew I had no one else to blame but myself. The motherfucker had TOLD ME exactly who he was.

Who knows how long I would have continued to create an alternate reality with this guy had he not done me the favor of doing something so batshit crazy that I couldn't ignore it. One night, when we were supposed to go out for Thai food, I texted him, "Hey, I'm really not feeling too great. What if we stay home and watch a movie? Maybe you could bring me tea ☺?" I waited for his reply and heard nothing. NOTHING. The entire night. As I lay in bed, I felt the acid reflux of *What the fuck?* gushing up my throat, making sleep impossible. The next day, I flew to San Francisco for a work trip, sure that I would hear *something* from him. I had been seeing him four nights a week at this point! Would he really just ghost me like this? Finally, late *the next night,* after I had spent the day kneading my knuckles over my tight, sick heart, he texted, "Sorry I disappeared. I had to talk to my therapist about the tea. I'm not sure I'm the kind of guy who can get tea for people." [*Drops the mic.*]

Not the kind of guy who can get tea for people? WHO IS *THAT* KIND OF GUY??? Who is so incapable of giving to others that they can't get *tea* for someone? And he needed to discuss this with his *therapist*? I laughed. I cackled like a witch over a cauldron about to cast a spell on all of man-boy-kind. It was just too absurd. There was nothing for me to interpret; I could finally see, in plain text, exactly who he was. When I called him to break up, I decided to do something in that conversation that I had rarely done before: listen. I grabbed my notebook and jotted down what he said so that the next day, when I missed him, I would not misremember things. I wrote down that he was on antidepressants and said he didn't feel like himself. I wrote down that he said he had body dysmorphia and that when we went out, he struggled with what to order and that's why he dodged restaurants. I wrote down that he said, "There is nothing personal here. I am an utter mess and need to deal with myself." I wrote it down so I couldn't play make-believe later.

If you are in a relationship where you are filtering and translating and acting like a fiction writer like I was, note the truth of what your partner says in your journal. It doesn't have to be a big to-do; you don't have to get *everything* down. But after a date, what if you took three minutes and jotted down the things they *actually* told you? That way, you won't make shit up. You can go back to the page and find out *exactly* what was said—not what you *wanted* them to say. This also works in the opposite direction. If they say, "I like you and think you're so sexy," no reason for you to hear, "I'm 'meh' about you." If they say, "I'd like to go on another date with you," no need to stress and obsess about whether this person is into you or not. They told you they're open to getting to know you better! Believe what you *actually* hear.

I think this holds true in most relationships. People can't help but tell us the truth about themselves. Your job is to pay attention. If your building manager tells you, "I don't have the power to approve that fix to your apartment," I would believe her. She's not intentionally thwarting your grand air-conditioning plans, she simply doesn't have the authority. No need to rail against her; instead, find someone higher up the chain of command. If someone you work with straight up tells you, "I am terrible with time-management skills," there is no cause to be perennially annoyed when her projects are predictably late. She has told you the issue! Maybe share your strategies for handling the workload or just shrug it off.

So remember: With their behavior, expressions, words, and attention, people show you, every day, exactly who they are. This holds true for you, too! If you don't hold the door open for people behind you,* you show that you are the type of person who thinks it's okay to shut a door in someone's face. *Is that who you want to be?* If you tell your friends, "I'm not ready to be in a relationship," don't be surprised when they don't offer to set you up with anyone. Why would anyone spend energy on something you already said you're not prepared for? If you tell people, "I'm not great at my job; I'm just *lucky* everything has turned out the way it has," even though you are fucking *killing it,* even though you are putting your heart and soul into your job and luck had NOTHING to do with the fact that your arduous, oh-my-God-will-it-ever-work project turned out STELLAR, why would you be surprised when your boss doesn't promote you? You've spent the past year downplaying your achievements and attributing them to dumb luck rather than grabbing on to the mantle of your victories. Guess what? Your boss *listened.* My advice to you is to pay attention to what impression you are making on the world and be sure it's one

---

* Whoa. I really have it out for people who don't hold the door open. Feel free to shame me if I don't hold the door open for you.

you love and adore, or at least don't hate. My advice to you is to be very careful about how you talk about yourself, because, very often, the people around you are listening.

But if we can, just for a moment, let's cut through everything in this essay and get at the larger, deeper, most important human truth: What is *absolutely essential* for all of us to understand is that *you can't date people who are unable to get you tea.* There is NO fucking time for that.

O Sister, Where Art Thou?
You CAN Stop Being an Asshole

OF ALL THE RELATIONSHIPS I wanted to figure out, my bond with my sister was the absolute most important. I yearned for the kind of rapport with her where we called each other our "best friend," where we talked on the phone EVERY DAY, where we knew exactly what was going on in each other's lives down to what flavor of froyo we had most recently consumed (cake batter; *pls, you know it's amazing*). Considering how much trauma, how much bullshit we had been through together, SHOULDN'T we be each other's support system? Shouldn't I be the Abbi to her Ilana? Shouldn't I be the Jane to her Elizabeth Bennet? Shouldn't we be like Thelma and Louise? (*Or maybe not Thelma and Louise. I can't exactly remember the plot to that movie, but I think they enter into a suicide pact after one of them kills a man?*) By the time I turned twenty-seven and she twenty-one, my sister and I were far from close. It was impossible to reach her by phone, which I found incredibly frustrating (just pick up the phone, Diana; I'm not your grandmother!), and on the rare occasions when we actually *did* spend time together, I somehow always managed to be an utter dick to her. Allow me to explain.

My little sister was born under extraordinary circumstances. She entered the scene at twenty-six weeks, which is now considered "extremely premature." In 1991, in the ancient times when smoking wasn't banned yet in restaurants and people didn't even have the INTERNET, this was thought to be a death sentence. She weighed two pounds and one ounce. She was TEENSY. She could literally fit in the palm of your hand. When my parents finally brought her home after four months in the intensive care unit, I, as a five-year-old, vowed to protect and take care of our miracle baby.* I would be her guardian. I would shield her from all of the chaos of our household and, together, we would fight against our parents and survive this mess as a single, unified front. JKJKJK. I wish TO GOD that had been the case. Instead, I was a terror.

I did all of the normal older sister things (being unbearably bossy, blaming *her* for anything *I* did wrong, painting bad makeup onto her face and then trying to remove it with flaxseed oil even though she hated flaxseed oil—like I said, *the normal stuff*), but I was also unforgivably cruel. I would pin her little body down and slow-spit on her face; I would play "dead" far past the point where it was funny. She, at an early age, fought back against my torture. Hard. I will never forget getting into a fight with her that was so physically violent that she ripped a sturdy silver necklace off my neck. I looked at her face, bright red and shining with tears, and then at the silver chain dangling in her clenched fist. *Man is she tough,* I thought.

Looking back, I see exactly what was going on. While I had no power or control over my parents, here was a little girl whom I could have TONS of control over. All of the violence and screaming and anarchy I had lived with alone for the previous five years I could now take out on my petite, sweet, inno-

---

* The *National Enquirer* actually ran a story calling her a "Miracle Baby." WHY DID WE KNOW SOMEONE AT THE *NATIONAL ENQUIRER*?

cent cherub of a sister. We might have eventually grown out of this dynamic were it not for the unfortunate fact that, as you know, my parents separated us in their divorce, when I was twelve and she was six. We spent our childhoods in different households and never got a chance to really *know* each other. I would love to have memories of her that weren't dramatic, memories of times where we JUST HUNG OUT together. Regrettably, though, most of my recollections are of bartering with my mom for time with my sister.

You see, my parents hadn't come up with a "plan" for how my sister and I would see each other, so in a parent vacuum at the age of twelve, I became the chief custody negotiator between my mom and dad. Before I could drive, if I wanted to see my sister, I *also* had to see my mom, which put me in a super-happy-not-on-the-verge-of-angry-tears-going-to-fling-myself-out-of-a-moving-vehicle mood every time we hung out. My sister's impression of me at the time must have been that I was exclusively either in a rage or *about* to be in a rage. IT WAS A FUCKING MESS.

Two years into my self-care odyssey, at the bright, bold age of twenty-seven, feeling a *hell* of a lot more stable and happier, I wondered what I could do to repair my relationship with my little sister. I had begun to catch myself journaling about how much I wanted her in my life but wasn't sure what I could do to lure her back to me. How could I trick her into *liking* me? Again: I was, historically and currently, mostly a dick to her. When I went to visit her at college in Connecticut, for example, I couldn't HELP but insist that she order *exactly* what I ordered at lunch (salad, Diana, not French toast!). Or I made it very clear that I was disappointed with her life choices. When she sublet an apartment without seeing it first, I interrogated her like a CIA agent confronting someone who had spilled state secrets. Was she so *irresponsible* that she would sign a lease and put down money on an apartment *sight unseen?* What if the whole thing was a fraud? What if she fell into financial calamity over this? Had she learned nothing from our parents over the years?! AND WHY DID SHE WEAR ONLY NEUTRAL COLORS? Couldn't she see they washed her out? When I bought her a bright pink handbag for her birthday, I was hurt that she didn't LOVE it.

At the same time I was trying to control her, I was also *begging* her to forgive me for how I had treated her as a child. In tears, at least once a year, I would plead for her pardon and then promptly forget I had ever done so. "Diana, I've *never* told you this before, but I should have been a better older sister to you. I'm sooo sorry I wasn't. I hate myself for it. Can you ever forgive me for the time I told you I was joining the Church of Scientology and you got scared and cried???" I desperately craved absolution. Diana would reply in a bored, exasperated tone, "Tara, we actually already went through this *last year.* I don't think you are evil or that you were even *that bad* of an older sister. We were in a super-fucked-up situation. I forgive you. *Forgive yourself.*"

But I couldn't forgive myself. I couldn't figure out what the fuck the next step in mending our relationship could possibly be if it wasn't endlessly blaming myself. I asked my friends what they did to be close to their siblings. They were mostly horrified to find out that Diana and I had been separated as children and had no advice to offer. A few were surprised to learn I *had* a sister. *That didn't seem like a good sign.* I tried to find books about mending sisterships, but no dice. Our circumstance was too unique. I asked adults in my life, I asked colleagues, parents, trainers at the gym who only made eye contact because they were trying to get me to sign up for their preposterously expensive sessions, but no one had any answers for me. I was left with only one option: Get my sister to take my call and see if she had any ideas about what in the holy hell we could do.

"Well, I guess this is a good start, just talking honestly about what happened," she said when we finally had the conversation. "Is there anything I do that really gets under your skin that I could change?" I asked, half-praying that she would reject this notion out of hand and say, "You are a perfect sister, Tara." HA HA, nope. "Yeah, I mean, the constant apologizing is pretty annoying. And all of the unsolicited life advice doesn't make me feel good." *Ouch.* Okay. So there were two things I could work on. "And," she added, "I feel like you have this vision of what we *should* be like as sisters, like we should be perfect and call each other all the time, but I just *hate* the phone. I don't talk to *anyone* on the phone. I hear how you talk about your best friends and how they are your support network, and I'm not sure I'm ever going to be that kind of person. It makes me really sad. . . . I'm afraid that I'm a disappointment to you." I felt my heart shatter into a gazillion shards. *SHE felt like a disappointment??? No, Diana, nooo.* It was no wonder she didn't want to talk to me on the phone; I was bossy, my apologies were selfish, and I had put such unrealistic expectations on our relationship that she felt like she would never be *good enough.* She had ALWAYS been good enough. She had always been *the fucking best.*

"How about," I said, "over your spring break, you come to New York and we have a sisters retreat? Just time to be together. I'll try my damnedest not to judge you or make weird comments, but will you please, for the love of God, help me? Like, tell me when I'm doing something annoying, please?" In the world's longest pause, a pause in which I had at least three heart attacks, my sister considered my proposition. Finally, she agreed. "Yeah, that sounds like fun."

My sister and I spent a week prancing around New York

City with the intention of getting to know each other. We went to the Boathouse in Central Park to have prosecco. We played our favorite childhood game of gin rummy in my apartment, during which I found out she was learning how to DJ. She liked *music*? I thought she was a science nerd with no other interests. "Will you play me something cool?" I asked. We spent the rest of the week listening to her favorite bands. We traded off picking activities. She chose seeing the new Uniqlo store in Midtown, and I chose drinking sangria in SoHo. She chose seeing the MoMA Sculpture Garden, and I chose going to brunch on my block. *My sister is way more interesting than I am, obvi.* Almost every day of the trip we got into some weird argument when I'd try to control her. But WE CAUGHT IT. WE CAUGHT IT, DAMN IT! We would find the little sore spots in our relationship and intentionally give them thought and care. That did not stop me from trying to control how she UNPACKED HER BAG. For some reason, she didn't want to unpack completely and just kept all of her clothes in a stack *on top* of her suitcase. *Can you imagine that?* I could not stop myself from suggesting a *different* way to unpack. BUT. As I gave her my thoughts, which no one had asked for, at least we BOTH KNEW what was happening, and we immediately started laughing about it.

That week in New York did not "fix" our relationship. But it gave us the basis for a new bond, untethered from the complications of our family. Since then, I listen to how I speak to her, and *if I catch myself being a dick,* I shut it down. I also tell her when something she does hurts *my* feelings. When I recently told her it hurt me that we never spoke on the phone, and she, for the millionth time, replied that she doesn't *like* the phone and it wasn't personal, she *also* went a step beyond and wrote me a year's worth of letters—one to be opened each month. That way, she is *always* communicating with me. Our relationship might not be the cinematic picture I always dreamed of, but it's so much better than that. It's very uniquely our own.

I have learned a lifetime's worth of lessons from my sister. I have learned that young millennials* hate phones, I have learned how to tie a square knot (it's a bow that will lie flat and look tidy if you're tying two ends of a shirt together; if you have questions, ask Diana—she watched one million YouTube videos on the subject), I have learned that there is no one way a relationship "should" look (and it probably *shouldn't* look like Thelma and Louise), but most important, I have learned that if you have fallen into a pattern of being a jerk-ass-dick, you can get out of it. The trick is to be honest with yourself about how you are treating the other person. Instead of thinking, *It's so rude that she never wants to hang out,* ask yourself, *Is there a REASON she doesn't want to hang out?* Be willing to face how you really treat other people and know that you have the power to change if you don't like what you are seeing.

One way to fast-track change is to *act* as if you are the best, highest version of yourself. What are all the best qualities you want to show this other person? Write them down. How do you want the other person to *feel* in your company? Write it down. What's something caring you could do for this person right now? Write it down. Look at your lists and see how, *today,* you could start enacting those "better versions" of yourself. Maybe even tape the lists on your bedroom door so every time you leave your room you see who you want to be. If you keep practicing, your best behavior will become more and more natural to you, until one day, lo and behold, the jerk-ass-dick in

---

*   I am an "old" millennial and, for some reason, think it's important that you know this.

you will vanish. And in its place, a more thoughtful, kind, and giving self will be born. It's not magic; it's practice.

Diana and I now have our own tradition of going to Disneyland every winter. We spend the whole year plotting how we will order the rides (get a FastPass for Indiana Jones, then *run like hell* to Space Mountain; your day depends on this!) and what food we will eat (Diana, clam chowder in New Orleans Square; me, churros until I get sick outside the Haunted Mansion). It might be a *little on the nose* that we go to Disneyland in an attempt to take back some of our childhood, but whatever. All I care about is getting to have unadulterated fun with my sister. I care about us getting to be kids again, if only for a day. I care about letting go of our past dynamic and letting *her* choose what ride we'll go on next. We sometimes get in fights at Disneyland—DISNEYLAND, the happiest place on Earth! But that's okay too. They are *our* normal sibling fights, and we learn from them. This year, as a Hanukkah/Christmas* gift, I plan on surprising her with a night at the Disneyland Hotel, because she once told me a story of how, when she was a little girl, she stayed there and thought it was the most elegant, extraordinary place on Earth. I LISTEN TO MY SISTER NOW. I might not have chosen to stay at that hotel on my own, but I am ECSTATIC to give her something she actually wants for a change.

Please don't tell her tho. It's a surprise.

A List of Ways to Heal a Wounded Relationship

Is there someone in your life with whom you would like to rebuild or fix a relationship? Maybe it's a friend, a colleague, an old mentor? Maybe it is your sibling, in

---

*   Why limit myself to just Hanukkah when there are other holidays to appropriate?

which case, oy vey! I feel ya! Trust, once broken, is hard
to rebuild. I wish I could give you a magic pill to make
it all better, but I can't. What I can offer are some steps
I have taken to heal relationship damage. Like all bruises,
it's going to take time, but I've used this remedy and it
gets the job done. Remember that you aren't necessarily
ever going to have the old relationship you are trying to
nurse back to health, or the one you always envisioned
having. But, most of the time, you can build something
new, authentic, and maybe even deeper.

1. **Write down your responsibility.** Don't be vague
   ("we lost touch") or lay blame ("she's being too sensitive"); what did *you* do? At work, did you keep your
   colleague out of the loop on *purpose?* Come on, *did you?*
   With your close-ish friend Becky, did you neglect to
   tell her that you were going on a date with her ex because you were too cowardly to bring it up? Write
   down what you are responsible for in the situation. If
   you did something you are ashamed of, FINE, we all do
   things that are embarrassing in retrospect, but only some
   of us have the wisdom to apologize and learn from
   these mistakes. YOU are one of those people.

2. **Be really honest with yourself.** Did you write down
   that you "aren't responsible for anything"? OH! ARE
   YOU THE ONE PERSON WHO NEVER DID
   ANYTHING WRONG IN A RELATIONSHIP?
   Wow! It's SO nice to meet you! *Ask yourself again.* Even
   in really bad, seemingly black-and-white situations,
   there is something we need to own up to. I once dated
   someone for way too long who screamed at me way too

much. I AM RESPONSIBLE FOR STICKING AROUND. If you are stuck, ask a friend who knows the situation for their opinion. The only way you are going to make *any* progress is if you can take an honest accounting of yourself. I KNOW, IT SUCKS.

3. **Think of what Future (i.e., Better) You would do.** Ask yourself this: *If I could go back and act differently, what would I do?* What would the highest version of you do? Not the version of you looking for convenience. Would you include your colleague on the email? Would you think about how your friend might *feel* if you went out with her ex-boyfriend? Would you call her before Date One and get a gut check from her? If she seemed distraught, would you cancel the date altogether? Write down what the highest version of yourself—the *you* you are totally and utterly proud of and in love with—would do.

4. **Ask to talk.** Warning: The person you are trying to mend a relationship with might not want to talk to you. Give them time. Try again. More than likely, however, the person will be willing to hear you out. Ask them to coffee or drinks or lunch or just for a quick chat on the phone. Choose a situation you think would make them most comfortable.

5. **TELL THEM ABOUT YOUR RESPONSIBIL-ITY!** Face the conflict head-on. Don't get lost in the weeds of a text that was sent, or an unclear voicemail, or the particulars of *why* you acted the way you did, step up and claim your responsibility. "I think I looped you out of the project because I wanted it to be seen as

100 percent 'mine,' which I now see was misguided. I'm not proud of that, but I do recognize it. I'm sorry." "I knew you would be upset if I went on a date with Jason, and I didn't say anything to you because I was too afraid that if I told you, I would feel guilty and never get to go on the date. I'm sorry." Apologize. APOLOGIZE. Apologize in a real way and tell them how you would try to react to a similar situation now. Use the wisdom of your highest self to guide you.

6. **Ask for forgiveness.** In most cases, you will get it. If you do get it, FORGIVE YOURSELF. No more dwelling on this! If you don't get it, you've done your best, so still FORGIVE YOURSELF.

7. **Ask for help.** Tell the person that you are open to hearing feedback. You might be surprised to find out you've done other things, totally unknowingly, that have broken this person's trust. BUYER BEWARE: The person you are talking to might take this as a cue to overreact and pile things on that you don't deserve. But it *doesn't even matter.* Just listen, compassionately, and take it in. You will then know what this person thinks of you, good or bad. No more guessing games. YAAAY!

8. **Ask for the benefit of the doubt.** One way relationships get in a rut is when one person *assumes* that the other person is acting maliciously. Then everything is seen under the lens of "Tara is trying to loop me out." Acknowledge that you fucked up, but ask for "the benefit of the doubt" moving forward. Tell them you will do your absolute best. You don't need the other person

to trust you immediately. You just want them to know that you're trying to change.

9. ***Give* the benefit of the doubt.** Don't dwell on what you *think* this person thinks of you or what *they* did wrong. You have approximately zero time for that.

You have a trip to Disneyland to plan.

That Time My Dad Almost Died
Nothing Is Personal. People Are Limited.

I AM GRATEFUL FOR THE love of my dad, the only constant adult I have had in my life. Because I was estranged from my mom by the age of twelve, was barely allowed to see my sister during my childhood, and had no supercalifragilistic babysitter or wise mentor to guide me, my dad, for a very long time, was the only family I had. When I was a little girl, on the occasions when he was home, he would tickle me and give me whatever attention he had available. In high school, he went into crushing credit-card debt so I could go to a private school where I was able to get a phenomenal education. At Brown, he walked me through my financial aid application when I couldn't figure it out, and then he spent the next ten years helping me pay off my (yet to be gone—WTF?) loans. He has been there for me both when I needed help on job decisions ("Am I being lowballed?") and when I desperately needed someone to replace the piece of shit showerhead that did not so much spray as it did trickle water onto my head in my tiny studio apartment (thanks, Dad!).

The problem with relying on him to be my support network was that I dismissed/ignored/erased/denied *any* amount of hurt or pain he caused me. When he chose weed over me in high school, I just started smoking, too, to dull my pain. *If you can't beat 'em, join 'em!* I figured. When my parents separated me and my sister, I channeled all of my rage toward my mom. I couldn't afford to see the chinks in the armor of the only man who *somewhat* protected me. Every time he disappointed me, I swallowed it down, hard, internalizing the sour taste of unmet expectations. And, in an incredible act of insanity and optimism, I kept hope alive that one day my dad would somehow turn into the nurturing, supportive father I'd always yearned for.

Instead of rebelling against him as I grew older or maybe just saying, "Fuck it; I have no reason to expect anything from my dad," I played into whatever expectations *he* had about me and did everything in my power to "protect" him from the truth of who I was. I wasn't an ambitious, emotional, sensitive, passionate, creative type who needed hand-holding and hugs. No, not at all! In my dad's eyes, I was a can-do, sensible, business-oriented adult who could take care of herself. I tried not to cry whenever I was upset, because he had told me my entire life, "I can't handle you when you cry." So I turned myself into a person my dad *could* handle. Do you ever do that? Do you ever hide things about yourself so you will make someone else more comfortable? By the age of twenty-nine, four years into my self-care expedition and finally healthy enough to see—and maybe, just maybe, for-the-love-of-God-PLEASE, *heal*—my deepest upsets, I saw that I had a *lot* of unresolved daddy issues.

The more aware I became of this, the more difficult it was to be around him. After I moved back to LA, my dad and I began a tradition of having dinner together on Sunday nights. In theory, this should have been "Oh!-that's-so-nice-your-dad-loves-you," but in practice, the moment I'd sit down to eat with him, I'd feel as if my skin had been lit on fire and I was ready, at any fucking moment, to nose-dive from the lip of a cliff into a lake in the canyon below. I guess you could say *I was on edge.* Any little thing he said could set me off. If he told me, for the millionth time, the story of how he lived alone on a mountaintop with his dog for a year and survived on only hot dogs, I would snap, "I KNOW, DAD, I'VE HEARD THIS STORY!" If he ranted about politics, I would cut him off with a "DAD, CAN WE *NOT*?" Even though I was a grown-ass woman, I was reacting to my dad as if I were a five-year-old throwing a hissy fit. In an unfair acrobatic trick, my dad, as he aged, was becoming a way more mellow version of himself, whereas I could *barely* hide the geyser of long-simmering, totally stifled emotions gushing to the surface of my conscience.

One Sunday night, I picked him up for our dreaded dinner, and he seemed totally trashed. UGH. *COME ON, DAD!* I watched him fumble with the car door. He could *barely* open it. He finally lumbered—well, fell, really—into the front seat, but he had so much trouble getting his right leg into the car that he had to pick up his pant leg and lift it in. "Dad, are you kidding me?" I asked, humiliated/mad/hurt/sad/about-to-shout-my-heart-out-of-my-mouth. *WHY COULDN'T I HAVE A DAD WHO COULD COME TO SUNDAY DINNER NOT FUCKED-UP?* He laughed to himself in a way that I found deeply troubling and cruel. What could be funny about this?

By the time we sat down to eat, I was ready to leave. *Fuck this,* I thought. If he didn't have the decency to be a *little* sober at dinner, then why should I have to eat with him? Our waiter approached the table to ask for our order. I watched my dad's mouth moving, but no words came out. I saw, through his darting eyes, that he was *looking* for words, as if somewhere, in the skylight of the restaurant, he could find them. *Oh-my-fucking-God-no.* My dad wasn't *trashed.* There was something much worse, much more dangerous going on. I shot straight out of my chair. I commanded the waiter to grab on to my dad and help him out of the restaurant while I raced for the car.

We flew through the streets of Los Angeles toward the hospital. In the moment, I felt no emotions. I was fixated on getting to the hospital NOW/ten minutes ago/HOW-ARE-WE-NOT-THERE-YET?! My dad, nearly unable to communicate at all, somehow choked out the words, "I'm sorry." I looked into his eyes, full of confusion, and suddenly felt more empathy for him than I had in all my life. "Don't be *sorry,* Dad! It's all going to be okay; you didn't *do* anything. We're getting you to the hospital." I put my hand on his shoulder and didn't let go.

In the ER, I was battered with questions I couldn't answer. "What's your family's medical history?" "Do strokes run in your family?" "Was your dad in a recent accident?" "Is he allergic to any medications?" "What medications is he currently on?" "Did he take any drugs before you came here?" *I DON'T KNOW,* I wanted to scream with embarrassment. I didn't know! And, I didn't know *whom* to ask! THIS WAS IT. THIS WAS MY WHOLE FAMILY, OKAY, MISS NURSE LADY? But also, thank you, Miss Nurse Lady; you're the only one who can help us right now. *Can you please tell me what is going on?!*

The night became infinite. It felt like we had been in that emergency room our whole lives and that we were never going to get any answers. At two in the morning, a new doctor, maybe the fifth we'd seen, asked if my dad had been in a car accident recently. "Um. I *think* my dad would have told me, but maybe not," I confessed. "Well, your father has suffered some kind of brain trauma. Perhaps from a fall, a car accident, something like that. He has a subdural hematoma." *CAN YOU SPEAK EN-*

GLISH PLEASE AND THANK YOU??? "His brain is bleeding. We have to perform emergency brain surgery." *EMERGENCY BRAIN SURGERY???* "Are there any other options? Can I get a second opinion?" I naively asked. In a grave, dramatic tone of voice that I thought was only reserved for TV medical dramas, the doctor replied, "There are no other options; this has to happen, *right now*. If you had brought your dad here any later, he would be dead."

Since my dad barely understood what was happening, I was the boss. This made me *seethe*. WHY WEREN'T THERE ANY ADULTS HERE TO HELP ME? But I had no time to entertain that chip on my shoulder; there were so many decisions to be made. I signed two billion documents. I initialed all of the lines in the universe. I asked as many questions as I could about what the surgery would do, what "success" would look like, what the risks of the procedure were, and I recorded the doctor's conversations on my iPhone as voice memos. That way, I wouldn't miss any crucial details. I researched the shit out of my dad's medical team.* The nurses walked us into the hospital room where my dad would rest until it was time for surgery. As he lay on the hospital bed, I sat on the cold linoleum floor next to him, my hand in his. There was a chair right by me, but in my intensely focused state, somehow the chair felt too luxurious, like if I sat in it, it meant I was relaxing.

I texted my friend network, my Lady Harem, all of the people in my life who made up my adopted family. I told them what was happening and asked if anyone knew doctors in the neurological world who could advise me. I called my aunt, who, while she didn't know much about my dad's medical history, either, and didn't have much contact with him, told me

---

*   THANK THE GOOD LORD FOR GOOGLE. How many times have you bailed me out? Infinite bailouts.

she would be there for the surgery. THANK YOU, AUNT ELAYNE. I hadn't seen her or talked to her since last Thanksgiving, but I was so fucking grateful that at least one adult would be with me. At five A.M., a nurse came into the room and told me I had a visitor. *HUH?* As far as I knew, I had no pending booty call scheduled for the hospital. (Tho that would have been very baller.) The visitor turned out to be one of my best friends' dad. Although Alexis lived in New York, when I texted her, she had immediately dispatched her dad to the scene. Paul didn't know my dad. He barely knew *me*. But the moment he saw me, he pulled me into a strong, loving, confidence-building embrace, his brown leather jacket warming my freezing body. I hadn't even realized I'd been trembling. *THANK GOD AN ADULT HAS ARRIVED!* I thought. After I laid out to him the plans I'd set in motion, the doctors I'd selected, what post-surgery preparations I was already making, I asked him if I was doing everything right. Was there anything I was missing? Any other way I should have handled this? He wrapped his hands around my shoulders and said, "You have this, kiddo. You've already done everything right." Paul was not the adult I had been waiting for. *I was.*

No one needed to come save me. There was, in fact, no person who knew better than I how to navigate this crisis. I was competent, I trusted and understood my instincts, I could handle this, but more than that, I would *get through* this. I had an incredible support network that I had built for myself, but at the end of the day, in the most dire, urgent situation of my life, I had *my own* back. I felt the feverish flash of a realization warm my icy skin and sink into my body: No matter what happened to my dad, no matter how the surgery went, I would survive. I had myself and I trusted me.

The morning of the surgery, my Lady Harem showed up. My Hilly, my Julia, my Lauren, my Fisch. Their moms showed up too. My sister, in Connecticut, *called*. She even made arrangements to fly home immediately. People who had never met my dad before arrived with bagels and lox and hugs and trashy magazines for me to read. My boss told me over the phone, "Don't worry about work. Be where you need to be. We totally support you." As the days wore on, friends stayed by my side, much to the dismay of the staff, who jokingly complained that we had set up "a refugee camp" in the waiting room. They gave us serious side-eye every time we laughed. *Oh, so sorry to break up the somber/anxious mood of the waiting room. Our bad!* I had spent so much of my time up until this point nurturing and growing my friend family because I wanted to create the tight familial bonds I lacked. I never dreamed, however, that they would show up with such force when I needed them the most. I was insanely grateful for the support and love that enveloped me. I had a caring family after all; it just wasn't the one I was born into.

I spent the majority of the next two weeks in my dad's hospital room, sleeping on a sofa that could *almost* fit me, my feet dangling off one end. Even though I lived close by, I wanted to be there when the doctors made their rounds at the UN-GODLY hours of four and six A.M. so I could get the updates on any changes in my dad's condition. Doctors: *What is up with this schedule?* Don't you want your patients to *rest?* In one of our last nights in the hospital, my dad and I ate spaghetti from take-out containers I had smuggled in. We watched the sun set. In a major turn of luck, his room had two massive, almost wall-length windows that made you feel like the entire room floated and extended into the sky. Some people think Los Angeles has epically pretty sunsets because of the pollution, but they are wrong and also probably cynical. The reason our sunsets beat all the others (gauntlet thrown down) is because as the sun's last rays filter through the atmosphere, the light has to bend, as if through a prism, and move around particles of dust and water in order to make it down to Earth.* This bend, this *willpower* to somehow make it to us despite the obstacles, is what turns the blue of the sky into watercolor streaks of purple and orange and pink. My dad and I watched in silence, transfixed by the light show as another day came to a close, another day my dad had survived. As the dark of night blanketed the sky, he asked me, "Tara, have you heard the song, 'Hope for the Best, Expect the Worst'?" I hadn't. I pulled it up on YouTube (turns out it's a Mel Brooks song from the movie *The Twelve Chairs*) and we listened. "Hope for the best, expect the worst. Some drink champagne, some die of thirst. No way of knowing which way it's going. Hope for the best, expect the worst!" As we listened, I noticed my dad's eyes misting up. "That's how I feel right now. Hope for the best, expect the worst," he said.

My dad was in the most vulnerable position of his life, lying in a hospital gown, his skull having been cracked open, eating pasta out of a box, sharing his fear with me in the form of a song. Sitting on my little sofa next to him, I realized that all of the anger I harbored toward my dad and all of the hurt I felt were *real,* but I needed to stop taking it so *personally.* My dad had not set out to neglect me; he had no intention of putting me in harm's way. He simply didn't have the capacity to treat me any differently. I didn't know much about his childhood, but I knew that there was no way on Earth this sweet man who was currently finding meaning in a musical number had any grand plan to cause me pain. Probably nothing my parents did in my childhood had much to do with me. It wasn't that they didn't love me, and it wasn't that they didn't think I deserved to be taken care of; my parents just didn't know *how* to love me or

---

*   At least this is what I *think* I learned from public radio. Maybe just go with me because it sounds so lovely?

how to take care of me. The most personal relationship I could think of, that between parent and child, was, in fact, not personal at all.

Maybe you don't have as troubled of a relationship with your parents as I do. Maybe you have it far, far worse. Or maybe you have the *best* relationship with them and count down the days till Sunday night dinner. Whatever the case, I think the sooner we can all learn the lesson to *not take anything personally,* the better off we will be. The boyfriend who is a total screamer and jealous of every dude you talk to is not really mistrustful of *you;* he is dealing with his own shit and taking it out on you. The boss who can't give you ANY amount of credit for a job well done isn't trying to make you feel small; he is so insecure that he *can't* share any acclaim with you—he simply does not have it in him. The boy you met on a dating app who has been stringing you along for months about how much he wants to "hang" but is "*so* busy" isn't intentionally being a jerk; he *can't* share himself with anyone else right now. The roommate who has yet to do the dishes as the sink becomes a radioactive nightmare . . . well . . . she should really clean that up. *You did make a chore chart, after all.*

My point is: We go through life thinking that other people's behavior toward us is DEEPLY PERSONAL. If the people close to us are acting in a hurtful way, we reason that it is *very specifically* about *us.* We then tend to internalize it and question ourselves. *What did I do wrong to deserve this?* We blame ourselves: They wouldn't have treated us in this fundamentally shitty way if we were worthy of better. But I'm here to tell you directly: This is madness. **The way a person treats *you* has almost *nothing* to do with you. It's about *them* and their limitations.** They are dealing with their own shit, and mostly that shit is so buried within them that *they* don't even know what's going on! It's like before they were about to throw a big party, they stuffed their overflowing garbage—their take-out Thai food and half-rotten bunch of bananas—in a bag way down in the basement. *I'll get to it after the party,* they thought. But years later, that bag remains, smelling up everything in the house and their life and they can't even find it! They give you what they have to give, but sometimes what they have to offer STINKS.

You can't govern how people treat you or the things they say, but you can absolutely decide what *you* will do with the gospel that nothing is personal and people are limited. Will you let that give you some distance in your relationships, a little breathing room to not react with anger or hurt when someone lashes out at you? Or even when they are just a *little* shitty? Will you let that information protect you from the slings and arrows of a family member who is historically unkind? How will you live your life if you start taking responsibility for how you *re-spond?*

That is where you have all the power in the world. Try letting go of the notion that anyone is mistreating you on purpose, and stand back as you watch resentment and anger float away. It takes time, it takes practice, but it does work. As you clear away all of those feelings that were holding you down, that were telling you, "This horrible thing is being done TO ME," watch as you find more room in yourself for love and compassion. It sounds a little cheesy, right? It is. But that doesn't make it untrue.

If he had the ability, I'm sure my dad would have been the best dad, the dream dad I always wanted, who encouraged my creativity, held me often, and made me feel safe and loved. I'm sure he wanted that too. But, for whatever reason, that side of him was not available, and I've learned to stop putting myself through the torture of expecting a version of him to arrive that doesn't exist. I'm done hoping for a different past and a better childhood. I can no sooner have those things than I can build a time machine. Now I'm getting to know my dad for the man he *is*. And the most delightful thing has happened: I have met a really sweet dude who is genuinely proud of me, who is passionate about boats and athletic gear, who (mostly) no longer puts me on edge. He's my dad and I love him, *just as he is.*

It's hard work to learn that these relationships are not personal. But you're good at hard work. You were probably the kid who did all the extra credit in grade school, right? Me too. That's why we get along.

Practice Taking EVERYTHING Less Personally

It would be unfair to say "nothing is personal" without giving you a way to practice that in your life. That would be like giving you the keys to your own Rolls-Royce but neglecting to tell you where I parked your ride. I'm not a monster. Get out your journal. Again, yes, you have to get a GD journal. Choose one clean page.

1. **Identify a relationship where you are feeling stung and like shit is v. v. v. personal.** Write the person's name at the top of the page. Is it a boss who keeps promising a promotion but every six months the goalpost seems to be farther down the field? Is it your friend who only ever calls to heap her emotional baggage onto your waiting lap? You never hear from her in good times, but you ALWAYS know when there is a crisis. When she starts talking, you begin scrolling through Amazon because you know you're going to be there awhile without being asked a single question. Is it someone you recently started dating where everything seemed like it was going GREAT (*five dates in two weeks; are we getting married?!*) and out of nowhere he

texted you that he started seeing his ex-girlfriend and "doesn't see this going anywhere"? What relationship are you taking personally rn? This can be some ancient shit too. An ex-boss, an ex-lover, an ex-friend, all of the exes, if you want!

2. **Write a scene describing a time you took shit v. v. v. personally and how it *felt* to be hurt.** What were the sensations in your body? "I thought this was the beginning of a real romance. I felt hopeful. We were talking all of the time and even had inside jokes. When he dumped me over text, I felt rejected and like a loser who would never find love. I was sitting in a café, eating twelve-dollar eggs, and all I could think was *What did I do wrong?* As tears streamed down my face, for all to see, I also felt like a loser/hot mess for not being able to finish my absurdly expensive eggs. THEY'RE JUST SIMPLE EGGS. WHAT HAVE YOU PUT IN THEM THAT MAKES THEM TWELVE DOLLARS?! I had no appetite at all. I felt sick to my stomach. I felt like I might throw up. I felt angry. I think that's why I was so mad at the eggs."

3. **Under your scene, make a word cloud of all the words that describe how you felt.** Rejected? Dumped? Taken for granted? Hopeless? Excited, for once, but now all things dashed? Woe is me? It's okay; get it all out there.

4. **Look at your word cloud and reframe how each one of these words is not YOUR personal fault.** Sure, you feel rejected, but is that what's really going on? Or is it clear this guy was not ready to be with you?

YOU *actually* had nothing to do with this. You feel hopeless about future romance? But why? If anything, there is so much to hope for! You met a dude you were excited about. There are more dudes—dudes who aren't low-key dating their exes. Look at each word and see if you can write out a reason why YOU ARE NOT TO BLAME.

5. **Now, under your word cloud, write the following:** "It's okay that I felt the way I did, but it's not the truth. The truth is that the way a person treated me HAS NOTHING TO DO WITH ME. Nothing is personal. People are limited. I refuse to blame myself." The way this person treats *you* is how they treat *everyone*. Including themselves. Your boss might not have the power to promote you, or anyone else, and that makes him feel weak. Your friend who is living crisis to crisis might not *even notice* that she is not so much calling to have a conversation as to give a monologue. She's not thinking about you *at all* rn. She's grasping for a lifeboat and does not have the mental space to understand that she might be dragging you down with her. The boy who dumped you prematurely didn't really "dump" you; he's just SO CLEARLY not the one for you. Write, "This was not personal," until you believe it. Sometimes it helps to write, "I am not to blame," over and over again, and every time you have a thought like *Yes, you are to blame—if you were better at your job, you'd be promoted,* then write next to that, "That's crazy; my boss isn't promoting me because he has no power. It simply doesn't have anything to do with ME." Keep writing, repeating, and reminding yourself that the way a person treats you has almost nothing to do with you.

6. **How will you protect yourself going forward?**
This is the time to pick what your line in the sand will
be, what new boundary you will set in this relationship
and possibly in others. "Going forward, I will protect
myself by looking for a new job. This has been going on
for a year, and I don't need to complain anymore."
"Going forward, I will try to explain to my friend that
I would love her to ask more questions about my life."
"Going forward, I will protect myself by not dating a
boy who tells me, up front, that he's 'not sweet.' That
was probably a warning sign and it turned out to be
true."

7. **Let go of expecting the person to act differently
and move on dot com.** Even if you tell your friend
that you often feel overwhelmed by her issues, she might
not be capable of making *any* changes (remember, people are limited), but what's important is that *you* stood
up for yourself and *created* a boundary that you can take
into the future. That's so dope. The next time she calls,
maybe don't pick up? Or. Let her vent for ten minutes
and then explain how you need to go to a "meeting."
No need to get mad at her, no need to feel hurt that she
acted the exact same way she always does. It has nothing
to do with you. With your well-defended borderline
behind you, do yourself a HUGE favor and let go of
your expectations around this relationship. What can you
do to move on dot com today? Update your LinkedIn,
stop expecting someone to morph into a new person,
listen when someone is self-declared "not sweet."

8. **Just remember: Do not blame yourself. This shit
ain't personal.** Would you blame yourself for bad

weather? Would you blame yourself for a fire that ravaged your house? Then don't blame yourself for how other people treat you, because you have zero control over that. Instead, the thing you have control over is how you react. And we are working on a reaction that is more loving, more kind, more generous toward yourself.

It's tough work to stop taking things personally. I actually don't think there is a self-care tool in this book that's harder to master. I struggle with this one and know it's impossible to do *all the time*. All I'm asking is that you *practice,* that you try to do just *a little* better, that you toughen up your skin a little bit. I'm asking you to build a little distance from the way people mistreat you and how you internalize it. I'm asking for you to develop a little perspective. I'm asking myself to do the same damn thing.

If You're Not in Love in Paris, You're Not in Love at All

Romance Yourself

THE YEAR AFTER MY DAD'S near-death experience, after another surgery, multiple visits to the ER, and physical therapy, after he had fully recovered and miraculously/somehow/thank-the-Lord returned to the land of the living unscathed, I decided it was time to take stock of my life. The realization that I would survive no matter what, that I *had*, in fact, survived so much already, that I was currently the adult I had always been waiting for, made me feel proud AF. It was a pride I could feel in my bones. I was stable, strong, firmly rooted in a life I SAVORED and in no way desperately wanted to flee. *Wow.* I no longer wanted to run away from my life; I wanted to run *into* it. I wanted to explore, headfirst, eyes open, wind in my face, my hair whipping wild in the gust, all of the places within me but also the bigger world that I was ready to relish.

One day, at the age of thirty, just as I had the afternoon after my twenty-fifth birthday, I began to write out the things I knew to be true in my trusty—now hundreds of pages long—Google Doc, the same Google Doc I had begun as a curriculum toward re-parenting myself. By now, it was a living document, a collage of passages from memoirs and magazine articles and little bits of advice I had heard from various people in my life. But I was no longer writing in a desperate attempt to save myself, and this time, when I sat down to write my truth, I didn't turn to the doc because there was vomit in my hair and alarming voicemails from my therapist on my phone. This time, it was because I wanted to recognize how far I had come. I was almost thirty-one years old, and I had been consistently journaling for almost six years. In fifty-four notebooks, I had written 21,580 things for which I was grateful. I had taken at least one hundred baths; I had burned countless incense pyres; I had a special drawer in my closet where I laid out my bras so I could see them fully and enjoy their lacy allure; I had written hundreds of thank-you notes; even better, I had *received* hundreds of thank-you notes; and I had climbed up so many mountains that I now considered myself an "athlete." An athlete! The girl who once miserably ran the mile in her gabardine uniform and saddle shoes now *liked* working out! My circle of friends had become my family and I now understood how to treat my own family like friends. I surrounded myself with things and people that made me joyful, and, from my vantage point, like Cleopatra before me, I could see that above the little problems of everyday life, there were vast lands just waiting to be conquered. I was my own person, my own royal highness. I respected the shit out of myself and felt ready to take on whatever new adventure would come next. *It was all so unlikely. It almost didn't feel real.*

I was not the only person stunned by my progress. All my life, adults, former colleagues of my parents, moms and dads of my friends, even my former grade-school teacher had told me they couldn't believe I had withstood my childhood. I once ran into my parents' former lawyer, who went as far as telling me,

"Can I just say that I can't believe you *survived* that house and that you're doing so well? Over the years, I thought about you and your sister and how sorry I was for you both. I can't believe you didn't end up in rehab . . . or worse . . ." Any time I heard something like this, I felt a little offended. If I had been in such clear danger as a kid, *why* hadn't this adult interceded? But I also kinda understood. I was just as surprised as anyone else that I was doing well. But I was! *YOU GUYS, I WAS.* All I had to do was look in my journals to see my progress. In the pages of the now dozens of notebooks I had been keeping, I saw that I re-parented myself into the person I wanted to be. There was something else that popped out at me in my journals: I read over and over that I had a desperate yearning for a trip to Paris.

In *every* notebook, in many, *many* entries, I wrote things like: "I want to go to Paris." "When can I go to Paris?" "I deserve to go to Paris." "Tara, stop stalling and go to Paris." On my blueprint of principles, there was only one photo—a postcard of the Eiffel Tower my dad had sent me when I was ten. On the back, he had written, "Paris is very beautiful. We spent the afternoon at the LOUVRE," in big, capital, important letters. The Looouvre. (Doesn't that WORD just make you want to fling yourself into the arms of a hot, scruffy-faced, scarf-wearing Frenchman?) My adoration for Paris had been a *coup de foudre*— love at first sight. From the very first time I watched Jean-Luc Godard's film *Breathless* in high school French class, I wanted to be the quintessential French Girl. You know the look: lots of striped sailor sweaters, lots of espresso, lots of running in the streets, lots of low heels clacking on the boulevards, lots of "I'm so effortlessly beautiful and I don't even *know* it," lots of mascara and red lipstick, lots of affairs and bottles of wine and— *ALORS*—was there anything more sexy, more chic, than a Frenchwoman? Moreover, many of the people I looked up to also seemed to feel a spiritual connection to the city. Joni

Mitchell had sung, "I was a free man in Paris, I felt unfettered and alive"; Gertrude Stein had become an expat in Paris; and, most important, perhaps my favorite book character from childhood, Eloise, had an entire scintillating edition that took place in the City of Light. Growing up the chubby-bespectacled-alt-kid in Los Angeles, a city with the cultural inheritance of Botox and freeways, I always felt out of place. I did not have the de rigueur stick-straight hair of the 2000s, nor the barely there eyebrows popular at the time, nor did I love *Dawson's Creek*. In Anna Karina, Jean Seberg, and Brigitte Bardot, with their gap-tooth smiles and disheveled independence, there was so much liberation, so much "I-don't-give-a-fuck-ness," that I dreamed I could emulate them and that I, too, could have a torrid love affair with Paris. I imagined myself at a table on the patio of my very own apartment, wearing red lipstick, reading the local newspaper, and sipping on a latte, the slanted gray rooftops of Paris my dramatic backdrop. *Dream big, kid, dream big.*

My junior year of college, with a signature black bow in my hair, a string of faux pearls, and four years of very poor high school French under my high-waisted belt, I enrolled in my college's study abroad program and moved to Paris to attend La Sorbonne. I felt like the world was my perfectly shucked oyster, perched on ice chips, ready for me to slurp down with a Kir Royale, *merci beaucoup*. I was sure that I was going to conquer the city and that maybe I would live there indefinitely, just reading Baudelaire and eating ALL the cheese. In Paris, I could be whomever I wanted. Who in Paris would care about what kind of childhood I had? Certainly *not* the French. Their *whole thing* (it seems to me) is that they don't care about *anything*, because they are just *so* aloof. They wear disinterest like a custom Dior dress; it hugs them in all the right places. And from what I had seen in the movies, French families were *super fucked-up*. I might even be normal in Paris!

That was the plan anyway. The reality was something far different. In Paris, I embarrassedly admit, I was a total mess. If I was sloppy at twenty-five, can you imagine how I behaved at twenty-one? I think the technical term is a "disaster of a person no one wants to be around in case they jinx us all and ruin our time." I spent my days in my apartment on Skype, arguing with my boyfriend in Providence, Rhode Island, trying to convince him that we were in an open relationship. My nights were spent cavorting around the city with a French sculptor named Julien. Fifteen years my senior, Julien had dark brown, curly, tousled, perma-sex hair and a girlfriend living in India. He explained that this was just the way it was in France. "It's natural, you know. I have my girlfriend, yes, in India, but you are also my girlfriend, here in Paris. It's not such a big deal." *How French.* I felt flutters of excitement when we made out, his rough olive-colored skin rubbing against my pale, smooth, inexperienced body. It was the first time I dated an actual *man,* and it was exhilarating that he knew how to do things like make a fire for me and cook, at all, *anything,* in his artist's studio in the countryside. I fell in with his circle of hipsters and writers, which included an ancient white-haired crêpe-maker-man named Hugo, whom everyone in the Marais seemed to know. One night, in our smoke-filled dive bar, Hugo barked at me, "You, mademoiselle, this city belongs to you!" "Oh, Hugo, you know just what I want to hear!" I cried out to him before sucking on an actual baby bottle of red wine, because, for some reason, this was a very hot trend in 2007. *SO CRINGEY, I KNOW.*

Living in Paris *should* have been a collection of glamorous yet scrappy (remember, this was all on my paltry student loan) memories, but I muddied everything by smoking too much hash. Paris is not a city known for weed, but I was entirely dependent and *immediately*—I'm talking within a *day* of being in the city—found a kind Senegalese drug dealer named Sowa to hook me up. When I wasn't fighting with my American boy-friend or running around with my French boyfriend, I was lighting up and drifting away before taking high-as-fuck walks through the Louvre Museum. That sounds way better than it should. Let me try again: The weed, the very shitty, low-grade weed—the kind of shitty that makes you cough after every hit and always gives you a headache—the weed that was likely laced with a lot of things I don't want to think about, robbed me of many of my memories. For example, I know I spent dozens of nights with Hugo the crêpe-maker-man, but what were his stories *about*? And what about Julien? My French had been horrible, and his English was almost nonexistent, so what did we do with our time together? *Well.* I know what we *did,* but I'd like to remember the details. My time in Paris felt less like a movie and more like a blur—the part after the credits have rolled where the screen becomes snow and fuzz.

I had lived in Paris, but I had not fully experienced or ap-preciated it. I had lived in Paris, but my life there had been ruled by men and bad hash. That's why I later wrote so exten-sively about the city in my journals. I wanted Paris to give me a second chance. But I had always found an excuse not to buy a plane ticket. It was far. It was an expensive trip. I was single. Wasn't it weird to go to Paris *alone*? Didn't you have to be *in love* to be in Paris? I told myself I would wait for a boyfriend who was worthy of Paris. But by thirty, he had still not arrived, and I was tired of waiting. And by this point, I had a deep faith in the power of my journal to tell me what to do. If it was de-manding I take a romantic getaway to Paris, who was I to say *"non"*?

I arrived in Paris under charcoal skies. The dark clouds looked like they could burst at any moment and unleash tor-rential rain onto the city, but instead, they just hung there, like a threat, casting a somber pall on everything. I loved it. Paris was exactly as I remembered it: a moody bitch. If my cardinal sin the last time I had been here was that I had been distracted by my own inner turmoil, then this time, I was going to be *present*. I would do nothing I thought I *should* do and only things I *wanted* to do. I thought this meant I would spend a lot of time reading in cafés and *really reflecting on life, you guys*. I packed a wardrobe of black clothes to match what I assumed would be my very serious, contemplative journey of the mind. But on that first day, as I looked at the pounds of heavy books in my suitcase, I realized I didn't want to read at all. I didn't want to spend one more moment *thinking* so seriously about things. *I wanted to shop.*

I AM NOT A SHOPPER. I hate trying on clothes; nothing ever fits right. AND, if something *does* fit, *oh boy* do I torture myself over deciding whether or not to buy it. I find the cost of women's fashion to be at best reprehensible, at worst conspiratorial. Still, for some bizarre reason, the only thing I wanted to do in Paris was SHOP. I purchased the perfect little black pencil skirt, something very understated but formfitting. I bought a black sweater with a white Peter Pan collar that made me look like a Parisian Wednesday Addams. I went from cheesemonger to cheesemonger in hot pursuit of the best, tangiest, smelliest, Frenchiest cheese I could find. I would haul my dairy discoveries back to my apartment, open a bottle of red wine, light a Diptyque candle, and stuff myself with baguette and brie. One morning, I stood in the most adorable bakery around the corner from the Canal Saint-Martin and eagerly watched as the baker pulled the fluffiest, most buttery, most melt-in-your-mouth flaky croissants from the mouth of a silver oven. As he heaped them into a pile, making a croissant mountain, I stood there eating one after another. "You would like another?" he kept asking, a little worried. "*Oui, merci beaucoup!* But maybe this time the one with chocolate," I exclaimed, crumbs sticking to the side of my mouth, not at all ashamed. I consumed Paris. In every shop, I tried in my broken French to communicate, to make friends, to connect, and, as I have always found, the French were super gracious in their responses. They appreciated that I was making an effort and were more likely to show me the brand-new spicy, rose-scented, limited-edition perfume that had *just* come in from India. I took the wax perfume and rubbed it on the inside of my right wrist, the balm melting into my skin, and breathed in. *Oh, Paris, you really turn me on!*

As I shopped and ate my way around the city, I kept up all the rituals I had been building for the past five years. I had told myself prior to arriving that there was no presh to keep up my routines, and that, again, I would do only things I WANTED TO DO. But, unpredictably, I very naturally kept my good habits. Apparently, I *wanted* to do them. One morning, after writing my gratitude list, I decided to run as far as I could. How far would that be? I wasn't sure. I began deep in the Marais at six-ish in the morning when the skies were still indigo blue, my headphones on, blasting OutKast. I found myself jogging down the empty streets—sans people, sans café tables, just me and the narrow cobblestone paths. In the early morning, the soft yellow light of the flickering streetlamps glinted off the dark dew-covered roads and cast a warm glow all around me. I ran to the Tuileries Garden, just next to the Louvre. Since it was November, the famous perfectly manicured trees in the garden had lost their leaves to expose the wild, spiderweb-like branches beneath. I ran circles around the reflecting pools, which were surrounded by empty green metal lawn chairs, each one curved down in a way that invited you to slink in and take a break. I could feel that soon these chairs would be inhabited by people, but for now, this was my *jardin*. I made a circuit through the Tuileries until I came upon the Louvre itself, grand, imposing, a building that when you look at it, it seems to say, "Yes, I know I am a very big deal, what of it?" What had started as a fortress to protect the little-nothing city of Paris in 1190* had grown into the home of kings and queens, only to be liberated and given back to the people during the French Revolution. There was so much history under my feet, I couldn't help but feel exuberated by how cool/strange/lucky/unbelievable it was for me to be casually running on such storied ground.

As Big Boi rapped for me through my headphones, I spotted another jogger. We both stopped in awe as the sun rose from behind the Louvre, bright yellow breaking through the clouds and lighting up pale blue skies, turning wisps of white clouds into a halo around the museum. The moment was so dramatic that the other jogger and I immediately looked at each other and with almost no words—just giant smiles—switched phones and took photos of each other in front of the Louvre, in front of the rising sun, in front of *fucking Paris* waking up for the day. Sweat poured down my face even in the cold morning air, my ponytail had fallen out miles ago, so my hair was a big, glorious mess, and my legs throbbed with pain, but my heart was fucking exploding with bliss. I was exactly the person I wanted to be, in the exact place I wanted to be.

For all of the Joni Mitchell "Free Man in Paris," "unfettered and alive" feelings I had, there was still one thing I wanted to do that felt too indulgent. Since high school, I had dreamed of buying the ultimate item in any Frenchwoman's closet: a classic quilted Chanel flap bag. Coco Chanel, the original boss lady, one of the very first women to build her own business empire, had created the purse for the modern woman. It was practical—

---

* One of my favorite places on Earth is the crypt of the Louvre. Deep underground, under the layers of tourists and art, you can actually see the ye olden-time foundation. It's damp and spooky as hell down there. I *highly* recommend it.

you could wear it either on your shoulder or across your body. Before Chanel's invention of a chain handle, women had to always hold their purses in their hands. The bag was mysterious in its charms, just like the French mademoiselles it was made for. Somehow, it pulled outfits together and gave the possessor an instant dose of style. In high school, to help myself cope with my parents' divorce, I made a photo collage of myself as a French girl that I kept in my closet. The centerpiece of that vision was a Chanel handbag. After college, I began saving for one. That was eight years ago. By now, I could totally afford it, but every year when I would think about pulling the trigger, I'd back down, afraid of what would happen if I owned it. Would I suddenly go broke because I had been so arrogant as to think I deserved something so beautiful? Would I immediately be robbed because no one should own something that decadent? But this trip was about doing the things I wanted, and my gut was screaming at me to go to Chanel's original store at 31 Rue Cambon, *maintenant!*

As I opened the heavy door to Chanel's vault of luxury, I felt a rush of history come in with me—the history of so many women who had admired Chanel before me, but also my own history. My own planning and longing to be the kind of person who went to Paris and had the life where she bought herself the things she had worked hard and saved for. I had expected the store to be glorious, and it did not disappoint. With a grand, sweeping staircase that elegantly connected Mademoiselle Chanel's upstairs apartment with the store, the shop itself was every bit as chic as I had imagined. What I had not expected was the line.

You had to wait in a line just to *talk to* a salesperson. And the line was *long*—at least seven people deep and cordoned off with a rope. And! You had to ask someone *else* if you could even *be* in the line. *Quelle horreur!* At the price point of Chanel, it did not seem possible to me that there could be enough people to even *form* a line. *Who were all these rich folks?* It had taken me almost a decade to save enough money to even *consider* buying this bag. I immediately began to berate myself. Why was I so superficial that shopping was so important? Why wasn't I reading a single book on this trip? And how *useless and stupid* was it to wait in a line to spend money? GODDAMN IT. But then it hit me: *That's my Frenemy Within speaking.* I actually had to say out loud, to myself, "Listen, *bitch,* I've worked hard, I've earned this, and you are not invited to this party." Luckily, no one saw my little slip into multiple personality disorder. And a moment later, a woman in white gloves and a tweed suit, holding a black lacquered tray, asked if I would like a cappuccino. *Oui, oui, I would.*

When it was finally my turn, some thirty minutes later, a perfectly coiffed saleswoman named Victoria escorted me to her display case. "What can I show the mademoiselle?" she asked. "I know exactly what I want. The medium flap bag in caviar leather, please." It had been the bag of my dreams *always.* I didn't have to look at any others. I KNEW WHAT I WANTED. "Mademoiselle, I am sorry, but that bag is sold out." *Sold out?* A bag that cost more than a month of my rent was SOLD OUT?! WHO WAS BUYING THESE FUCKING BAGS? I felt like the wind had been knocked out of me.

Victoria asked if there was anything else I would like to see. "Sure," I lied. "Have anything more *classique?*" I snidely challenged her. "Actually, yes. I have something the mademoiselle may like very much." Victoria walked away as I eyed the exit.

She returned with a white box. "This has not been out yet," she almost whispered as she took the lid off with her gloved hands, unpacked mounds of delicate white tissue paper, and then slipped off the dustcover to reveal the jumbo flap bag. I had never seen this bag before, and it was HONEST TO GOD love at first sight. Does that sound intense? It should. *It was fucking fierce:* THE BAG TOOK MY BREATH AWAY. The shape was so sleek, so sexy. Yes, it was large, *jumbo* even, but the lines were so perfect that it looked like it was *just* the right size, not at all ostentatious. Well, ya know. Not ostentatious *for a Chanel bag.* The gold clasps were so shiny that they refracted the light of the store. I felt the butterflies of infatuation, like I had met a boy with whom I was about to have a very serious fling. I nervously touched the leather. I held the bag gently and pulled the gold strap to convert it from a shoulder to a cross-body bag. I loved the way the chain cl-cl-clinked as it moved. I took the bag and hung it across my body like I was anointing myself with a sash. I looked in the full-length mirror and, like a bride who had just tried on her destined wedding dress, I knew I had *the one.*

Victoria showed me the secrets of the bag. The tip pocket that Coco had created so she could easily reach for a few francs to give a valet. The secret pocket designed to house love letters and correspondences. I wanted love letters and correspondences. I hoped that having a place to store such delights would hasten their arrival. She explained to me that the interior of the bag was burgundy because Coco thought if it were black, one would never be able to find anything. *Good thinking, Coco.* The bag was indeed both practical and magical, and I didn't hesitate for one moment to buy it. It was time. Victoria served me a glass of champagne, and after I was charged (in a totally separate room, by the way, where I *also* had to wait in line), she took a series of photos of me standing on Chanel's staircase. That part was a little embarrassing; we took, I'm not kidding, maybe thirty-five photos of me posing with the bag on that staircase. But I wanted something I could always look back on to remember the victorious independence I'd achieved. To remember that I had endured my very-un-fun-nearly-feral childhood and made it out of my reckless-self-hating-let's-just-destroy-ourselves twenties, but that I was *grateful* for what those experiences had taught me. I knew it was silly, but in that moment, all I wanted to do was drape my body all over that damn staircase and roll around on the carpet like an unrepentant child— gleeful, awed, thankful that I had arrived.

I walked out of Chanel's store and strolled down the rue Saint-Honoré, practically skipping with my extra-jumbo-size shopping bag slung over my shoulder. For so long, I had wished to be the kind of person who went to Paris simply because she *wanted* to go to Paris, and now I WAS THAT PERSON. The fact that I was done denying my innermost hungers was cause for celebration. I remembered that the Ritz was just around the corner. I had never been to the Ritz before, but this seemed like the perfect time to have an aperitif in the fabled and glamorous hotel. I floated through the formal and imposing Place Vendôme, a square that is so striking, so startling in its precision, that I took a stutter step in my white Converses. I looked around at the perfectly uniform, meticulously designed gray façades and wondered what went on behind the closed doors. I waltzed through the square and looked up at the Ritz, the old stomping grounds of F. Scott Fitzgerald, Ernest Hemingway, Mademoiselle Coco Chanel herself, and now, by some miracle, me. I strolled into the hotel like I belonged, like I had been there a million times before, and made my way, Converses and all, to the warm, wood-paneled bar.

In a romantic little nook, I sat at a table with two chairs. One for me. One for my bag.

THE WELL-BEING RITUALS

Time To Create Your Own Shiny,
Joyful, Inspired, HELLLL YES Life

It's Your Turn

You might think it's a little frivolous to end this book with a story about buying a luxury handbag in Paris, and to that all I can say is "THANK FUCKING GOD. That story *was* frivolous and whimsical and that is entirely the point, k?" I wanted to leave you with a story that wasn't painful, that wasn't difficult, that was, in fact, a victory lap of re-parenting. I wanted to leave you with that, because I want you to have your *own* "trip to Paris." I want you to get your *own* "bag." The purse, for me, was just a symbol that I had survived a rough start at life and was now thriving, that I had turned a painful story into a delightful one—one that I could call my own. It was the material manifestation of many years of working on becoming the kind of adult I had always wanted to be. It was my talisman. A declaration of my own independence, of trusting my gut, and of letting myself enjoy the fuck out of my life.

I think that a lot of people lead their lives never having really lived them at all. They play the roles they were assigned early in life, without questioning if they even *want* to be this way. They get comfortable, even with really *uncomfortable* circumstances. They let the days and weeks and years wash over them and never see that they have the power to change IT ALL. But I don't see that for you. If you've made it this far with me, if you've taken on the work of nurturing yourself, then you are not going to become one of those people who, on their death-beds, complain, "I wish I'd had the courage to live a life true to myself, not the life others expected of me." You are not going to think, *I wish I had let myself be happier.* Do you know that those are two of the top five things people regret when faced with death? I do because I googled "What do people regret before they die?" and found that Bronnie Ware, a palliative nurse in Australia who had spent years sitting with people who were dying, wrote an entire book on the subject: *The Top Five Regrets of the Dying.* She saw over and over just how much people regret not living the life they wanted, not letting themselves be *happy.*

I just don't see any of those regrets for you.

For you, I see something grander: I see a life that you *consciously* live. That you curate and cultivate and create for yourself, a life in which you are self-aware AF, grateful for the luck that you are here at all, a life in which you love and also let yourself be loved. I see you engaged to your life, holding it firmly yet tenderly by the hand like it's your soulmate, bringing it in for the deepest of make-out seshes. I see you feeling up your life in the most passionate of embraces. *That* is what I see for you.

It's been really lovely spending time with you. I felt you here with me the whole way. I felt your warmth and presence and smelled the delicious perfume you are wearing. Or maybe it's just your dope shampoo? Whatever it is, keep it—it's working for you. Thank you for encouraging me along the way, for supporting me when there was something I felt scared to share. I gotta say, I was super fearful at times, but you made me feel safe and strong and like I *belonged*. You were right here with me when I needed you the most, and I will always be right there with you. All you have to do is pick up this book.

So, my darling friend, what's your Paris? What's your sunrise run? What's your bag? What are your lilies? What are you waiting for?

It's your turn.

With all of my heart, with all of the glitter in the world, with tears in my eyes, with a kiss for you that is sloppy and wet and definitely covered in too much lip balm . . .

I love you.

Is that cheesy?

Yes, but I don't give a fuck.

LOVE AND KISSES,

TARA

A.K.A. T$ (STILL TRYING TO MAKE THAT A THING)

ACKNOWLEDGMENTS

I AM ETERNALLY GRATEFUL TO:

1. Anyone whose path has crossed mine and who appeared in a story in this book. THANK YOU for being a part of my life, the good moments, the not-so-good moments, the so-joyful-my-heart-might-explode moments. You gave me a story to share, and I have the deepest gratitude to you for that.

2. My agent, Monika Verma. There would be no book at all if it were not for you. Thank you for being patient with me and taking me on when I told you I had a "soup of an idea." Thank you for spending the next nine months figuring out the ingredients. Thank you for being so kind, so smart, for holding my hand, for helping shape the narrative, for your advice, for the phone calls, and oh-my-God-thank-you-Monika for your partnership over these years.

3. My editor, Annie Chagnot. Thank you for being my saint, my defender, a part of my brain from the pitch to now. I blacked out the first time I met you because I was

so blown away by your intellect, your heart, and your belief that I had something worth saying. I will never forget seeing my sample pages, all marked up, in your able hands and thinking, *Yes, this is my person.* Thank you for whittling this down when I sent you way too much, for the wisdom of your edits, for your understanding of exactly what I wanted to make, for promising to be gentle with me and my story and for following through every step of the way. Thank you for answering my insane emails and for protecting me in all senses. Dearest reader, if you read this book and you liked it and it made sense, Annie Chagnot is the reason why.

4. My publisher, Whitney Frick. Your passion for telling stories driven by the heart, your belief that books can change lives, your enthusiasm to launch the voices of women and to further the way we see ourselves, all inspire me. THANK YOU for believing in the mission of the book, for your wise leadership, and for your utter support. I am thrilled I get to learn from you.

5. Julie Grau and Cindy Spiegel. Thank you for giving me my first literary home. Your wise presence in that first meeting alone gave me more confidence than anything else had in my life. Just to be seen by you made me see myself. Cindy, I hope I followed through on being "the friend" you spoke about, and Julie, I hope I made you proud. You both changed my life.

6. My family at The Dial Press and Penguin Random House. Thank you, Jess Bonet, for dealing with me even when it was way too early and for all of your excellent-

right-on ideas; Dhara Parikh for your tenacity, collaboration, and all the hard work you do—I see you, lady!; Maria Braeckel for your enthusiasm from the jump; Barbara Fillon for getting your hands dirty with me; Melissa Sanford, Avideh Bashirrad, and Kelly Chian for all of your production work (sorry for all the slang!); Matthew Martin for being gentle and protective; Anna Kochman for the excellent design; Jess Phoenix, thank you for the best, most me, most oh-my-fucking-God cover of all time. You nailed it.

7. My Comedy Central family. I simply would not be the person I am today, nor would I have been able to re-parent myself, without the stability and love you have given me. You were my first safe home. Thank you to my mentor, friend, and person-I-would-most-like-to-be-like, Kent Alterman. You make everyone in your orbit feel seen, quite possibly, I think, because you actually *see* them. You are so authentically you, so curious about the world, that I aspire to be as comfortable and open as you are one day. Thank you for helping me grow even when it took too much of your time. I am beyond lucky to have you in my corner. Sarah Babineau, thank you for being the first person to take me seriously when I said I wanted to write a book. That magical dinner and your continual encouragement made this possible. Thank you to Jonas Larsen for always going to bat for me and for making me feel valued in your kind actions and words. Thank you, especially, for embracing my mush-ball ways. Monika Zielinska, you are a saint on this planet and I thank you for all of the years of friendship and guidance and for the many times you let me cry in your office. The kindness and dignity

you show to everyone around you is a model to us all. Thank you to Kaiti Moos for always keeping me sane, organized, and well fed.

8. Adam Grant. It's kind of hard to believe that you are *such* a giver. How do you do it?! Thank you for being a generous supporter, an early reader, for giving me such invaluable advice from the moment we first met. *Originals* inspired me to let go of my fear of risk and tackle this project. You taking me seriously helped me take myself seriously.

9. Sarah Hurwitz. SARAH! WE ARE DONE! CAN YOU BELIVE IT?! Thank you for all of the writer-sympathy emails and calls, for the early read, for the thoughtful, incisive notes. Thank you for sharing this process with me—the good, the bad, and the oh-my-God-how-are-we-not-done-yet?!

10. Beck-Dorey Stein. Thank you for the incredibly helpful early read, for the amazing Sylvia Plath quote, and for your encouragement. Now please move to LA.

11. Julia Cameron and her book *The Artist's Way.* Your book made it possible for me to breathe, for me to reclaim my creativity and come out from the shadows. Thank you for the gift of your writing. If you, reader, are currently stuck in your creative process, stop reading now and DO Julia's book.

12. Jennifer Flanz and Elise Terrell at *The Daily Show.* Thank you for giving me my first opportunity to be the best at the worst.

13. Jordan Peele, Keegan-Michael Key, Jay Martel, and Ian Roberts. Thank you for giving "the digital girl" way too much rope and for your faith that I could somehow make "the Internet work" for the show. From you I learned the importance of having a point of view and sticking with it. In particular, thank you, Jay Martel, for encouraging me and editing my earliest work.

14. The surrogate families who have taken me in and taught me so much over the years. Thank you to the Pollares for always coming through, the Newmans for all of the advice and delicious food, and Tim Forbes and Anne Harrison for always encouraging my creativity, and for the best Sunday night dinners of my life. Special thanks are due to Sam and Leah Fischer for being my role models and friends, and for legit giving me shelter when I was at my weakest. Thank you for teaching me what family looks like.

15. Liz Glotzer, Matt Jacobsen, Michael Glotzer, and Elayne Glotzer. Thank you for filling in family history when I had no clue. Thank you for being honest with me. Thank you, Liz and Matt, for Thanksgiving.

16. My Hype Men: Kevin Seals, Jules, H-San, Deme, Alexandra Panzer, Lindsay Safran, Khoby Rowe. My Road Warriors: Sarah Walker, Sam and Leah Fischer, Alex Murray, Matt Levy (the best lawyer a gal can have), Anna Wenger, Mike Farah, Susanna Fogel, Alexis Beechen (who makes a marketing deck for a friend?! You do!). My extended Lady Harem: Jessica Kerry, Jana Schottenstein, The Seven, Naomi Nevitt, Evan Krenzien. Thank you to Jessica Kerry and Isabelle FitzGerald for being my OG editors. THANK YOU for reading and editing

all of my garbage essays over so many years. Jess, I *almost* believe you that I am a writer.

17. A serious friendship debt is owed to Lauren Fedman for guiding me back to myself whenever I get lost. You are my soulmate friend and there would be no functioning person, much less a book, without you. I am also grateful to Lauren Pollare for giving me the opportunity to have a little pink office that night at Cedars, and for listening to versions of all of these essays from day one, even when you just wanted to go to bed.

18. My dearest sister. We had different childhoods, and the greatest sadness in my life is that we weren't able to share more of that precious time together. Thank you for letting me back in, for your honesty, for that day you picked me up from the airport and helped put my life back together, for your letters. Thank you for being so kind and thoughtful: It turns out you really are a miracle baby. Thank you for letting me share our story and for your support throughout the process, even when it was scary and weird and brought up uncomfortable memories. Thank you also for always laughing at my jokes, even the bad ones.

19. My dad. I know you love me. I know you wanted to be a different kind of parent. I know you were doing the best you could. Your greatest gift to me has been your unwavering support in the process of writing this book. Thank you for validating my memories, for telling me "Don't change a word," even when those words were difficult for you to read. Thank you for telling me that there was nothing I could write that would make you stop loving me. Thank you for showing me I had nothing to be afraid of.

ABOUT THE AUTHOR

TARA SCHUSTER is vice president of Talent and Development at Comedy Central. She is the executive in charge of *Lights Out with David Spade* and was the executive in charge of the Emmy and Peabody Award–winning *Key & Peele* and the Emmy Award–winning *@Midnight*. Her numerous other shows have included *Another Period*, *Not Safe with Nikki Glazer*, and *Hood Adjacent*. Her plays have been performed in the New York International Fringe Festival and her writing has appeared in *The New Yorker*. She lives in Los Angeles.

taraschuster.com
Facebook.com/tara.schuster.3
Twitter: @taraschustar
Instagram: @taraschuster

ABOUT THE TYPE

This book was set in Bembo, a typeface based on an old-style Roman face that was used for Cardinal Pietro Bembo's tract *De Aetna* in 1495. Bembo was cut by Francesco Griffo (1450–1518) in the early sixteenth century for Italian Renaissance printer and publisher Aldus Manutius (1449–1515). The Lanston Monotype Company of Philadelphia brought the well-proportioned letterforms of Bembo to the United States in the 1930s.